Top Producer Secrets

Top Producer Secrets

*Digital Marketing Strategies to Stand Out and Take Over Market Share
Any Agent. Any Market.*

Krista Mashore, B.A. Psychology, M.A. Education

Published by Game Changer Publishing

Paperback ISBN: 978-1-964811-61-1

Hardcover ISBN: 978-1-964811-02-4

Digital ISBN: 978-1-964811-03-1

www.GameChangerPublishing.com

FREE GIFT: BONUS RESOURCES & TEMPLATES

TOP PRODUCER
TOOLS UNLOCKED

My **pro tips** and *expert insights* on how to get started using these strategies and tactics in your business *right away*. Plus you'll receive access to over **25** additional tools, resources, templates and bonus trainings for FREE. Get started now, go to:

KristaMashore.com/TopProducer

SCAN ME

Top Producer Secrets

Digital Marketing Strategies to Stand Out
and Take Over Market Share
Any Agent. Any Market.

Krista Mashore

B.A. Psychology, M.A. Education

www.GameChangerPublishing.com

Table of Contents

INTRODUCTION 1

**BECOME UNBEATABLE THROUGH
NEIGHBORHOOD FUNNELS** 5
by Krista Mashore
Tracking... 14
Using Funnels for Old School Marketing 15
How Funnels Support the Sales Cycle 18
Benefits to Your Clients 20
Getting Started... 21
Does It Really Work?... 23
Takeaways.. 25

WIN BEFORE YOU ARRIVE 27
by Sabrina Shaw
Before the Listing Appointment: Listing Packet..................... 29
Follow Up 30
At The Listing Appointment 31
Getting the Home Show Ready 33
Presenting Their Home 33
Takeaways.. 37

THE UNSTOPPABLE LISTING PROCESS 39
by Shanara Carter
The Initial Call.. 41
CMA Box 43
At the Listing Appointment... 47
Takeaways.. 49

HOW TO OWN A NEIGHBORHOOD WITH THE CMA DROP-OFF PROCESS 51
by Joe Seamon
Your Typical CMA...55
Start With Your Farm and Your Ideal Client 56
Create Your CMA..56
Drop-Off #1: The CMA..58
Postcard #1 58
Drop-Off #2: Seller's Guide...59
Postcard #2 60
Drop-Off #3: Stats and Tips..61
Postcard #3 61
CMA Box Drop-Off...62
Does It Work?...64
The Complete Package...65
Takeaways...66

HOW A NEW AGENT CAN CRUSH IT 69
by Haley Jones
Step By Step Guide to Getting Started....................................71
Taking It to the Next Level 75
Up Leveling Even Further 78
Takeaways...82

WANT TO MAKE MORE SELLING LESS? 85
by Windy Goss
Start By Believing It..86
Putting the Pieces Together 86
Connecting with My Ideal Clients 87
Beyond Facebook 89
Educating Them About the Market...89
Learning From Blowing It 90
A Great Support System...92
Takeaways...93

FINDING YOUR AUTHENTIC VOICE IN VIDEO 95
by Alisha Collins
Where I Started 97
Finding My Voice 98
What's Your Voice? 103
Making Mistakes to Get Better 106
Removing Excuses...................................... 108
Videos That Serve Your Community 110
Do the Hard Things 111
Takeaways... 113

LEAD WITH VALUE... 115
by LaToya Latimore
Leading With Value.................................... 117
Using Video to Lead With Value 118
Using Marketing Updates to Lead With Value 121
Using Omni Presence to Lead With Value 124
Using Niche Marketing to Lead With Value 126
Leading With Value Means I Win Before I Arrive 128
Takeaways... 130

BECOMING A COMMUNITY MARKET LEADER© 131
by Chris Pesek
What's a Community Market Leader©? 132
Community Date Night.................................. 134
Twelve Days of Christmas.............................. 136
Live Here, Give Here 139
Digital Marketing Mastermind 142
How Being a Community Market Leader©
    Impacted My Own Business 144
Find Your Own Passion 146
Takeaways... 148

FACEBOOK: THE NEW MEGA MALL 149
by Cheryl Fowlkes
Facebook: The New Mega Mall.......................... 150
The Scary Power of Video.............................. 157
How My Business Has Changed 160
Takeaways... 162

HOW TO GO FROM ZERO TO BEING A TOP AGENT 163
by Sarah Stone-Francisco
Video as a Problem Solver.. 167
Get Started Creating Videos 168
What to Talk About 170
Getting It Out There 172
What It Looks Like.. 174
Takeaways... 175

THE WORLD HAS CHANGED AND SO MUST YOU 177
by Carlos Zapata
Out of My Comfort Zone and Into the Digital Age................. 178
Being a Latino Professional... 180
Personal and Professional Transformation 182
From Local to International 183
Impact on My Clients 184
Recommendations for New Agents...................................... 185
Takeaways... 187

FACEBOOK ADS DONE RIGHT... 189
by Betsy Flores
Earn the Right to Ask... 191
Facebook Pixel Power 194
Retargeting... 196
Adding a Sales Funnel... 197
Takeaways...200

HOW TO GET YOUR TIME—AND YOUR LIFE!—BACK 203
by Alex Mayer
Differentiating Yourself...206
Be a Marketer, Not Just a Salesperson 207
Time Management..210
How Videos Save Time...211
Support of Great Colleagues 212
Takeaways...214

THE SECRET IS IN THE SYSTEMS 217
by Jenn Sells
Starting in a Nightmare 218
Do or Don't Do. There is No Try............................220
Start with Your CRM 223
Keeping Your Transactions On Track 228
Systems to Keep on Top of Your Finances............229
Branding and Marketing Systems...........................231
Marketing Systems...235
Time Management Systems: 236
Takeaways..238

DAILY SHEET MAGIC 239
by Lani Belcher
Start with Your Vision 240
Accountability 241
Gratitude...241
Tasks 242
Pay It Forward 245
Acknowledge Your Wins and Successes................245
Calendar Your Day 245
Takeaways..246

HABITS THAT SET YOU UP FOR SUCCESS 249
by Pamela Terry
Habit #1: Manifesto 250
Habit #2: Preplan Your Day 252
Habit #3: Pomodoro Technique............................252
Habit #4: Stick to Your Strengths and Your Niche 253
Habit #5: Get Good at Social Media 254
Habit #6: Share Your Knowledge 255
Habit #7: Keep Building Your Business 255
Habit #8: Find Your Tribe...................................256
Habit #9: Strengthen Your Mindset 257
Takeaways..258

BIG AND SMALL THINGS LEAD TO SUCCESS 261
by Heather Jones
Friendships 262
Routine 263
Digital Location Domination 264
Getting Started..266
Google Photos..266
Coloring Contests 267
Community Funnel 269
Takeaways...270

WHAT'S YOUR RETIREMENT STRATEGY? 273
by Jesse Zagorsky
Agents' Typical Retirement Plans...........................275
You Need Leverage...276
Takeaways...281

THE DECISION THAT CAN CHANGE EVERYTHING 283
by Lenka Doyle
Before I Made the Decision 284
The Decision to Invest in Myself 285
Results from Deciding and *Committing* 287
How My Decision Saw Me Through Hard Times....................288
Do You Need a Coach?...290
Takeaways...291

A FINAL WORD FROM KRISTA... 293

Introduction

In this book, you'll get to meet some of the top producers in my coaching program. You'll see that some of them are pretty new to our industry and others have been around for a long time. I'll tell you from knowing them personally that the people writing chapters in this book are awesome, but they are no different than you. They aren't smarter or harder working or better looking. The markets they work in are not healthier than the market you're in. They didn't succeed because the real estate market was doing great. In fact, many of them had their best year ever in 2023 when interest rates were higher than they had been in 24 years, when we seemed on the brink of a recession, and inventory was low because people were afraid to make a move.

As you read this book, you won't find all the traditional things that agents are taught to do, like cold-calling, door-knocking, brokers' tours, and open houses because that's not what I've taught these top producers. I'm going to ask you to keep an open mind to strategies that are *totally different* from what you've been taught. In fact, that's one of the main secrets to the success my students have achieved. They had an *open mind* when they came into my program. They weren't glued to doing just traditional things they'd been doing. In fact, most of them had come to realize that traditional methods, especially in marketing, are no longer effective. They were willing and open to learn something totally new—and sometimes out of their comfort zone.

And they got to be top producers because they not only learned the things that I taught them, but they *implemented* those things. They are consistent and persistent. They know that the system I teach them really works, and they work it. Some of these people have been in my program since the beginning in 2018 and some have been with me for just over a year. And all of them have seen huge increases in their business and their confidence.

I put together this book because I thought it would be helpful for you to hear directly from some of my students about some of the strategies, techniques, and routines that helped them succeed. So, I asked some of my top producers to share what has made the biggest impact on their business. It was a big ask because none of them are professional writers who write *New York Times* best sellers in their spare time, and all of them are super busy. (Spare time? What's that?!?) Still, they were excited to write their chapters because they are all "Go-Givers" who genuinely want others to succeed. Several of them wrote about the same things, like how they use Facebook ads, video, or the CMA (comparative market analysis) process I taught them. But they all talk about it from their own unique experience and perspective. Many of them took what I taught them then got feedback and collaborated with me and others in the program. Then as they implemented the strategy they'd learned, they put it on steroids making it even more effective.

Don't get intimidated that this book is 300+ pages long! Just take it a chapter at a time and jot down any ideas you get that you could use for your business before you read the next chapter. The great ideas my students wrote about here can make a huge difference to the way you do real estate *if* you implement them into your own business. That said, I want to warn you that you need to have a full game plan that goes from A to Z. You can't just implement one piece without thinking ahead.

For example, one agent (I won't give her name because she *hates* when I tell this story!) got all excited about the idea of sending postcards to the market she wanted to dominate. She paid $900 thinking it was for 9,000 postcards but it was only for the list of addresses. Then she paid another $9,000 to actually have the postcards made and sent. Might sound expensive but it's still okay because she got 400 responses from the postcards asking for information. Woohoo! The only problem was that she had *absolutely no plan of what to do next with them!* When people say they're interested in you, you need to get back to them quickly, right? Well, there was no way she could call all 400 people quickly and she didn't have any follow-up material to send them or a funnel to direct them to. (Even so, I'm proud of her for doing *something* rather than nothing. Yes, she made mistakes, but she's still ahead because she *took action.*)

This same agent, still very enthusiastic, decided to do the CMA box (comparative market analysis) drop-off process that you'll learn about in this book. She ordered enough giveaways (branded pens, cups, etc.) for 5,000 CMA boxes and spent about $20,000. That's probably more than you need to spend on these, but the main issue was that she ordered 5,000 calendars for these boxes. If you think about it, calendars are only good if you send them in January of that year or December of the year before. You can't send them out in September when most of the year is already gone, right? Unfortunately, she didn't have the team or bandwidth to deliver these 5,000 boxes (with their calendars) quickly. She finally hired someone and got them delivered by March, which wasn't great and created another expense she shouldn't have had.

I'm telling you this because you need to have a full strategy that keeps your leads interested and following a journey that you've put together for them. That's what I teach my students, an A to Z strategy not just single clever ideas. Students are always telling me that my coaching program is like getting a doctorate in real estate!

I hope that hearing from these top producers will inspire you and help you see that you can do what they've done and create a business you love.

Wishing you great success,

Krista Mashore

P.S. If you'd like to take action right away, make sure you unlock your **Top Producer Tools** that accompany all of the secrets unleashed in this book: **KristaMashore.com/TopProducer**.

Become Unbeatable Through Neighborhood Funnels

by Krista Mashore

I'm going to tell you about a strategy that can make your business boom very quickly if you do it right. It's something I haven't seen anyone else do (except me and my students) which is crazy because it is so incredibly effective! By investing some time in creating neighborhood and community funnels, other agents won't be able to touch you. Let me explain how and why I started using this strategy.

Back in 2008, when the market totally crashed, I ended up becoming a short sale and foreclosure agent. Before the crash, I knew something was off in the market, so I'd started educating myself around short sales and foreclosures and marketed my services to asset management companies and banks. I ended up with the Freddie Mac account, Wachovia, Wells Fargo, a bunch of other banks, which added up to a total of 13 different asset companies and banks. For five or six years, it was great because I'd show up at the office and have all these homes (short sales and foreclosures) just sitting there waiting for me to sell. Every day, I'd get a new bunch of properties. And at that time, they sold really quickly. I didn't have any time to do much marketing because investors were just swooping in and buying them. (And in fact, because of the condition of many of the properties, you didn't *want* to market them. People left their homes dirty and in disarray. I totally understand it because these homeowners felt the banks did them a disservice—which they had, by loaning them money that they couldn't actually afford using Stated Income Loans.) In my best year during that time, as a solo agent, I sold 169 foreclosures.

So, it was wonderful for five, six years, and then the market got better, which was amazing for the economy and the community, but it destroyed my business. Suddenly, my business went from selling 153 to 169 homes a year down to about 12. It seemed like almost overnight, foreclosures disappeared. I realized, "Oh, my gosh! I am screwed. Nobody knows me. I haven't been marketing myself. Nobody knows my name. Nobody even knows I'm in real estate." I knew I had to 100% change how I was doing business and how I was landing listings. It was almost as if I had to start from scratch as a brand new agent. I had to totally change how I was doing business—or I would have been *out* of business (and many of you need to do the same right now!!).

You might be one of the many agents who are struggling right now or maybe you're brand new or maybe you just want to do better. Well, I'm going to explain a strategy that I used back then to transform my real estate business from being 100% foreclosures and short sales to primarily being nearly 100%, normal traditional sales. Plus, this strategy helped me get back up to selling over 100 homes within a 12-ish month timeframe. (I wish I could tell you exactly how many months it took but as I'm getting older, numbers and dates just don't stick the way they used to!)

I knew I had to do something different, so I met with my lender, Debbie, and said, "We are going to start dominating certain neighborhoods." Together, we picked two specific neighborhoods and focused on spreading good information to them. Back then, no one did a lot of marketing on places like Facebook on the internet. We had websites, but that was pretty much it. I started creating postcards that had market updates: what was new on the market, what was active, and what was pending. I used Every Door Direct from the U.S. Post Office to distribute these postcards. Every ten days for three months, I would show up in their mailbox. Anytime I had a listing in the area, I would do massive, massive marketing and blanket the neighborhood with postcards and flyers. I didn't just do it when I had my own listings. I kept researching what was happening in those neighborhoods and telling them all about what was going on. I let them know about everything from new listings to what was sold, in addition to all that was happening in the development, new businesses and restaurants coming in, even things that were controversial (like a new golf course or one that was about to go under).

The thing is that I was *consistent.* I didn't just get postcards out once or only when I had a listing. People in that neighborhood got something from me at least every 10 days for 3 months. After the first 3 months, I sent something to them twice per month. (The reason I did it every 10 days for the first 3 months is that I wanted them to keep seeing me and not forget.) It worked so well that I ended up dominating those two neighborhoods. Then I started doing the same thing in other neighborhoods until eventually I covered almost my entire city in this manner. After that, I went to the city adjacent to it, which is Oakley and started marketing in specific neighborhoods there.

About two years after I'd started doing this strategy, I started doing digital marketing as well. I started running Facebook ads and campaigns and creating video content. I created videos about the communities and their local schools. I videoed my interviews with businesses in the neighborhood. I made videos where I talked about things to do in the area, the best dog parks, the best places to eat anything and everything you can imagine. Then in conjunction with doing all the digital marketing, I added that information on the back of the postcards that they were seeing in their mailbox. (Doing this not only helped me and my business but it also helped my local community and its businesses which was an added bonus.)

Now people were seeing me both in their mailbox and digitally with Facebook ads. By using Facebook to run your ad campaigns, you can target your local community and make sure you end up in the newsfeed, so they actually *see* your content. It got to the point that anywhere I went in the area, people would see me and just start talking to me out of the blue as if we were friends. (It's called a parasocial relationship, where you see someone so often, like a celebrity or performer, that you feel like you know them even if you haven't actually met.) I completely transformed my business. When I was active in the business, I sold hundreds of homes every single year by utilizing this marketing strategy. It works and is the main strategy that I teach all my students.

So fast forward. I had done this for years and years, and then I learned about funnels. Funnels are different than websites in that they are designed to attract people who are interested in a specific topic or area. A website can be like a department store where people wander in, but you have no idea what they came for. Maybe they want new underwear or a vacuum cleaner, but the store's owner has no way of knowing as they walk through the store. A funnel is more like a specialty shop, like a fly fishing shop or a place that sells wedding dresses. People are attracted to it specifically because it has what they're looking for. You know for sure that the gal who walks into the wedding dress boutique isn't looking for a vacuum cleaner and the person who walks into the fly-fishing shop isn't looking for lingerie!

Your website might have all kinds of information and content but it's usually pretty general, not focused. But a funnel has *specific* content that speaks *directly* to the potential clients you want to attract. You're speaking their language and giving them information they really care about. Research shows that the more that your content speaks *directly* to somebody, the more likely it's going to convert them.

When they go to your website, are they looking at your reviews, searching for properties, learning about who you are and why you got into real estate, or looking for information about buying or selling? The point is, when they go to your website, you have NO idea why they are there. This is important because if you don't know why they are there, you don't know what they want and what to give them next. You don't know how to put good content in front of them or how to give them *relevant* information that they are interested in and seeking out. Let me repeat: The more the content (aka information) speaks directly to someone the more they will convert.

For example, I'm going through menopause. If I see an ad on how to sleep better or how not to have hot flashes, I am definitely clicking on that. But if I see an ad or information about how to bulk up muscle as an 18-year-old young man, I'm swiping left. It doesn't pertain to me. I'll ignore it. That is why having a funnel versus a website is so important. With a funnel, you *know* what they want and can give it to them. With a website, you don't have a clue.

When I learned about funnels, I thought to myself, *Oh my gosh, now I want to take location domination, both digitally, through Facebook ads, creating video content about my community to a whole new level. I'm now going to take all that information that is specific to each neighborhood and put it into a neighborhood funnel. Then I'll do the same thing for the whole city.*

One of the things that makes marketing really stick is proximity. The closer you are to someone and what they're specifically interested in, the more they'll pay attention. For example, if there's a fire in New York and you live in California, you shrug and think, *Yeah, okay, there's fire in New York.* Then if there's a fire in your city, you're thinking, *Wow, there's a fire in my city.*

But if there's a fire on your street, you really pay attention! You check out that fire every five minutes and look for any news you can about it because it's so close to you. The more that you can make your marketing have proximity and speak directly to your audience, the more attention you will get. Your content becomes prolific, and the topic people are talking about.

The content can be anything that is important about the neighborhood. For example, in one of my neighborhoods we had a golf course that was going to be shut down. Some people were for it, and some people were against it. I used the golf course issue, but I didn't take a side. Instead, I became somebody that was like the reporter. I started going to all the meetings in the neighborhood about it. I reported on what the developer was saying and what the homeowners were saying, the pros and cons of having the golf course or not. With that information, I would create videos on and do Facebook ads, and all that information went into the neighborhood funnel.

Basically, a neighborhood funnel is where you pick a specific neighborhood. The funnel is everything about the neighborhood, from the school scores to the crime report to videos about local businesses. It has information of what's nearby, as well as an updated monthly market update specific to that neighborhood. When you run ads or create postcards or flyers, or if you do an open house, you can have a QR code that basically directs people to the funnel.

One reason these neighborhood funnels are great is that once I create the content, it's done, and I can use it over and over. I can create a seller's guide for sellers because I have a seller funnel for a specific neighborhood. I can create a buyer's guide because I have a neighborhood funnel for buyers. It's actually the exact same funnel. I just tweak each funnel slightly so that it speaks to whomever I'm speaking to (i.e., buyers or sellers). I'll have a buyer's book or the seller's book depending on which funnel it's going into. I'll have a marketing plan for the seller's funnel, or

I'll have more information about the neighborhood for buyers. I have buyer-related videos that talk about the buying process, so buyers can binge-watch that. I have seller videos for the sellers that sellers can binge-watch all the information about selling. For most of the other content, I'll use the same videos, but I'll just tweak them a little bit to speak directly to buyers or sellers. Still 90% of it is the same exact thing. You create the work once, then modify it slightly for different purposes. For instance, I put the neighborhood name right at the top of the funnel aka (website) for a specific neighborhood. So "ABC Neighborhood Market Update" shows right at the top so people know the info on the page is all about that neighborhood. Everything is named within the funnel to that specific neighborhood, then I just change a few things depending on whether it's a funnel for buyers or sellers.

It's great because something that took you 15 or 20 minutes to create will get seen over and over by people you haven't even met. Even while you're asleep, people will be binge-watching your content. It works even when you aren't working! You'll get views while you snooze, and every time someone sees your content, they are thinking of you as the expert and authority in your community. You are no longer just a commodity. They feel a connection to you, and they trust you before they ever meet you. Is that powerful or what? This is my unique value proposition differentiator. This shows that I know what I'm talking about, that I specialize in this neighborhood. Think about it: If I'm competing with another agent for a listing and I send the prospective seller to my specific neighborhood funnel with tons of info about the neighborhood, who do you think they will pick?

There are so many different things that I can do with this neighborhood funnel and content. I can do a "Just Listed" card with a QR code that directs traffic to the funnel. I can put the QR code on the flyer of the home. I can do a Facebook campaign where I'm driving traffic to the specific funnel of a neighborhood. And if I choose to do an open house, I have a QR code, one for sellers and one for buyers, that drives them to the specific neighborhood funnel. So now I'm utilizing this content many times but creating it once. I can repurpose each video and any other materials in the funnel as an individual ad and put it on Facebook, Instagram, my website, TikTok, Twitter, YouTube, Instagram reels, and YouTube shorts. I'll create content about the general community then, just by tweaking a few things, I can use that same content on a number of different neighborhood funnels as well as using it as single piece content. So, I end up with multiple funnels for neighborhoods that look like the content is specifically for this neighborhood, when in all reality 75% of information is just repeated in different areas.

Once I create it, I can house it forever and I can use it over and over again. Once the funnel has been populated with great content, all I have to do is a quick two-minute local market update every month. People want to go back to this funnel because they're curious about the latest happenings in their neighborhood. They are curious about the value of their home and I am updating them regularly. What's the first question somebody asks you when you go to a party and they know you're an agent? It's "How's the market? What's happening?" Right? Our job as real estate agents is to be that local authority, tell people what they want to know and keep them informed. Updating your funnels every month lets people know that they can expect to get good current local information from you all of the time.

The beauty of having the funnel is that when a buyer or seller calls me from a specific neighborhood or about a specific neighborhood, I can send them directly to the funnel specific funnel (buyer or seller) they need to see. It automatically elevates my authority and my status. It shows that what they're looking for is in my niche and that I'm fully knowledgeable. It completely positions me as the expert to both buyers and sellers and gives me a competitive advantage over my competitors because no one else is doing this. And because my competitors aren't doing it, they are viewed as a commodity like every other agent, right? What's a commodity? It's replaceable. It's interchangeable. When you're a commodity like gas or cellular service and you've got what everyone else has, the only thing you can do is lower your price. But when you are seen as an expert and an authority, it's the difference between a brain surgeon and a general practitioner. An expert and authority can make more and work less.

That's what these neighborhood funnels do for you. When a seller calls me and says, "Hey, I'm interviewing three agents and I'd like to interview you too," I'll say "Sure." Then before I get there, I send that seller to my neighborhood specific funnel that's talking about their neighborhood. Before I even step through the door, I've elevated my authority and my status. I've shown them that I specialize in that neighborhood, and I'm going to win the listing, period. I do the exact same thing before I meet with a buyer. I am winning before I arrive.

I always use this example with every Realtor® who is new in my course: "What's the first thing that you do when you see a listing go up in your neighborhood? First thing you do is you get upset because they didn't hire you. Well, I'm sorry but if you're being honest with yourself, it's your fault because you let them forget about you. And trust me, I understand! In the past I let this happen to me before too (though not since I started utilizing this strategy). You weren't marketing appropriately, and you weren't staying top of mind. The second thing you do is you either pull the flyer, if there is one, or you go home, and you pull up the MLS to find out who the agent is and what the house listed for. You do this because you are curious. You want to know what's happening in your neighborhood because you live there and, even as an agent, you care about the prices, what is active and sold because you live in the neighborhood, right?" Then I have them imagine, "Let's just say somebody calls you and says they're interviewing [XYZ] agents. You send them to your neighborhood funnel and the other agent does nothing. Who's going to get that listing?"

Tracking

It's important that you keep track of visitors to your funnel so that you can market again to the people who have shown interest in the neighborhood you're featuring. Why? According to research from the National Association of Realtors, most buyers start looking anywhere from 3 to 12 months before they actually take action and decide to move. If you're set up to track visitors to your funnels, you can go back to people that were looking at homes in the neighborhood three to 12 months before. You can retarget them on Facebook and other advertising methods so that when they're ready to pull the trigger, you're still top of mind for them. You can use this data and information to show prospective sellers what differentiates you from your competition.

To do this, you need to include pixels in your funnels. A pixel is a tiny bit of code (HTML or JavaScript) or tiny invisible image. These pixels can gather information about visitors to your funnel and track their activity on the site. Once you have this information, you can then retarget them with more content that would interest them. And you would know what they want because if they were interested in a similar funnel in the past, you can assume that they are still interested in similar content. You can send them new current content (aka the funnel) when they are more likely to buy. You can create whole marketing campaigns because you know that this person just looked at this particular funnel, so they're probably interested in this community, or they live in this community. You can create ads specifically targeted to people that you pixeled who already engaged with that neighborhood funnel. If somebody just came into the website through something like Facebook, you may or may not have a way to track who it is specifically. But with the information from the pixel, you can retarget them, and you can re-advertise to them. And when you have a new listing that's in that same neighborhood, you can go back to the people you previously pixeled that were looking at similar neighborhoods and retarget them with more current updated information.

If you want to go beyond that, now we also have *dynamic* QR codes. You can get a dynamic QR code through a QR code generator. (To learn more about dynamic QR Codes you can go to **KristaMailbox.com**). When people click on these dynamic QR codes, I can see who that specific homeowner is, and I get their basic information. I know that this specific person clicked on my QR code and that they're reading my market update or watching my market update video. I know that this person is in my funnel. Why is that important? Because now I can call and say, "Hey, this is Krista. I specialize in digital marketing, and I noticed that you just watched the video about the market update in [XYZ] neighborhood. I'm not a stalker but I just wanted to know if you have any questions. Can I help you in any way?" Now, it opens up direct conversations that are not salesy or pushy. We are just adding value by checking in to see if we can help them in any way. With this approach, people can let their guards down with you.

Using Funnels for Old-School Marketing

I'm a real estate coach who focuses heavily on digital marketing, utilizing social media and video. The strategy is to show up where people are looking, and people are looking online. But you may still do old-school techniques. Funnels can still help you. For example, imagine doing an open house. Most agents have a couple of brochures and their business card to hand out. And what happens to those? Tossed in the trash as soon as people get home.

But what if when you do an open house, you invite the neighbors or you invite the neighbors to the pre-party? At the open house or pre-party, you give all the neighbors a QR code that's specific for that neighborhood funnel that has great content specific to their neighborhood. You've now driven those neighbors to the neighborhood funnel, and because you did, you've positioned yourself as the authority. You let them know to come back every month because they'll have an updated market report on what's happening in their area. You're educating them, you're adding value, and you're also staying top of mind and showcasing yourself as the expert in the neighborhood.

Each time you list a house, you can do that. You can put the QR code on your "Just Listed" cards and your "Just Sold" cards. You can put it on your flyer and your lawn signs with a great big arrow that says, "Scan here for more information about your neighborhood." Or "Scan here to find out what's recent, what's happening in your neighborhood!" People are curious and they're going to do it. And with their one click, you've elevated your authority. You now stand out from the pack, and they'll remember you.

If I were going to do older school techniques like open houses or knocking on doors (which I don't do), I would use a similar approach and get people to the funnel. I would say, "Hey, I'm Krista and I've found most people I meet in your area are super interested in what's happening in real estate in their neighborhoods. Every single month I do a two-minute video talking about what happened in [XYZ] neighborhood. Would you be interested in me adding you to my list so that I can just send you the link every month? Then you can know what's happening, too." Most people will say "yes" to that. Then it's not like you're cold calling just to let them know about the open house or to try to get listings. You're doing it with purpose. You're adding value and you're inviting them to learn more about something they're interested in without asking them for anything in return.

Again, thinking old school, how do you even take it a step further? You can create a cute little magnet or something they'll keep that has a QR code that directs them to your neighborhood funnel. You can use the dynamic codes or a QR code that's more general (which will save you some money in the printing). "For a current market update for [XYZ] neighborhood, click here every month." This directs them into that neighborhood funnel where they can get all sorts of information about the neighborhood along with the market update. Even if you're a brand new agent and never sold a house before, doing this would make you look like a seasoned pro. Perception is reality.

For buyers and for sellers, I've got eight different funnels that cover four different neighborhoods. In addition to that, I do funnels for the entire community: one for the city of Antioch, one for the city of Oakley, one for Discovery Bay, and one for the city of Brentwood. The whole city funnels are very similar to the neighborhood funnels with the same types of videos about schools, restaurants, things to do in the area, etc. And these broader community funnels also have seller videos and buyer videos. These are a little more general but it's still providing 99% more than any other agent. You may not be able to do a funnel for every single neighborhood or subdivision. But even doing a more general community funnel will position you as an authority and make you stand out from the competition.

How Funnels Support the Sales Cycle

The old statistic was that 87% of agents fail within the first five years. I think it's much higher now. In my mind, the main reason they fail is that they don't pay attention to the entire sales cycle of their business. Marketing is the first phase. If you market and brand *appropriately*, you're going to generate leads (which is the second phase), not just any old leads, higher quality leads.

Nurturing those leads is the third phase. You've got to nurture those leads, especially in real estate. If you do, you're much more likely to convert those leads to listings or active buyers. If you don't, odds are that they will forget all about you when the time comes for them to buy or sell their home.

The fourth phase is conversion. If you've done everything right, this should be a no-brainer. When they are ready to sell their home or buy a home, you are the obvious choice to represent them. They already know you and trust you. You just have to show them a little bit more about what you will do for them that is totally different—and better!—than your competition.

The fifth phase is fulfillment and delivery. Here, of course, you want the process to be the best experience ever for them. This is where good systems and processes are important, like having a good CRM (customer relationship manager) with automations and workflows. (If you'd like to learn more about mine, The Mashore Method, go to **MashoreMethod.com**.) But even if you are a rockstar in this phase, they'll forget you unless you do phase six, which I call the six R's (refer, retain, resell, rituals and routines, retire).

Your neighborhood and community funnels work for every single aspect of the sales cycle. My funnels work to help *market and brand* me and help me *generate higher quality leads*. They help me *nurture* the leads which helps me *convert* the lead. Once they hire me, they also help me *fulfill* my promise because I can utilize those funnels to market the home for a seller. I can also utilize those funnels to educate a buyer about the community and the neighborhood which makes a buyer more solid and less likely to fall out of escrow (which hurts both buyer and seller, costing them time and money). And when the transaction is done, I can also use that funnel for the *six R's*. The funnels will help them remember me and refer me.

Most agents fail because they don't think about their entire business model. They might be really great with customers in the fulfillment and delivery phase and their clients love them. But if they don't know how to market properly, they're not going to get as many leads which means they're not able to get as many clients. Or maybe they're great at marketing, but they suck at nurturing. That means they're not going to convert the leads they get because you need to nurture the leads that you're marketing to. All of it goes hand in hand. If you miss one piece of the sales cycle, you have a huge gap in your business, and you simply aren't going to be as successful as you could be. The funnels help you cover all the bases.

Benefits to Your Clients

When we explain funnels and their impact to sellers, we take it one step further. We actually show them how we take that same neighborhood funnel, and we add their home at the top. Their home then, is the focus of the neighborhood funnel. Now the funnel has a video of their home, a 3D virtual tour of their home, and tons of pictures in addition to all the information that the seller loves about the property and the neighborhood. This is all part of our listing presentation process.

I've never seen anyone else do neighborhood funnels like we do. It's never been done. This is my invention and concept. People try to copy this strategy, but they usually miss essential pieces so it's not as effective. I'm the originator and I teach my students to do it so that will really give them results. Other agents have got a website, and then they may even make a website for the home. But because they don't know how to market them, we all know no one even really sees those websites. They may put their listings on Zillow or Realtor.com or some kind of other real estate website. Doing that still doesn't even come close to producing the results that our marketing does. When we market our way—running Facebook ads and paying for attention, paying for exposure—we completely crush the results of Zillow. When I show sellers the difference, then they really understand the power. I'll tell them,

"Attention is currency, attention turns into money. So, the more attention I can get here to your home, the more money I can get you and the better terms I can get you. More exposure will equate to better terms for you and more money in your pocket."

Another important way the neighborhood funnel helps both buyers and sellers is by educating buyers. Educated buyers who make an offer are much more likely to close. For example, let's just say there's an HOA and a buyer doesn't know they can't put their boat in the side yard until they get the documents during the due diligence period. This could definitely be a deal killer and a lot of time wasted when the buyer backs out. Or what if the school scores in the area are very low? Some buyers might not care but a family with young children might back out of the deal when they find out. Much better for buyers to know all of the good, the bad, and the ugly up front *before* they make an offer! Good information up front means fewer buyer cancellations, less risk of the buyer losing their deposit, and less risk of losing time on the market because somebody got into contract and then backed out.

This truly gives us a competitive edge. It helps me "win before I arrive" with sellers and buyers. It gets me more referrals because people are continuing to go back to these community funnels over and over again. They care about what's happening in their neighborhood. And because I keep them informed about their neighborhood, it's impossible to forget me!

Getting Started

Okay, so this may seem like a lot and you can't get it all done immediately. Just get started with lead magnets. A lead magnet is basically providing something of value in order to get somebody's contact information. Getting contact information used to be a lot easier to do than it is now. People are more skeptical these days. So now, we create valuable content pieces that we give out to people without even asking them to opt in. They get the content, and we don't even ask them to give us their contact information.

The more information and value that I can give without asking for anything in return, the more they will be likely at some point to want to give me their contact information by opting into whatever I'm offering. The idea is that we give them such awesome, valuable information that when we finally offer a lead magnet (another piece of great content), they're happy to opt in.

The information you want to create is specific to the neighborhood or broader community. We'll do a national market update then we'll do a local market update and I'll put it on the neighborhood funnel and community funnel. Then I'll do an update specific to the neighborhood and put it on the neighborhood funnel. So now they're seeing what's happening nationally, they're seeing what's happening in their local area and also in their neighborhood. These updates are the only thing that you have to recreate every month. You don't even need to get fancy with graphics or anything, you can just use Zoom. I've been doing my national and city updates for a long time. So, I have graphics and a green screen and all that. But for my monthly neighborhood updates, I just jump on Zoom and record them. If I need to, I just edit them but it's very, very quick. (To see an example of a neighborhood funnel, go to **KristaMashore.com/TopProducer**.)

The beauty of this is that you can do all of those things, or you can just do one of those things to get started. If you just did a city update, or you just did a neighborhood update you are doing what 99.999% of other agents are *not* doing. It's elevating your authority, your status, and your brand just by doing that one thing. I tell my students, "Just start and then let's build it. It doesn't matter if you don't have tons of content yet. Create your funnel and start!" (People can purchase my software that has everything they need to build their funnels. They just have to do a few things to make it their own.)

So initially, you could just start off with the community and neighborhood video updates. Then to build up your assets, you can add in other things, like guides for sellers and buyers. I've got guides on selling your home in Shadow Lake and in Deer Ridge. I have guides for buyers. You can do interviews with local businesses. You can feature everything a dog owner would want to know like where the dog parks are, local veterinarians, places to buy dog supplies. You can feature restaurants that are great for date night, or places to take young kids for fun. You can come up with a million ideas for content that people would appreciate. It's not that big of a deal. I can use most of those videos for multiple neighborhoods.

Even if you just start with a little bit, it's so much more than the average agent does! I help my students set a three-month plan to commit to getting their neighborhood and community funnels. When it's complete, they have that asset forever and can reuse it and repurpose it by using it on their website, using it for ads, sending it to sellers or buyers, nurturing leads, etc. etc.

By the way, though most of my students create neighborhood and community funnels, others do them for different niches. For example, one student does hers for rural properties where she gives all kinds of content about the ins and outs of rural properties. Another student has done one for divorce where she specializes in divorce and talks about the issues in a divorce regarding property. You could do them for a specific Ideal Client like single women or first-time home buyers or investors. You could do them for certain kinds of property like condos or homes on the water. If you do your funnels and market them properly, you'll be able to dominate whatever niche or market you want. Check out an example of one of our neighborhood funnels so you can see how it works at **KristaMashore.com/TopProducer**.

Does It Really Work?

We met with a guy in Discovery Bay, and he said, "Look, I'm just interviewing you because I see your marketing everywhere. But I have no intention of hiring you. Because I want an agent that specializes and lives in Discovery Bay." I don't specialize in

Discovery Bay, but I do have a Discovery Bay funnel. So, he interviewed us and we sent him to our neighbor funnel. Guess what? He ended up hiring us and said, "Wow, like, I've not seen anybody do this."

One of my students, Heather Jones, had a similar experience. She created her neighborhood funnel. She created a QR code for it and put the code on a brochure she had created. She was doing an open house for another agent and brought her brochures. A man came in and told her, "I never ever work with anybody except the listing agent. I always go to the listing agent." Days later, he ended up calling her and said, "Hey, I've got to tell you that I'm hiring you because you look like the real expert in the neighborhood." When he saw her funnel, he knew that she was the expert and the authority in that neighborhood.

I can give you another example. Basically, I wanted to prove to my students how well this process works. So I went on the MLS, and I showed them that during the previous 12 months, I had not sold one home in Discovery Bay. I live in Discovery Bay, but I didn't ever specialize in it. I specialized in Brentwood, and I didn't really want to specialize in Discovery Bay. I pulled up the MLS (multiple listing service) for Discovery Bay for my students and said, "Look, I've not sold anything in 12 months. You don't see my name anywhere as the selling agent, right?" I started my Digital Location Domination strategy, and I built a neighborhood funnel. I started creating content about how close different areas and homes are to fast water in Discovery Bay and the different sun exposures they have. I interviewed businesses and talked about Madelyn's, a local clothing and gift shop in Discovery Bay. I did a video at the Boardwalk, which is a restaurant down there. I talked about the boat storage place and anything else I could think of that would be interesting. I also ran ads. I took this content that I was creating, and I created Facebook ads with the videos. Then I targeted those people and directed them to the funnel. When people would call me about selling their home,

I would then send them to the funnel before I met with them. Within four months, we had closed four transactions, when the year before we had done zero in that market!

Takeaways

1. A neighborhood funnel positions you as an expert and authority, even if you're brand new to the business.
2. A neighborhood funnel will support you in all six phases of the sales cycle (marketing/branding, lead generation, lead nurture, conversion, fulfillment & delivery, 6 R's: refer, retain, resell, relist, rituals/routines).
3. A neighborhood funnel can work with old-school real estate practices as well as digital marketing.
4. A neighborhood funnel benefits your clients by creating educated buyers (who are, therefore, more qualified) and by giving your listings exposure to the buyers who would be most interested.
5. A neighborhood funnel gives you the ability to track and retarget people who have shown interest in the area.
6. A neighborhood funnel shows sellers how you position yourself and their home as unique and different. It shows them the unique value proposition differentiator of yourself and their home.
7. You can create a funnel for any niche you wish to dominate.

KRISTA MASHORE
Homes By Krista - eXp Realty
Founder, CEO - Krista Mashore Coaching

📞 925-325-4663
✉ Krista@KristaMashore.com
📍 East County, California
🌐 https://KristaMashore.com

Krista Mashore (Owner of Krista Mashore Coaching)
www.KristaMashore.com

Free Gift: Bonuses
Time To Take Action!

Information alone is not enough. I've put together this **free expert resources member's hub** to help you get started now. Customize the strategies and tactics from this book to *your* business and marketing plan, with guidance, top producer tools and extra trainings.

KristaMashore.com/TopProducer

To learn more great strategies and tactics, sign up for my free 3-day event at: **KristaMashore.com/Masterclass**.

To order my books that are mentioned in different chapters, go to Amazon.com and search, ***"Krista Mashore Books"*** and you'll see all of my best-selling books now available.

Win Before You Arrive

by Sabrina Shaw

I am going to share with you a strategy that will give you the power and confidence to win any listing! I don't know any other agents in my area who are using this strategy to win listings. And when you follow the steps, even if you are a new agent, you are sure to win the listing before you even get to the listing appointment. Plus, you will show up with the confidence to know you are the absolute best choice for the seller. There is definitely work on the front end, but the hustle is worth it. Other agents won't come close to doing what you are doing. The great thing is that this is a duplicatable process that anyone can follow. I am going to share with you the listing process I use, that I learned from Krista, from start to finish! I have never lost a listing since I started doing what I'm about to share.

Prior to real estate, my husband and I both had good careers making mid-six figures combined. But we were living paycheck to paycheck. So, when I gave notice to my school district that I did not want my contract renewed as a high school principal and assistant superintendent, we weren't sure how it was going to turn out. At that time my husband and I had a couple of rental properties. I had been reading about flipping and wholesaling so that was the route I was planning. It was scary and there were a lot of unknowns. My husband was worried, but he believed in me. I was working part-time and made just enough money to cover my bills, but nothing extra.

I found Krista because I had listened to a podcast she did on *Real Estate Rockstars* (I think that was the name of it) and found her book *Sell 100 Homes a Year* on audio. Her book was a gold mine and opened my eyes to the power of social media in real estate. I started implementing things from the book and it helped, but I wanted more. Then Krista started popping up on my Facebook. I clicked on her stuff and started researching her (plus I wanted to learn how she was able to target me on Facebook). You know that feeling when you know you have found something great and you are craving more and you know if you could just have access to it, it would change your life? That is exactly what I was feeling! I wanted the coaching so badly, but it was expensive. I didn't have any extra money to afford it. But I kept seeing her and I couldn't shake the feeling that her coaching would change my financial trajectory. So, I made it work. I just figured it out. And it has completely changed my life mentally and financially.

When I started coaching with Krista, I was in my first year of real estate as a part-time agent and was on a team. After I went through Krista's coaching program, I went from selling a few homes per year to being a top-producing six-figure solo agent. I have stayed in the top ten percent of Realtors® in my MLS region for several years in a row now. I can tell you for sure that the listing process she taught us which I am outlining in this chapter has been one of the big keys to my becoming a six-figure agent. It is a strategy that is seriously gold. Anyone can do it if they put in the work and time. I am going to tell you exactly what I do to win the listing, how we get the home market-ready, how we create buzz around the listing, and how we prepare to go live and get the absolute most eyes on the property. When you use this strategy, you can dominate listings in your market!

Before the Listing Appointment: Listing Packet

The first thing I do when I have a listing appointment is create a video for the seller. I use Zoom (recording the screen) and walk them through the neighborhood comps, along with a quick, broad market report over the city and county. I don't suggest a price for their home yet. I then create a QR code for the video and add it to my listing packet.

In the packet I include a "Why Work With Us Flyer," a Community/Neighborhood Market Report with the QR code to the video I just recorded, and a flyer that talks about our strategy for pricing and selling. I add in my marketing plan, my seller homework checklist, my prepacking and getting ready for staging guide, and a handwritten card.

All of these materials are aesthetically pleasing and high quality (plug-and-play of what Krista provides us). I put them in a decorative box that has me and my brand on the outside and client pictures and testimonials on the inside. I am telling you this box and the documents inside it are pure gold when it comes to impressing clients. Once, I walked into a seller's house after dropping it off, and she had it displayed in her closet. It was that great! She didn't want to throw it away because it was so nice. Have you ever had boxes you didn't need, but wanted to keep? Kendra Scott, Tiffany's, Louis Vuitton. It is all about branding and messaging and already showing that you think about details and quality. Presentation is everything and you are planting the seed already that you are different and what you do is extra. I drop this off to their doorstep before my scheduled appointment day as soon as I can.

Of course, all of my materials are prepared ahead of time so I can put the packet together quickly. Anybody can do this. If you are new and you haven't even sold a house yet, you can still do this. You may just have to word things a bit differently when it comes to your experience. You *never* want to lie about what you have done or what you will do to market a home. But you can partner with people and use their expertise and experience until you have their own.

Follow Up

Once I drop off the listing packet, I create a video text message standing in front of their house. I thank them for the opportunity to interview and let them know I just dropped off my listing packet with a Home Equity Analysis specifically prepared for them, along with my marketing plan and materials to help them with a successful sale of their home. I tell them all this will help them have a successful sale *whether they use me or not.* This is important! I never worry about giving away too much information for free. I completely believe there is enough business for everyone, and houses are being bought and sold every day. Krista always says, "Serve, don't sell," and I always try to live by that mantra. My goal is to give value. Whether this particular seller chooses me or not—though they always do since I started doing this process!—I know that the value I give away will come back to me tenfold. Have you read *The Go-Giver*? I strongly recommend that book! Krista recommended that book to us and it is woven into every aspect of her coaching and real estate organization. Doing the video text message ensures they will know you left the box at their door and that again you are going the extra mile to have great communication with them.

A few hours after I drop the seller package off, I send a pre-written email thanking them again for the opportunity to interview. In it, I send a link to my marketing listing video that Krista taught us and helped us put together. I am telling you if the seller packet is gold, then the listing/marketing video is diamonds and treasures! This video showcases what makes me different and unique and why I'm not just a commodity. It talks about the non-traditional things we do. It explains why marketing, innovation, social media, geo-targeting, retargeting and so much more is what they need to maximize the return on their investment when selling their home. It shows them the stats and data that prove how effective the digital marketing process we use is. Anybody can do this. You just have to do the work and invest in marketing, but you'll stand out because no other agents are doing this.

In the email I tell them it's so important they watch the video because it goes over everything I do to market their home. In this pre-recorded video, they see me again and they are getting to know me. **And this marketing/listing video, doesn't just tell what we do. It shows what we do.** It is seriously amazing! If I could only keep one thing from Krista's program, it would be the marketing/listing video, hands down. A little later, I send a text saying, *"Hi! I hope you were able to dig into the listing packet I dropped off. I also just sent you a super important email. Please let me know if you didn't get it."* My listing appointment is usually a day or two later. I want the listing packet dropped off as soon as I know I have an appointment (this is essential if they are interviewing other agents) and send the email with the marketing/listing video right after that.

> *And this marketing/listing video, doesn't just tell what we do. It shows what we do.*

At The Listing Appointment

When I show up for the appointment, I ask them if they had time to go through the packet and watch the listing video. Most people have gone through the packet a bit and watched most of the listing video. Because of this, their mind is already made up that I have the listing. So, I just go through the appointment as though they aren't even interviewing other Realtors® and that I have the listing. Commission rarely comes up because, as Krista says, I have "Won Before I Arrived."

I ask them questions. I want them to have "the time of possession." I want them talking because when people have time of possession, they feel more connected, and they like the conversation better. I don't need to go on and on about me and everything I do. I have already shown them. My job is to take notes and to *really listen* to their needs.

I have a questionnaire I go through that is designed to build rapport and to find out what they need from selling their home. Some of the questions I ask are:

1. How many properties have you sold? (If this is their first, I go to question #2.)
   a. When did you sell your last one?
   b. What were your experiences with that sale?
   c. How did it go for you?
   d. What did you like the best? What did you like the least?
   e. What would you like to do the same or different on this sale?
2. If you could wave a magic wand and have this sale go just the way you want it, what would that look like?
3. Why are you selling your home?
4. Where are you going?
5. How soon do you need to be there?
6. Do you have any other properties that you need to sell?

> *I have never lost a listing when I do this.*

These are just a few of the questions. I also have the listing paperwork with me and ready to go. I am telling you, you want to show up to the appointment like you know you will be leaving with the listing because if you do these things, you will almost every time. **I have never lost a listing when I do this.**

Getting the Home Show-Ready

Based on their timeline and the condition of their house, the next important step of the listing process is to get the house show-ready. People have different personalities and different mindsets. Some sellers will do everything you say and are on top of it! Other sellers are stressed and busy and don't have the capacity to do much of anything. It's important to get them to understand that pre-packing (getting rid of clutter) and pre-staging make a huge difference. I give them a pre-packing and pre-staging guide that I created with a stager. So instead of my telling them that they need to get rid of all their pictures and knick-knacks and loud colors, I am putting that on the stager who does this for a living and specializes in preparing homes for sale. Homes that are staged sell faster and for more money. We want to make the home more neutral in style so that it appeals to a broader audience of buyers. The guide also talks about the importance of cleaning and making sure everything is spic and span along with the buyer psychology of these things.

I go through the guide with them and make a plan for what they can and can't do. Then we put together a timeline. Now I offer semi staging with all my listings (but I didn't do this when I first started out). I have a storage unit full of staging items that I use for my houses. I pay a stager to meet me at the house after the sellers have followed the guide to the best of their ability.

Presenting Their Home

When the semi-staging is done, I schedule media. I work with Vast Media (the absolute best real estate media company in the Tulsa Metro, hands down!). I am telling you my media rocks! We *always* do professional photos and drone photography. If my listing is over $250,000, I do a Matterport 3D tour and a listing video. One copy of the video is branded and one is not so I can put it on the MLS and Zillow and the other sites. I use the branded video and 3D tour to distribute to buyers through target marketing on social media. Digital marketing is an entirely different topic, but very important. After you have been diligent in getting the house market-ready, now you need to present it to the masses in its absolute best light.

The goal is to *stop the scroll* on social media and to get the most eyes on the property by properly distributing outstanding listing videos. On each branded video I do, I am purposely getting viewers' attention with me in it to stop the scroll and build my brand. In the Tulsa market, I am known for how I market my listings. Agents know when a listing is mine because I have differentiated everything. From the first photo I use on the MLS, to my *Coming Soon* marketing, to my *Just Listed* marketing, to my listing videos, and target ads. What I do gets my sellers' properties in front of a massively larger audience (thanks to Krista's Facebook Ads strategy). You can see this by going to my Facebook page @homesbySabrina or by going to my YouTube channel @ livinginTulsaOklahoma. I have templates that I use for *Coming Soon* and for *Just Listed* that I use on Facebook and Instagram specifically designed to target buyers in my area. Then I use a different format for my YouTube channel that is designed to attract relocation buyers.

In 2020, 2021, and the first part of 2022, agents were not getting homes ready or doing premarketing campaigns. I never stopped doing those things because it didn't serve my seller in the best way. I also knew the market wouldn't stay like that forever so I wanted my community to remember me for my marketing. Now in 2024 as the market has shifted and homes are staying on the market longer because of decreased competition and an affordability problem, I know that the marketing part in my listing process is more important than ever!

Just this last weekend I had a listing go on the market. This house was built in 2021 in an area where we have the largest new construction inventory in the Tulsa Metro. We knew it would be a hard sell because we were going up against brand new construction with builder incentives. So, in a market with a 3.6 months' supply of inventory and an average of 73 days on the market, by using our listing process we got the house under contract within the first three days. This was also during an arctic blast with temperatures in the single digits! Not only that, the price per square foot from this sale would be the second highest in the city in the past six months compared to all the other newer constructed homes that aren't brand new construction. We created that "fear of missing out" through the marketing portion of the listing process and it works!

Again, properly distributing the marketing (meaning making sure you as an agent and your properties are actually being seen) is a whole topic in itself and I won't try to cover it here. Through the digital marketing I learned from Krista, I am getting tens of thousands of eyes on the property and hundreds of hours of watch time from potential buyers! She is a master at digital marketing. In the listing video, I explain the impact of digital marketing using the example of an open house. With an open house you might get a handful of buyers in and a lot of neighbors. But with buyers watching my videos, it can be the equivalent of doing 40 or more open houses with each open house having over 100 people. When you do the stats it is crazy to think about! When Zillow used to show your views compared to similar property views, mine always outranked the competition by gazillions (including massively outranking Zillow) again because of the marketing from the listing process and digital marketing campaigns.

You might be thinking, *I can't afford to do all this.* I didn't integrate a lot of this until I was having more success. But even doing a handful of the things I mentioned, you are going to be leaps and bounds above other agents. You are going to be valuable, you are going to be amazing! People are not going to question your commission because you are *earning* it!

Confidence sells! It doesn't matter if you are just starting out. If you *know* that you can do the best job for your seller, your confidence will show through. By following this process, you will have the confidence to know you are the best choice. My confidence has literally gone through the roof using this. When I show up, I know that I am the best choice because I am not a commodity and doing what everyone else is. In fact, as I talk about things that showcase why I am the best choice, my sellers start to think, *Why isn't anyone else doing this?* And therefore, I win the listing at a full price commission!!!

So again, from start to finish it's about winning the listing and representing the seller by doing things no other agents are doing. By utilizing this process, you can go in with the belief that you are a seller's absolute best choice to get the best price and terms with the least amount of headache. And that you are doing things to sell the property the majority of agents are not doing. What I just shared with you is something that will make you money and make you a better agent.

I think people are put in your life for a reason and Krista Mashore was an absolute godsend to me on a business level, empowerment level, mindset level, freedom level. She is one of my all-time favorite humans and I am blessed to have her as a mentor, a business partner, and a friend. And I can say without a doubt that I would not be where I am now without Krista's coaching. She took me from a new agent to a consistent six-figure earner. My health is better, my friendships are deeper, and I am a better person. And along the way I have found a tribe of agents across the country who are now some of my very best friends. We travel together, share life together, and help each other when we have real estate questions and need life help. I also have access to a huge network of amazing agents throughout the United States for referral business.

Takeaways

1. Don't show up to a listing appointment cold. Give them a ton of value and information before you arrive.

2. Always use quality materials in your listing packet. It will show them the level of quality they can expect from you all through the process.

3. Don't just tell them what you will do. *Show* them through your stats and data, examples of your marketing, your follow-up, your consistency.

4. Don't just give them written information but use lots of videos before you arrive. That way, they'll already feel like they know you and can trust you.

5. Walk in feeling confident that, if you do what I've talked about in this chapter, you will be giving them more value than any other agent.

SABRINA SHAW

Homes By Sabrina - eXp Realty

918-637-7826

SabrinaShaw0102@Gmail.com

Tulsa, Oklahoma

Free Gift: Bonuses
Time To Take Action!

Information alone is not enough. I've put together this **free expert resources member's hub** to help you get started now. Customize the strategies and tactics from this book to *your* business and marketing plan, with guidance, top producer tools and extra trainings.

KristaMashore.com/TopProducer

The Unstoppable Listing Process

by Shanara Carter

In my journey through the challenging landscape of Chicago's real estate market, I've adopted an amazing, unique and highly effective approach to landing listings as taught by my extraordinary coach, Krista Mashore. In using her approach, I also brought in my own personal experiences, especially those early in my career. This approach centers around meticulous preparation and providing customized materials *before* the actual listing presentation. Krista calls it the Unstoppable Listing Process.

This has been a game changer in my career. It is the epitome of "Winning before you arrive!" By offering detailed a marketing plan, insightful guides, and a captivating prelisting marketing video *beforehand*, I set a standard of professionalism and thoroughness that distinctly sets me apart from my competitors.

Let's dip into a little history about me, how I started, and how I began using this process. My early days as a real estate agent were a time marked by some challenging yet transformative experiences. Back then, I was juggling my roles as a buyer's agent, a divorced mother, and a registered nurse. I encountered setbacks that profoundly shaped my professional outlook. Losing listings due to issues like overpricing or property imperfections was disheartening. But these weren't just setbacks, they were invaluable lessons.

I soon realized I did not have the confidence to convince my sellers to respect my opinion and I just agreed with what they wanted. This often led to losing listings even though I had known what they wanted would cause difficulties in getting the home sold. I didn't have the authority to convince them otherwise. These experiences were pivotal, prompting me to seek a new direction and adopt a more structured and confident approach to listings.

In the beginning, I thought my long-term experience as an investor in real estate was enough to set me apart from other agents and give me credibility with sellers. I believe it helped me from a knowledge perspective. However, it was not nearly enough to build my authority with sellers and, trust me, I learned this the hard way. The truth is that losing those listings did more harm than good. It broke my confidence with listings. So, I focused on my buyers, pouring all of my energy into them. I remained scared of listings even during the time that I was in a previous coaching program.

I did not know it then, but I soon discovered through my new amazing coach, Krista Mashore, that I was mired in the "analysis of paralysis." What is insane is that although the Krista Mashore Coaching program provided all the tools I needed to set myself apart, unfortunately the *fear* of listings was still real. I was damaged like people in relationships, afraid of possible rejection and failing again. As you grow, you learn. Failure brings knowledge, strength and perseverance. I realized my competition was not more skilled than I was. They had more experience with listings on their side. But guess what? They did not have this golden process that I learned from Krista!

Today, my method of getting listings is more than a series of business transactions. It's about fostering a conversational and trust-building experience with my clients. I make sure they are thoroughly informed and understand that their best interests are my utmost priority. Incorporating my personal experiences of losing listings into my current strategy of the Unstoppable Listing Process has not only set me apart but also redefined my approach to real estate. It allows me to truly *Serve, Not Sell* while giving personalized service. This process allows me to *win before I arrive*. The value of learning from past experiences, and the ability to adapt and evolve in a dynamic and competitive industry, my friends, is priceless!

Let's dive into the Unstoppable Listing Process and how we make magic happen.

The Initial Call

There are several methods to expand your sphere of influence and generate leads. Let's assume you've been successful and you get a call from a potential client who wants to sell their home. On this initial call, whether it is a warm lead, past client, referral, friend or family member, I am gathering as much information as possible. We know that the initial call is *crucial* before setting the actual listing appointment. It is the perfect opportunity to gather as much information as possible, get to know them better or learn more about their motivation to sell. This process is essential for understanding the seller's needs, expectations, and the specifics of the property. This enables you to tailor your approach and presentation effectively. Here's how I navigate this step and my recommendation of how you might navigate it:

1. Understanding the Seller's Motivation: Begin by asking *why* they are selling. Are they upsizing, downsizing, relocating, or seeking investment opportunities?
2. Property Details: Inquire about the specifics of the property. Even if I sold them the house, I ask them about

any unique features, recent upgrades or renovations, and any known issues. This information will be crucial for preparing the Comparative Market Analysis (CMA) and marketing strategy.

3. Timeline Expectations: Ask about their timeline. Are they looking to sell quickly, or do they have a more flexible schedule? Do we have to find a home before they sell? Will they need to rent back? This information will guide the marketing plan and pricing strategy.

4. Previous Listing Experience: If the property was previously listed, find out what went well and what didn't. This insight can help you avoid past mistakes and leverage successful strategies. Do not talk trash about the previous listing agent! Your expertise and how you handle things moving forward will set you apart. Your client will see it without you getting your hands dirty!

5. Financial Considerations: While delicate, understanding any financial constraints or expectations is important. This includes their thoughts on pricing and seller credits plus any openness to negotiations with potential buyers. This is especially relevant in your work with investors.

6. Preparation for Sale: Discuss any preparations they have made or plan to make before listing. This could include home improvements, staging, or repairs.

7. Expectations from You: Clarify what they are looking for in an agent and their expectations from the selling process. Understanding their expectations can help you effectively communicate and avoid any misunderstandings before they happen.

8. Contact Information and Availability: Ensure you have all necessary contact information, preferences as to *how* they prefer communications (by phone, email, text, etc.) and that you understand their availability for future meetings and communications. Be sure to schedule the

listing appointment on the initial call. This is crucial, and this is also when you notify them that you will be sending them materials (both physically and digitally) to review before you get together.

By thoroughly gathering this information, you not only prepare yourself more effectively for the listing appointment but also demonstrate your professionalism and attention to detail, setting the stage for a successful partnership.

CMA Box

Now that you have scheduled your appointment, it is time to drop off the CMA (Comparative Market Analysis) box. What is a CMA box? Before any appointment, I prioritize delivering my marketing materials to showcase my preparation and commitment, regardless of whether the client is a

> *I view each interaction as a job interview, striving to demonstrate my uniqueness and professionalism.*

referral or a past client. **I view each interaction as a job interview, striving to demonstrate my uniqueness and professionalism.** The irony here is that everything I call marketing materials is in this CMA box (all of which Krista provided and taught me to do), *except* for the actual Comparative Marketing Analysis. Let's briefly describe the amazing tools in this box that help me win before I arrive:

My Marketing Plan: The marketing plan can be in a booklet form or printed and placed in a binder or within a report cover. Either way, it is an invaluable asset in your real estate business, serving as a comprehensive outline of your marketing strategies. Your marketing plan should go far beyond basic videography and photography. It needs to encompass a broad spectrum of your services and unique approaches. This marketing plan is a critical tool for showcasing your value and differentiating you from competitors. It outlines exactly how you intend to market the home, highlighting how the property will be showcased through various channels like online listings, open houses, and social media. The marketing plan showcases what traditional agents do *not* do and how your digital marketing sets you apart from the competition.

The marketing plan includes accolades from former clients, closing stats, neighborhood statistics, and makes comparisons to what typical agents do (which showcases our competitive edge). It also highlights our experience, education, credentials, and other achievements relevant to the specific client and the area. Your marketing plan's importance is amplified in a competitive market. It shows your seller, through evidence of past listings, why they should hire you and why your competitors are not competition at all, despite the length of time they have been in business.

Seller's Guide: The Seller's Guide and the What to Expect While You're Listing guide is an invaluable resource for homeowners looking to navigate the complexities of selling their property. It offers a comprehensive overview of the selling process, starting with the preparation of the home for sale, including tips on staging and necessary repairs or improvements plus tips on curb appeal. The guide also outlines the importance of pricing the property correctly, utilizing market analysis and competitive pricing strategies. It also educates sellers on the legal and financial aspects of the sale, including understanding the terms of the contract, negotiations, and closing procedures.

Finally, it provides insights into the roles and responsibilities of the real estate agent, emphasizing the importance of communication and collaboration throughout the selling journey. This guide serves as a roadmap, ensuring sellers are well-informed and prepared for each step of the process, ultimately aiming to make the sale as smooth and successful as possible.

Personal Touches: In the competitive realm of real estate, standing out is crucial. That's why, in addition to a comprehensive suite of marketing materials, I include a touch of personal flair in my custom, personalized CMA box. This box not only serves as a tangible representation of my commitment to each client, but it also contains carefully selected swag items that leave a lasting impression. Among these are personalized pens from my attorney's office, symbolizing professionalism and attention to detail. There's also a custom bag embedded with my logo, serving as a constant reminder of my brand. Perhaps the most delightful surprise is the custom personalized lip balm—a small but thoughtful token that resonates well with clients. These items, while seemingly minor, contribute significantly to a memorable experience, enhancing client perception and setting me apart in the highly competitive real estate market.

Examples: My CMA box includes examples of Just Listed cards, flyers, and postcards to demonstrate the high quality of our materials and to highlight our distinctiveness from other agents. Here we showcase previous listings that received drone photography, 360 tours and complimentary basic staging.

I've also embraced the power of free resources to enhance my marketing efforts, one of which is List Reports. This platform has been a game changer for me, particularly because I'm connected with a lender, granting me access to an even wider array of resources. The platform provides detailed information about local schools, parks, restaurants, and other amenities, enriching my presentations and demonstrating my thoroughness and attention to detail. I use these to create personalized marketing pieces that not only highlight the property itself but also its surroundings, including nearby medical facilities, ATMs, gas stations, coffee shops, gyms, pharmacies, grocery stores, and movie theaters.

Seller Homework: Another valuable asset that I got from Krista is the Seller Homework document which is a comprehensive checklist designed to streamline the listing process for homeowners preparing to sell their property. Yes, I give my sellers homework. The Seller's Homework: A Key Tool in the Listing Process is given *before* the listing goes live. It's crucial for sellers to prepare certain items. This checklist ensures that all necessary details are in place, contributing significantly to a successful listing. The list includes details such as:

1. Key Copies: Providing two copies of the front door key and any other keys for areas like storage sheds.
2. Family Information: Details of family members' birthdays and anniversaries, if relevant.
3. Alarm and Showing Instructions: Instructions for the home alarm system and any specific showing instructions for agents, such as advance notice requirements or pet instructions.

Additionally, sellers are requested to complete several documents available in their packet:

1. Excitement List: Highlighting the unique features of each room.
2. Room-By-Room Marketing Form: Detailing the specifics and appeal of each area in the house.
3. Neighborhood Hot Spots List: Showcasing local attractions and amenities.
4. Utility Information Data and Provider List: Providing essential utility details.
5. Review of Showing Instructions: Ensuring clear communication on how the property should be shown.

The checklist is very detailed (Hardwood floors or laminate? Gas or wood fireplace? etc.). It covers things like upgrades as well as what is and is not included with the home so we can market it properly. This allows us to get the seller's personal experience and connection with the home, such as their favorite feature of the house, the best aspects of its location, and any upgrades or renovations they have done. The Seller Homework is more than just a checklist. It not only streamlines the listing process but also ensures that the unique characteristics and strengths of the property are effectively communicated. It's a strategic tool you can use to transform a listing into a compelling narrative, enhancing its appeal to potential buyers.

Listing Presentation Marketing Video: This is probably the most important piece of my listing process and I credit this video alone for my success in winning listings almost every single time. Krista put this video together to showcase all of the unique things we do to market and highlight their home. And here's the kicker: to highlight all of the amazing things, you have to be trained in the highly comprehensive digital marketing strategy that she taught us. An agent could try to emulate that video, but it would be impossible without the experience and education on how to do it. Clients are encouraged to watch a listing video *prior* to my arrival, further establishing my dedication and distinct approach. A personalized QR code in the CMA box directs them to the video and I can see if they have watched the video and the length of time they spent with it.

When I drop off the CMA box prior to the listing appointment, I send a video text message while still in front of their home. I detail the importance of reviewing the materials in the CMA box as well as watching the listing presentation marketing video in its entirety. This is a very important step to the pre-appointment strategy which is designed by Krista to create a positive impression even before I walk through the door (Win Before You Arrive). I also follow the professional practice of making a phone call the day before our meeting as a friendly reminder and to confirm they have reviewed the materials. This not only reinforces the appointment but also contributes to building a professional image. All of these steps are in my CRM, the Mashore Method.

At the Listing Appointment

I avoid sending the Comparative Market Analysis in my CMA box beforehand, instead choosing to deliver it in person during the appointment. The CMA has a personalized letter attached as well as a Strategy for Pricing and Selling handout on one page with details of all the amazing services they will receive. The CMA itself is presented on high-quality paper with high-quality materials, including colored brochures and detailed information like the absorption rate, which reflects the pace of the real estate market in the client's area. This comprehensive approach ensures clients are well-informed and impressed by the level of detail and professionalism I bring to the table. I do not want them to be discouraged by the value in the CMA. In addition, I do not want another agent to get the seller to sign because they offered a higher listing price.

With this Unstoppable Listing Process, I establish a strong presence by ensuring I stand out from the start. My goal is always to position myself distinctively in the market, and these strategies have proven effective in setting me apart from the competition. This facet of my approach is not merely a business tactic. It's a reflection of my commitment to nurturing long-term relationships and valuing sustained partnerships over short-term financial gains. This practice has earned me respect and a strong network of loyal clients.

Prior to Krista's program and utilizing the Unstoppable Listing Process, I primarily worked with buyers. Now, my business has shifted, and I primarily work with sellers. This process has given me a competitive advantage that I didn't even think was possible. The thought process behind it and the way all of these materials are systematically designed to convert uncertain prospects into eager clients has been a complete game changer in my business. I am no longer just another agent, a commodity. With this process, I am seen as the authority and expert, and I literally have no competition. And the best part is that the "commission" conversation rarely comes up. It's more like, "Where do we sign? You're our girl."

Takeaways

1. With the Unstoppable Listing Process, you actually win the listing before you even go to the listing appointment!

2. Every interaction with a prospective client, from the initial call to the listing appointment itself, should be treated as an interview.

3. By preparing all the materials in the CMA box in advance, clients gain confidence in you and your authority. It also helps you gain confidence in yourself!

4. Your CMA box materials should all be high quality and should reflect how you are distinctive from your competitors.

SHANARA CARTER
At Home with Shanara - eXp Realty

312-219-3200
AtHomeWithShanara@Gmail.com
Chicago, Illinois

How to Own a Neighborhood with the CMA Drop-Off Process

by Joe Seamon

In this chapter, I'm going to go into detail about one of the processes I learned in Krista Mashore Coaching (KMC) that has made a tremendous difference in my business. Recently I did the math and within a 12-month timeframe, we got 48 listings between April of 2022 to May of 2023, practically 1 listing per week all from the process I'm about to share. I'm not saying that by doing this one thing you will all of a sudden have a ton of business. No, that's not how it works. You need to do videos and distribute them correctly on social media. (My latest TikTok has 5 million views on it!) You need to get your mindset strong and be accountable every day. You need to have a good CRM (client relationship management system), etc., etc., etc. That said, the Comparative Market Analysis (CMA) drop-off process I learned from Krista is one of the most powerful tools in my toolbox. It could be in yours, too. (By the way, I know that a bunch of other coaches have copied it and started teaching this since Krista came up with it three years ago. But she's the first one who originally created it and continues to improve on it.)

I'm a real estate agent in the Augusta, Georgia/Aiken, South Carolina market. Yes, two states and two different real estate licenses. I have enjoyed (almost) every second of real estate since I began in March of 2018. And on average over the last three years, I have sold 200 homes a year—all from being a part of Krista's coaching group.

I came into real estate in 2018 and was very excited to jump in with both feet. I ended up joining a team but three months in, I realized that the team and I were not the best match. After leaving the team, I didn't do much business. All in all, I had sold eight homes total and made a whopping $11,000 the whole year of 2018. I was really questioning, "Is real estate really the right path for me to go down?" I've got a degree in accounting and a minor in marketing and small business management, so I started applying for corporate jobs. Every corner I turned I just struck out. Offers were not coming in. I passed out literally over a hundred resumes trying to find a job.

In late 2018, a friend of mine called and asked if I was still doing real estate. Of course, my answer was, "Yes, I'm still in real estate. What can I help you with?" He said that he and his wife were interested in selling their house. I immediately jumped into action and set an appointment for the very next day. I had never been on a listing appointment. I met with my broker, and she helped me pull some comps and actually pull together a listing presentation.

I won that listing and we ended up closing it in early 2019. 2018 had been a very rough year, but that first closing in 2019 allowed me to see that there was actual light at the end of the tunnel and that this real estate gig might not be such a bad thing. In 2019, I ended up closing 54 homes. It was still a rough year financially for my wife and me. We have four kids at home and the money we made in 2019 mainly helped us catch up from 2018. Then in 2020, I ended up selling 113 homes.

The business just kept growing and growing. Being in marketing, I knew that in every market there are cycles. That's taught on day one of every marketing class. No matter what industry you're in, you're going to have cycles. I knew that 2020 and 2021 were such great years of real estate that the cycle had to slow down at some point. I was on a high in 2021 and I had joined different coaching groups. Every coaching group was great, but I just felt like there were so many different pieces missing. Myself, I'm a processes and systems guy. I was trying to find a coaching group, a platform that just had everything in it. I didn't see it. Again, these other coaching groups are great, but they were very pieced together.

I ended up coming across Krista Mashore's coaching group (KMC). I found her (or rather she targeted me) on Facebook. I ended up going to a three-day event that Krista presented and signed up right after the event. That was in September of 2021. That was when the real estate industry was just booming. You put a house on the market and four hours later it was under contract.

That year I ended up selling close to 200 homes. Even though I was selling a lot of homes, I still felt the need for coaching. After Krista's event, I realized that she is giving way more than just the tactical things that the other coaching groups were giving. I realized, "Hey, this is going to be an investment." It was a little scary for me to do, but I just felt very sure and very confident that this is what I needed to do.

There are so many pieces to the KMC coaching group, and it is the most robust real estate system you will ever come across. Krista is constantly adding to the coaching group and the coaching platform. By November, I was trying to keep up with my current business, my family, my sellers and buyers, and trying to go through Krista's program. By November, I was ready to just hang it up because it was a lot to take on. I felt like I was going back to school and getting my master's degree in real estate and digital marketing (which, if you go through the KMC program, is essentially what you're doing). I was overwhelmed.

In KMC, you are assigned an accountability coach. I would meet with my accountability coach, and she would be behind me pushing and pushing. "Joe, do the videos. Joe, all I'm hearing are excuses. Joe, everyone is busy. Joe, just do the system. It works." And so, I had a meeting with my family. I sat them down at dinner one day and said, "Hey, Dad is essentially going back to school and so I'm going to need y'all to understand that I am going to be doing this coursework. I may be up in the office on my computer early in the mornings and I may be on my computer up in the office late at night. I just need that time and I need y'all to understand that I am basically going back to school to make our business better, to just make it an ironclad business." My kids and my wife understood and supported me fully in it. I am so glad that we had that meeting and that I stuck with it and that my accountability coach through KMC was behind me pushing the whole time. Had I not had the accountability and the coaching group, I do not think that we would be where we are today.

So today, fast forward two years, two and a half years, I'm still part of the coaching group. I still love to contribute greatly to the coaching group and through it we have just been able to add different things and systems and pieces to the group that no other real estate agent in my area or in my region is even coming close to. This is absolutely setting us so far apart from the average real estate agent that it isn't even funny. We have local real estate agents coming to me almost daily. "What are you doing? How can I do what you're doing? I don't understand how you're doing so much."

Out of the average 200 homes we sell a year, we list about a hundred homes. I run a small team now and currently we have myself and five agents (3 full-time and 2 part-time) plus a few administrative people. I'm still about 80% of our production. Out of 200 homes, I still sell about 160 of them myself every year. It is doable to sell that many homes by yourself if you put the work towards it and have the right systems in place.

Your Typical CMA

Okay, so I think all real estate agents use CMAs. A CMA is a *comparative market analysis* that estimates a home's price based on recently sold similar properties in the immediate area. Real estate agents and brokers create CMA reports to help sellers set the listing price for their homes and help buyers make competitive offers. Typically, when a seller calls wanting to know the value of their home, an agent prepares a CMA and shoots it off to them or tries to set up a meeting to bring the CMA to them. Not much effort to it—and not much impact either.

What we have implemented and strategized and created is a system of CMA drop-offs based on what Krista taught us. These are *unsolicited* CMAs that we prepare for certain neighborhoods or farm areas. And it's not just a one-time drop-off. It's a specific series in a specific sequence. It keeps you top of mind for people in that neighborhood. If someone is thinking about selling, you want to be the agent always dropping something off, always giving value, always in front of them with something about their home or their property or what they can do to update or upgrade or spring tips or something like that. You also do this to get people who are just thinking, *Hey, I may have this much equity in my home, and it may be time to sell.* You always want to be in front of those people because typically they start thinking about selling six to nine months prior to actually calling a real estate agent or thinking about selling. You want to be that agent in front of them six to nine months before they even think about selling. There's an old saying in the business that "you need listings to last." That's why the CMA drop-off system is so imperative. Over the last 3-4 years, having lots of listings has sustained our business.

Start with Your Farm and Your Ideal Client

To begin, you need to think about the areas you want to farm. What areas does your Ideal Client want to live in? My particular Ideal Client is a move up family, a family that has a husband and wife with one to five kids who are moving up from a three or four-bedroom and now need a four to six-bedroom. With that, typically we end up listing their starter home. My second Ideal Client is a first-time home buyer. So, they fit hand in hand. My team and I farm an area of over 3000 homes, and we have gotten many, many, many listings off of our CMA process. This year, 2024, is going to be off the chain! We have dropped off over 3,000 CMAs in the past six months and I'm going on 2-3 listing appointments a week!

Create Your CMA

Once you've figured out your farm area, you need to create a CMA. We create CMAs through Realtors Property Resource® (RPR) from the NAR or through Cloud CMA. RPR and Cloud CMA are just two programs that make it very easy to create a neighborhood CMA. If you don't have access to either one of those, you can do your own homework and create a CMA using your MLS. It'll take a little bit more time, but it is doable.

Please note: **You never ever, ever, ever want to give someone a personal property value without standing in front of them.** That is why we create neighborhood CMAs with average and median home prices for that particular neighborhood. The CMA we drop off is about eight pages, including the sheets that we create plus the pages that come off of Real Property Reports.

> *You never ever, ever, ever want to give someone a personal property value without standing in front of them.*

Our neighborhood CMA is 8 ½" by 11" with a cover on the top and a cover on the back. The very first cover page has my team's logo at the very top and the title of the cover page is *"Curious about your home's value?"* Then it says *"Scan me now"* with a huge arrow pointing to a QR code that leads to our funnel that we created through Krista Mashore Coaching. The cover page also has a picture of me, my brokerage and some accolades that I've been able to achieve over the last six years.

Page two is a letter to the homeowner which says, *"I'm sure you've been hearing all the buzz around the craziness of the real estate market and if you're anything like me, you may be curious how all the real estate news affects your property's value."* Then the next three short paragraphs go on to explain that I am giving them a free CMA, which is a comparative market analysis, and that home buyers do a lot of shopping by comparison. *"In today's market it's very important to price your home right and to get it show-ready."*

The last paragraph of the letter says, *"This is a very condensed copy of my personal marketing plan. I can absolutely give you a free copy of my 14-page marketing plan and my 28-page seller's guide."* The very last sentence says, *"My goal is to help you sell your home quickly and at fair market value. I look forward to meeting you soon and hearing how I can help you accomplish your goals."* And then I personally sign it in blue ink.

The next page is tips for selling your home with eight suggestions. We have a little block that explains how these will help you sell your home. Then some more accolades down at the bottom.

Next comes the CMA itself. We use the one right off of RPR. There's a tab on RPR that you can hit and run a neighborhood CMA. It's about eight or nine pages and we take out four or five pages of it. It's all neighborhood stats and charts. It shows median estimated home value, estimated home values, 12-month change, median list price, percentage of own versus rent, the median home age price range of comps sold.

Price per square foot of comps sold is on the next page of the neighborhood CMA. Then it gives some area stats like the population density per square mile population change, the median age, then the male-to-female ratio. Then it gives more information on the size of home sold, the age range of comp sold, number of bedrooms in the neighborhood sold and population of children by group, population of adults by group, so on and so forth. It just gives a lot of information but *nothing* specific to the property address. That comes at a later stage.

Drop-Off #1: The CMA

In the first step of this six-month strategy, we go and door-knock each property and drop these CMAs off. Now 90% of the homeowners in our area are not typically home. We rarely get someone to come to the door, but when we do, that is a really great conversation for us. We're able to provide them with something of value, the CMA. If they are not home, we drop it off in a plain 11 ½" by 15" cellophane bag. The CMA fits nicely in here and we will drop some kind of trinket (a notepad or a refrigerator calendar magnet for the year or a pen or stickers, any of our branded stuff). We then hang the bag on their door.

After this first step, we know the addresses of the CMA drop-off area. We know who we've been able to talk to, and we know who we left a bag for. We wait four weeks before we send out the next piece.

Postcard #1

Step number two is sending out postcards (so you're not having to door-knock every single time). We mail a 6" by 9 ½" big glossy postcard that says, "What's your home worth?" It has a picture of me and a big QR code that says, "Scan me." This QR code goes to our home valuation funnel. Once they scan that code and they put their information in, they're dropped into our home valuation funnel. I get an email and I'm alerted that "Bob Jones at 123 Main Street would like a home valuation." The back of the postcard says, "What our clients are saying about us" with a well-written testimonial from one of our previous clients.

Drop-Off #2: Seller's Guide

After we mail that postcard, we wait another four weeks before we do anything else. Then we go back into the neighborhood door-knocking again. I don't know that we have ever had the same person answer the door twice. Typically, we get a whole different round of people that answer the door. A great tip is to do this on the weekends because you will catch more people then. As you're door-knocking, be sure to have the mindset that you are *providing value*. You are not being a nuisance. You are not just giving junk. You are absolutely providing value to these homeowners because everyone is interested in real estate. Everyone wants to know what their home is worth. You're providing value as the local real estate agent expert. You're providing value as to what their home is worth.

This time we drop off an eight-page little booklet. We have taken all of these pages right out of our seller's guide and just made a smaller booklet with a snippet out of our seller's guide. The very first page is "Meet Your Agent." You want to keep saying that "I'm your agent, meet your agent, I am your agent." Subconsciously, this ingrains in that potential seller's mind, "Oh, Joe is my agent. Mary is my agent. Krista is my agent." This page gives a short little bio of who I am, who my family is, and a picture of me. The second page of this booklet is the strategy for pricing and selling. As one of Krista's students, you can get this right off of Krista's Canva and it is chock full of information on our strategy on timing, preparing pricing, marketing, negotiating, disclosure, and showing to get your house sold. Pages number three and four show the four stages of selling your home, also straight off of Krista's Canva link.

Page number five is "Before You List" tips. Again, this is right out of the seller's guide which is 28-pages. We condensed this down to a little mini seller's guide to be only eight pages. Page number six is "Enhancing Your Home Interior/Exterior" tips. Pages number seven and eight is a "Prep Your Home for Photographs" checklist.

We print these and bind them to make a nice little booklet. We put them in the nice white cellophane bag if they're not home and we hang it right on the door.

Postcard #2

We are on step number four. After dropping off the "Meet Your Agent" booklet, we wait four more weeks then send out another 6" by 9 ½" glossy postcard. People ask me all the time, "Do you think it's worth the extra money to send the big postcard out compared to a smaller postcard?" Absolutely! Always, always send out the bigger postcard! If I could find an 8 ½" by 11" postcard, I absolutely would send that out. The 6" by 9 ½" absolutely is a much bigger attention grabber. You want to grab people's attention when they're pulling it out of their mailbox.

By now we're 12 weeks into the 6 month program. For the front of this second postcard, we have "Is your Z-estimate correct?" I didn't want to get in trouble with Zillow, so we say, "Is your Z-estimate correct?" By now as you're marketing to these homeowners, they've probably looked up their home's value on the big national websites. This postcard is created to plant that little seed of doubt: "Is my Z-estimate correct or do I need to get a local's opinion of what my home's value is?"

This postcard shows one of the houses that I've sold in the background with me in the forefront and my website. Then it's got a big QR code that says, *"Scan the QR code for your home's value. Joe Seaman 803-270-7583."* On the back of this postcard is another testimonial, somebody different than the first postcard. Using testimonials is social proof that people are using you and giving you reviews. You also want to show that people are reviewing you on Google because if someone is thinking about using you, they're probably going to look you up on social media and Google. They'll see that, "Oh, so-and-so did leave Joe a Google review, and this is a true review that's on the back of his postcard."

Drop-Off #3: Stats and Tips

Step number five can be optional. We use pieces of our marketing plan typically showing how many views we get on social media. One of my TikToks is at 1.3 million views right now. One of our sponsored Facebook ads is at over 140,000 views (because we learned how to distribute it properly through Krista). We use that as social proof that we are who we say we are. We also drop off something that fits whatever time of year it is, like tips for getting ready for Spring or summer. In Fall you might give high school football schedules or baseball schedules in Spring. All of it should be on glossy paper or laminated or put it in a little booklet or a brochure. Again, we're going back around door-knocking and if they're not home, we leave it on their doorknob in a cellophane bag.

Postcard #3

We wait four weeks, and we send our last glossy 6" by 9 ½" postcard. At the very top, it says, *"Free, no obligation, no pressure home valuation. Scan the QR code for your home's value."* On the back, we have another 5-star review.

If you don't have a home valuation funnel ready, you need to have your QR code to go to some type of Google form that emails you whenever someone scans it and requests value. Ours goes to our home valuation funnel so the homeowner will drop into our CRM and can work their way through the funnel with all the videos. If they are going through the videos in your funnel, more than likely they are a pretty serious seller.

CMA Box Drop-Off

Once I get that alert that someone has requested a home valuation from our CMA drop-off efforts, I stop everything I'm doing. Whenever I get that email or text that *"Bob Smith at 123 Main Street is requesting a home valuation,"* I look at it as though he raised his hand and wanted more information about his home's value.

I immediately go to my office and call Bob Smith to talk to him about his home's value and set a listing appointment for me to come by for us to discuss his home's value. Typically, that appointment is two days to a week later. Right after getting off the phone with Bob Smith, I get a CMA box ready and take it to his house to drop it off (thank you Krista for this amazing step by step and plug and play blueprint).

So, what is in the CMA box? It's a beautifully printed box inside and out, very glossy, high quality. My particular CMA box measures 10" wide, 12" long by 2" inches deep. On the very top, it is big and bold with a beautiful, translucent picture of the interior of a home with big, bold words on top of it: "Who you work with matters." Along the sides of this box is our website, some information about me, and where you can find us on social media. It also has another QR code on the bottom that says, "What's my home's value?"

When you open the CMA box, the top has more about our team and a little bit of bio about who we are. In the very bottom of the box, we have even more Google reviews for them to look at and read. Social proof, social proof, social proof! You want those reviews. You want the homeowner to know that you are who you say you are, and that other people are using you. I don't think you can ever have too many reviews in the CMA box or in any kind of marketing material.

The very first thing that we put in the box is our full 28-page home seller's guide. We also have our 14-page marketing plan, which is an 8 ½" by 11" magazine-quality booklet. Every page is glossy and has a very nice texture to it. Then we give them examples of our "Just Listed," "Under Contract" and "Just Sold" postcards. These are also 6" by 9 ½" with a lot of testimonials on them. We give them an example of the full-color brochures that we put in each home after we list it. All of these are showing them what we do for marketing and proof that we really do it.

These are all materials I got from being a part of Krista's coaching program. The thing that makes them so good is that they are strategically crafted and designed to elevate my authority, show how different and unique I am. So, I'm showcasing the unique digital marketing abilities that I learned from being in Krista's coaching program. We also put the book that I co-authored with Krista in there. And, of course, some of our branded little trinkety stuff. I will also put another copy of the neighborhood CMA in that box.

When the box is ready, I immediately take it over to Bob Smith's house at 123 Main Street. If he's home, great. If he's not, I leave it on the porch and will immediately video text him to say, *"Hey Bob, I know our appointment is not until four days down the road, but I just wanted you to know that I dropped you off something and left it on your porch. And just by reference, I want you to make sure if you're interviewing other agents, that they are an author like I am and are able to provide you with the materials that I have provided you with prior to our listing appointment."* This creates a win before you even arrive to the listing appointment. This is such an absolutely strong tactic that when we use it, I don't even have to hardly go through the listing presentation. I do just because it is a service that we provide. But it's almost like the seller has made their mind up before I even get there.

Does It Work?

I've got many stories of how this particular system of CMA drop-off and CMA box drop-off with all the materials in them have worked. In one example, I was up against three other agents for a listing that was in my farm area. The seller called me up and said, "Hey Joe, you don't really know us, but we're looking to sell our home. We would like to interview you." She was very transparent and upfront with me and said, "Just so you know, we are interviewing three other agents and these are the agents that we're interviewing, [XYZ]."

What did I do? Immediately, I stopped everything I was doing. Nothing else in the world mattered at that point. I got a CMA box together, pulled together a neighborhood CMA, got all my trinkets, the seller's guide, the marketing plan, the book, the magazine, the notepads, everything was in the box.

I went to the house and knocked on the door. They happened to be home. I said, "Ms. Smith, I know our appointment isn't until Friday, but I just wanted to give you this CMA box. I wanted to drop this box off to you and your husband. I want y'all to look through the information. And as you're interviewing these other agents, I just want you to know that they need to be compared to everything that I do.

"You want to make sure that they have a seller's guide. You want to make sure that they're able to give you their marketing plan. You want to make sure that they are a true legit author and that they are going to do your house a service and not a disservice. Just look through my stuff and I will see y'all on Friday."

So, a few days went by and our appointment time came up. I went to the house. I gave my listing presentation. I knew that one agent was going to be a low-commission listing just because that's who she is. I wasn't sure what the other two charge for commission, but I knew out of all four of us, I charge more commission than most agents do in my area. And so, through this interview, I let them know that I am probably *not* going to be the cheapest in commission.

But we didn't discuss that. We discussed how to price their home. We discussed how we were going to market their home. They had it all in the box with proof of how we were going to accomplish all of that.

I called the seller the next day. She said they hadn't made up their mind. I called her the following day. She said, "Yes, we've made our minds and we're going to go with you."

So, I asked her, "Why did you pick me? Because I know I was charging more commission than the other three." She agreed that I was the highest in commission, but she felt it was worth the extra commission dollars for everything that I was doing because no other agent came prepared with a marketing plan or anything else that I did prior to even going on the listing appointment. Now that's "winning before you arrive!"

No other agent came prepared with a bound CMA. No other agent came prepared with a seller's guide. No other agent was an author. No other agent dropped a CMA box off. No other agent did the legwork that I did *prior* to the listing appointment. And that's what allowed us to win that listing. I ended up double-siding that listing and bringing the buyer, and we sold it for more than list price and closed on it within 30 days. That is just one of the many, many stories that I could tell of how the CMA drop-off process works. However, I say this about everything: it only works if you work it.

The Complete Package

The thing is, you can't just say, "Okay, I'm going to start implementing the CMA drop-off process," and you all of a sudden have all this business. No, that's not how it works. I've learned from Krista that you have to do everything: videos, social media, paid ads, strategic digital marketing, etc., etc. People ask me all the time, "I'm a brand new agent. What's one thing I need to be working on?" My response is that you have to do *everything* to make it work. The process I've shown you is just one piece of what is going to set you apart in the real estate world. It works for us. I know it will work for you too if you implement it the correct way.

The other thing I've learned at KMC is that a big piece of the puzzle is mindset. It's not just the tactics that will get you there. You also need a strong mindset. We have tried to think of different ways to say it because mindset sounds so cliché, but there is just no other word for it. I just love the mindset piece of the coaching group and Krista is a master at it. Having a great mindset is needed in our industry because the work can get very lonely sometimes. It's very easy to compare yourself to other agents in your area or other agents across the country. "I'm not doing as much as they are. How do they get so much business? Why do they sell all the big, beautiful houses and I'm selling all the little rinky-dink things?" Krista has a way to absolutely help you change your mindset whenever you get stuck in one of those ruts. I love her mindset calls and she's always bringing in top-of-the-line guest speakers to come to her summits and train us and to feed us what she has been fed.

When Krista teaches us something, I try to implement it fairly quickly. Through implementation and the coaching group, our business has absolutely soared above any other real estate agent in my area. I am the number one agent in my town, in my brokerage, and I am aiming towards being the top agent in our area. Through this coaching group I know for a fact that I will get there, and it will not be too much longer before I get to the number one spot.

Takeaways

1. A typical CMA doesn't do much for your business. But creating a great CMA process with all the bells and whistles and using it strategically is what makes you crush the competition.

2. Start the CMA process by knowing your farm and who your Ideal Client is.

3. When you're dropping off material and knocking on doors, make sure to do it knowing that you are providing service, not pestering people.

4. Never give a homeowner a specific value of their home if you aren't face-to-face.

5. The CMA drop-off process will let your farm know that you are the area expert. It will also keep you top of mind with them.

JOE SEAMON
The JProperties Group
Brokered by Meybohm Real Estate

📞 803-270-7583
✉ JoeSeamon11@Gmail.com
📍 North Augusta, South Carolina

SCAN ME

**Free Gift: Bonuses
Time To Take Action!**

Information alone is not enough. I've put together this **free expert resources member's hub** to help you get started now. Customize the strategies and tactics from this book to *your* business and marketing plan, with guidance, top producer tools and extra trainings.

KristaMashore.com/TopProducer

How a New Agent Can Crush It

by Haley Jones

In this chapter, I want to show you how a rookie agent can go from closing on only 8 transactions per year to doing 53 transactions per year less than four years later. I know it can happen because that's what I did. And if I can do it, you can too, whether you're new to the industry or have been in real estate for many years.

Prior to getting into real estate, I had been a successful high school math teacher, instructional coach and district-level leader. My aspiration was to eventually become a school superintendent and change the face of education. However, over time and after working at the district level on major education projects, it became abundantly clear that that world had become way too political. I left daily feeling angry, and that is *not* how I wanted to live life. Long story short, I had thought about becoming a real estate agent for a long time and finally just decided to go for it and got my license in March of 2020.

As a new agent, I felt completely overwhelmed and frankly terrified. I was so worried that I would mess up the biggest purchase or sale of someone's life! I started reading books and taking as many additional classes as I could. I felt absolutely desperate to understand what I was doing and how I could best serve my clients. This led me to a small real estate conference in DC. There were several speakers at the event, and one of them was Krista Mashore.

From the stage she was this giant ball of energy, and I was completely locked in. I vividly remember her talking about how to essentially use videos and ads to follow people online and how to show up in front of them over and over again. This sounds completely insane, but that night I was buzzing. I could not sleep. I knew I had to figure out a way to work with her. I returned home from the conference and signed up. I had literally no idea how I would pay for it, but I just knew I had to learn from her. I was basically a brand new agent when I decided to join Krista's coaching program. I had gotten my license in March of 2020 and enrolled in Krista's mastery program in November. Here is the timeline of what happened:

March 2020: Got my real estate license.

March to November 2020: Closed 3 transactions.

November 2020: Joined Krista's coaching program.

December 2020: Started running monthly marketing campaigns including ad spend through Facebook.

Year 1 in real estate (March 2020 to March 2021): Closed 8 transactions (started working with Krista and running ads about 7-8 months into that first year).

Year 2: Closed 33 transactions.

Year 3: Closed 44 transactions.

Year 4: Closed 53 transactions. (Note that in years 3 and 4, interest rates were high, inventory was low, and most real estate agents were *not* doing well.)

Obviously, working with Krista had a HUGE impact on my business and my ability to grow my business and serve more people. How?

Step by Step Guide to Getting Started

First off, I was able to learn exactly what to do every day to grow my business. Before I met Krista when I first started as an agent, I had signed on with a "coach" at my brokerage for my first several transactions. She helped me to know how to go about transactions in general, but when it came to what I needed to actually do every day, there was not a ton of guidance. I remember I got handed a "First 30 Days in Real Estate" calendar and it went something like this:

Week 1: Call 50 people, host 1 open house, pass out 100 flyers about the open house.

Week 2: Call 100 people, host 2 open houses, pass out 100 flyers about each of the open houses.

Week 3: Call 150 people, including everyone you have met at the open houses, host 3 open houses, pass out 100 flyers about tech for the open houses...

Week 4: Okay, so you get the idea. By Week 10, was I supposed to call 450 people and host 10 open houses?!?

This seemed... dumb. But I was desperate, so I did it. During the first two weeks while walking neighborhoods, I kept thinking, *Is walking to mailbox after mailbox really the best use of my time?* All the while, I posted homes on social media and did live home tours each week on my social media as well. That seemed to have more reach, especially to people that knew me, but gaining momentum felt so *s....l....o....w...*!!!!

Fast forward to beginning to work with Krista. From the very start, I had some immediate wins, and most importantly, I knew *specifically* what to do every day. I know this step-by-step guidance made a HUGE difference for me as a new agent. But I've also heard my experienced colleagues in the program say that it's been critical for them too. Here are the first things I've learned to do each day and week to grow my business:

Video Text Messages

One of the first things we were taught to do is to reach out to 10 people every single day via video text. We could video text Facebook friends on their birthdays and anniversaries. Rather than leaving comments on people's posts when they had something to celebrate, we send them a video text. Rather than commenting directly on people's social media posts who were looking for a recommendation, we reach out to them directly via video text. We were taught to just video text anyone that pops in our mind and just say "hi." When you send a video text message, you want it to be personalized. Say their name, and *don't* ask for business or referrals. It's just a friendly check-in, but it reminds them of you. They'll remember that you are in business and they'll think about giving you referrals. The more you do this, the easier it gets to know which 10 people to message. Video texting becomes easy because you become so used to doing it that your brain gets on board and you just do it.

Daily Sheet

The beauty of doing the Daily Sheet every day is that it not only helps you focus, but it also helps you acknowledge what is going well. It is *very* easy to focus on the feeling that you are not doing enough. Using the Daily Sheet has helped to transform my mindset around being/doing enough. It has shifted me so that I now celebrate and acknowledge wins. The Daily Sheet includes:

- Daily Quote/Affirmation
- 6 top things you need to focus on and accomplish the following day
- Naming your wins
- Things that you are grateful for

(To get your own copy of the Daily Sheet, go to **KristaMashore.com/TopProducer**)

Video and Plan Monthly Marketing Campaigns

#1 Decide on your content: Videos are absolute GOLD. Many people join Krista's programs and do not make videos for a while. That is a mistake. As Krista always says, "Do it now!" And the monthly marketing campaigns literally changed the game for me when it came to knowing what to say and how to say it. Because I was doing the monthly marketing campaigns, I was up to date on national and local real estate market data, which meant that when people asked me what was happening, I knew exactly what to tell them. Period. These monthly marketing campaigns are not just about making the videos. They are about *how* to talk about real estate. As a new agent, this helped my confidence soar!

#2 Edit scripts and press record: I already knew how to edit so I actually edited mine myself for a while until I was ready to hire an editor. Krista advises hiring an editor and I agree. Looking back, despite knowing how to edit, I could have better spent my time repurposing content that was already edited rather than actually editing raw footage.

Skin in the Game

Skin in the Game is a call you get on every morning with other agents in the program. On the call, we each make one personal and one business commitment. It can be something like "Today I commit to working on my marketing video for at least 30 minutes, and I also commit to exercising for 45 minutes." We focus on being well-rounded human beings, not just business. The primary purpose of Skin in the Game is to help you hold yourself accountable and commit to action. But it has a lot of other benefits as well. For one thing, you get to grow your network of like-minded agents. Through my Krista Mashore network, I have closed over 10 deals in the past three years in the program, one of which was my biggest transaction to date!

Skin in the Game is also a gold mine for great ideas from others including ideas around client closing gifts, past client reachouts and value adds, how to partner with local businesses, etc. The sky is literally the limit here. Another benefit is that it encourages you to up your game. When you get on this call and hear people say, "Yesterday I did what I committed to, and today I commit to [XYZ]," coupled with hearing their wins, you learn very quickly to take action, build momentum, and get results. When the people you most admire are getting stuff done, you don't (or at least *I* don't) want to be the "loser" on the call that didn't follow through with your (my) commitments.

Video Repurpose

Once you are making content consistently, now you want to get the most out of it across multiple platforms. Learning through Krista helped me to set a vision for this on my own content. This is something I continually do and remind myself as Krista says, "It's about getting views while you snooze." Basically, the more placements I make and the more people I reach through content, the better. Just like video text messages, repurposing content is an example of a "low-hanging fruit" type action and is something I can always be doing that moves the needle of my business forward.

Weekly Krista Calls

I love these calls! They provide a ton of value and ideas on things I can take action on. Most importantly these calls serve as anchors for the week. The whole spirit of working with and learning from Krista is a "do it now" mentality. For example, on one of these weekly calls, the CMA (comparative market analysis) drop-off challenge was born. As a result of this challenge, and taking action on it, I got a $900k expired listing, which I double ended, and which has since turned into two new $1M+ transactions! Literally, taking action on the ideas that come from these calls yields sales and raving clients.

Running Ads

I believe this is one of the main reasons I scaled from 8 closed transactions in my first year to 33 transactions Year two. Running ads exposes your videos and content to the masses literally. The ads help you retarget (get back in front of) people who have engaged by watching your videos and seeing your content. For me, this includes getting in front of people relocating to my area by targeting locations nationally where I know a high concentration of people are moving to my area.

Office Hours

Simply put, these hours give you the support you need to get started. The hours are set at certain times with Krista's team, and you know you can call in and get help and answers to questions. I know this support was critical to me as a new agent, but I also know that many of the very experienced agents in the program take advantage of it too. My cycle became: Feel the overwhelm, get on an office hours call and ask for help, take action accordingly, repeat.

Taking It to the Next Level

Okay, everything I've just mentioned is related to day-to-day and weekly action I learned through Krista's program. Once you are doing all of this and your phone is ringing with people that want to work with you, what the heck are you supposed to do and how can you continue to up level? (At least that is what I asked myself).

This is now when ninja strategy comes in. Let's break this into some key ideas and processes I learned that helped me continue to grow.

Listing Presentation Marketing Video

About six months into the program, I completed the listing presentation marketing video Krista teaches, which is a video you share with potential sellers. I send it to them prior to my listing appointment and it shows them how I'll expose their homes to the masses using video and strategic online marketing. This is a POWERFUL video that shows potential clients what I can do. It talks about all the things we do that are much different than what a typical agent does and this positions me as an expert and showcases my value add. For me the script alone also helped to solidify my confidence when talking with sellers about how I will market their properties and why I am the best choice to sell their home in order to get them their most desired results.

Seller Funnel

Now that I was making videos consistently, I started compiling a "seller funnel." Once I had a large enough retargeting audience from people that watched my seller-based videos, I could now route these viewers to a seller funnel, which was a collection of videos solely about selling your home to get the most money and the best terms. This funnel gives me a way to provide continued value, but also a way to collect seller lead information through my own funnel rather than through a lead generation ad directly on Facebook.

This is just one example of a funnel you can create. You can create buyer funnels, luxury funnels, relocation funnels, probate specific funnels, investment property funnels, neighborhood specific funnels—all as a way to provide value, capture people's information, continue to stay top of mind, etc. Literally endless possibilities.

Listing Process

This is essentially how you win a listing before you even arrive at the listing presentation at your potential client's house. This is the go-above-and-beyond of acquiring a listing to help your clients sell on their terms and for the most money. This process includes dropping off information such as your marketing plan, seller's guide, local market update, sample listing brochures, possibly a book you've written book if you have one (I've co-authored a book for sellers with Krista that I include), and any other number of items *prior to the listing appointment.* This also includes giving them access to the listing presentation video.

Seller's Guide

The seller's guide is a high-quality printed magazine-style booklet that you provide to sellers, ideally *prior* to arriving for your listing appointment. This guide shows them that you are the authority in providing valuable information to your seller and that you know how best to guide them in the process. This guide is basically an overview for them about what to expect when selling, general market information, etc. This is a staple tool I make sure I have stocked and ready to share.

Marketing Plan

Like the seller's guide mentioned above, the marketing plan is a high-quality printed magazine-style booklet that I use as a staple in my business, especially when it comes to the listing presentation. You will often go to potential clients' homes and see materials from other agents, but they may be on simple black-and-white paper with poor copy quality. My marketing plan stands out as a hard copy supplement to my listing presentation video. In my opinion, it is a great tool to use during your actual listing presentation as you can directly point out and provide proof of concept as you describe how you will strategically market your client's home online. I suggest ordering these in the 100s at a time and keeping them handy.

Property Brochures

All of my listings get a 4-page color brochure, which I use during showings, open houses, etc. I order extras and include them as sample marketing materials when going on listing presentations.

Buyer's Guide

Same idea as the seller's guide but geared towards buyers. I always have this on hand the first time I meet with buyers.

Seller & Buyer Book Co-Author

This is a supplemental option I had the opportunity to take advantage of through Krista's program and is another way to stand out. It not only gives prospective clients a full book of valuable tips on how to choose an agent, how to prepare their home for showing, etc., it also positions me as an expert. These books are strategically written to go against the grain (in a good way!)

and talk about comprehensive digital marketing strategies that most agents don't even know how to talk about. And how many other agents will show up with a book they've written?

Up Leveling Even Further

By being a part of Krista's programs and learning all I've learned, my mind has massively expanded in terms of how I think. This has meant using ideas and concepts I have learned from Krista and others in the program and then adapting them to be used in a multitude of other ways. Here are some examples of what I mean:

Buyer Consultations and First-Time Meetings

Now I bring something personalized when meeting buyers for the first time. For example, if we're doing a day of multiple tours, I will print out a fun cover page with "Mike & Sue's Home Search" and the date. I often include an image of the map for the day or a fun visual that shows that they are moving from their state to Tennessee with clipart of the two states and then an arrow pointing from one to the other.

I put together a package for them that includes my printed buyer's guide and a market update (which is often a simple one-pager). For people relocating from another state, I also include a relocation guide. If I'm showing them properties, I bring the property MLS sheets. They are put in order in a binder, so they don't have papers flying everywhere. I also include swag like branded pins, stickers, koozies, branded M&Ms, etc. I now put these in clear bags that have my branding. My goal is to make it special, make it nice.

Mailing Property Brochures.

In addition to sending out postcards to the neighborhood when I get a listing, I also send the 4 page color brochure of my listing to the neighborhood. Also, in the envelope, I send a very specific local "market" update that compares the neighborhood to the larger community. I typically make this update a one pager that has a QR code that takes them to my listing presentation video on one side (or the seller funnel, or my YouTube – etc.), then neighborhood sales stats compared to the larger market. Once the property is closed, I send a "Just Closed" postcard, usually in collaboration with my preferred lenders. (When I collaborate with my lender, I ask them to order 50 or so extra postcards so I have them on hand for listing process packets, etc.)

CMA Packet Drop Offs

If the area you service is small enough, you can drop these off by hand. I actually do this by mail as the area I service is incredibly spread out and mailing allows me to reach more people. In these packets, I include basically everything I have (all of which I created by being a member of Krista's coaching program): marketing plan, seller guide, sample brochures, my "menu" of services, market update 1 pager, QR code to my seller funnel, QR code with a video message of me going over the actual home valuation, my branded swag, and QR code taking them to my listing presentation video.

I've gotten leads for this mailing in a number of ways. Some lenders provide programs such as HomeIQ or Homebot which you can run ads behind and collect potential seller leads that request home valuations. You could also choose a niche like probate, for example, and target potential seller leads that way. I have also targeted expired listings. The main key with expired listings is *speed*. You want to get CMA packets to them ASAP.

Becoming Community Market Leader©

The idea of becoming a Community Market Leader© is to become that go-to person that everyone in the community turns to. The easiest way to get started is to make content about your area. Yes, this can include local market updates but also make content that people are searching for locally. For example, you can make a pumpkin patch guide graphic as well as a video overview of local pumpkin patches.

For me this has morphed into highlighting local businesses. My husband and I love to eat so I will make videos highlighting local restaurants. Also, when new businesses open, I create content about the business. We have a ton of outdoor activities and things to do where I am located so I make content on our parks, rivers, lakes, etc. To find content, you can use tools like GoogleTrends, Google Search Bar, AnswerThePublic and TubeBuddy to see what people are searching for in your area and make content on that.

Partnering with/Supporting Local Businesses

From one of my colleagues on a Skin in the Game call, I got the idea to interview local businesses. This led me to spotlight one business a month in the newsletter I mail to past clients. This has since evolved into sharing a weekly interview with a local business owner on both my YouTube channel as well as in an audio-only podcast. I also share shorts and reels of these interviews on my social media channels.

I also do branded Google reviews of local businesses. This is an example of an awesome idea I learned on one of Krista's weekly calls. Essentially, I write Google reviews for places I already go to locally. Then I make the review branded by putting my logo in the corner of photos and videos in the review. This is another example of low hanging fruit that helps people to see you everywhere but also provides value to businesses and their potential clients.

My Monthly Newsletter

I have been sending out custom newsletters to past clients and my sphere of influence since year 2 in business. These newsletters have evolved, but the entire purpose is to provide something fun and valuable in the mail. I always have a small snippet about something current in the real estate market. I also include something related to things happening in the world at large and/or local events to look forward to. On each cover, I share a note or thought. I also provide a link to my podcast. Sometimes I might also include a link to a recent video I made with some "fast facts" and then a screenshot of the video on YouTube with a QR code to the video.

Supporting What I Love

As a former teacher, I love to spoil teachers and send them all the positive energy I can. Past clients who are teachers get flowers at the beginning of every school year. My sphere of influence teachers get a gift or card right after Fall Break and then again around Valentine's (these are times when teachers are right in the thick of things).

I also support local schools by sending a letter to the principals at the beginning of the year offering to partner with their school. One year I made coupon books that principals could redeem, but I actually found that mailing the principals directly with an overview letter got better response. I'll provide a breakfast, making it really nice and adding in a goody bag of fun stuff that also includes some of my swag. I also provide teacher of the month and student of the month gifts to schools I partner with. And I provide staff or student t-shirts.

Putting together a silent auction basket for local schools simultaneously supports small businesses in the community as well as the school. I go to various stores and shops around the local school and purchase gift cards. The basket is advertised as the "Rocky Hill Experience" because the school and area are both called "Rocky Hill." I create a graphic with logos of all the businesses whose gift cards have been included in the basket along with my logo. There are gifts ranging from $25 - $100 in the basket and the total value is about $800.

Well, there you have it. This is how I went from brand new agent to top producer in my area in a very short amount of time. It may sound like a lot to do, and it is. But you don't have to do all of it at once. And if you compare the results you get to the results you get from making hundreds of calls every day and walking mailbox to mailbox, you'll see that it's well worth it. The bottom line is that whatever you do, you have to be consistent, and you must work on believing that the action you take is going to work, meaning you need a positive mindset. Whatever it is you choose to invest in to grow yourself and your business, go into it with the attitude that it will work. Acknowledge your doubt, change the thought, and keep it moving (Krista teaches great ways to do this in her book *Stop, Snap, and Switch*. Download it now from your Top Producers Resource Area: **KristaMashore.com/TopProducer**.

Takeaways

1. In my experience, the old way of launching yourself as a new agent is a waste of time. Even if you work very hard at it, your results will be very *s...l...o...w* in coming (if they come at all).

2. The best thing you can do as a new agent (or even one who's been in the business for years) is to establish daily/weekly routines to do the things that will really move your business forward.

3. Creating videos and learning how to properly distribute and repurpose them is one of the key things every agent should do.

4. If you want to succeed, you need to stand out. One of the ways you can do this is by having high-quality materials to give to your sellers and buyers.

5. One of the most powerful videos you can make is a listing presentation video. It not only helps you win clients before you even meet them, it also adds to your confidence in presenting yourself and your qualifications.

HALEY JONES

Haley Jones Home Team - eXp Realty

📞 865-242-9821
✉ HaleyJonesHomes@Gmail.com
📍 Knoxville, Tennessee

Haley Jones

SCAN ME

**Free Gift: Bonuses
Time To Take Action!**

Information alone is not enough. I've put together this **free expert resources member's hub** to help you get started now. Customize the strategies and tactics from this book to *your* business and marketing plan, with guidance, top producer tools and extra trainings.

KristaMashore.com/TopProducer

Want to Make More Selling Less?

by Windy Goss

Are you a Realtor® who would like to make more money selling fewer houses? If so, this chapter is for you! Before I met Krista, I was stuck making $500K-$600K GCI for almost ten years. No matter how many lower-priced homes I sold, I could not hit my $1M GCI target. I wanted a change, and I knew that change only happens if something changes—so I changed! I took the leap and joined Krista's coaching program. I started making better videos and marketing them correctly. Then I joined eXp Luxury and hit my first million GCI in 2022. Since I started focusing on luxury homes and learning how to market to high-end sellers, I have landed an $850k, $950k, $1.2M, $1.4M, $1.6M, $5M, $7M, $11.7M, and a $12M listing in just eight months! In this chapter, I'm going to share what I learned and what I did to inspire you to reach outside your comfort zone to achieve your goals like I did.

Start by Believing It

I have been helping people buy and sell houses in the Las Vegas area for almost two decades, and I have always treated all my clients like luxury clients. But it wasn't until I joined Krista's coaching program and eXp Luxury that I truly believed I could be a luxury agent. Whenever you decide to make a big change, it starts with mindset. It's not just about thinking bigger, it's about overwriting the stories you tell yourself inside your head. Thanks to Krista, my marketing skills were on fire! But I was still intimidated to go up against the "big dogs" and scared to talk to high-end sellers. Like, who would even want this Jeep girl in jeans selling their $10 million dollar home?!?

I started using Krista's Stop, Snap, and Switch technique to change my thoughts, and it changed my life. I went from thoughts like, *Who am I to think I could do this? It's way out of my league!* to *Heck, yeah, I'm going to go up against the big dogs! I have everything I need to win! Heck yeah, I'm going to talk to high-end sellers! They put their pants on just like me!* I stopped thinking about not being good enough, and I reminded myself:

1. I have a kick-ass team of photographers, videographers, and stagers.
2. Thanks to Krista, I know how to digitally market any home to the entire world.
3. Thanks to eXp Luxury, we market our luxury listings to The Wall Street Journal, Robb Report, Unique Homes, Mansion Global, UPMKT, Luxury Estate, Barron's, Market Watch, and run 80+ ads to over 100 countries for international exposure. Of course, they'll want to list with me!

Putting the Pieces Together

After I got past my mindset issues, I acknowledged that I had the tools and knew it was time to utilize them. I started by making

Krista's Listing Presentation Video, knowing I was going to show luxury homeowners something amazing they couldn't unsee. In this video, I talked about my teams and tools: My staging team was going to get their home looking amazing. My photography team was going to showcase every detail of their beautiful home. My soft-touch 4-page brochure was going to highlight all the special details of their home. My digital marketing strategy was going to reach high-end buyers—not just locally but nationally. This video turned out so well! I now put a QR code on all my luxury marketing materials that leads to this video.

Let's talk about marketing materials. Of course, my marketing materials had to represent the high-end market I was targeting. I bought custom black soft-touch hard covers with my gold and white foil logo across the front to contain my luxury presentation. I added a cover letter in the front of the presentation on effervescent cardstock that includes the QR code linking to my Listing Presentation Video. The back page is on the same cardstock with a QR code that goes to my new luxury website. I also ordered large, padded shipping envelopes with the eXp Luxury logo across the front. In each envelope, I put the presentation book, a Raiders/Vegas Golden Knights magnet schedule, and my metal business cards to FedEx them. Everything was made especially for high-end sellers—who were soon to be my new clients!

Connecting With My Ideal Clients

Krista taught me how to run "reach" ads through Facebook, how to create and master a Luxury Funnel, and how to retarget luxury buyers and sellers that you capture. This is exactly the kind of knowledge I paid big bucks for because I knew it would pay for itself many times over! I started targeting homeowners of expired listings over $1M. I went back two years, making sure those homes had never returned to market. I just started sending my luxury listing presentations to them via FedEx. Homeowners raved about my presentation. They even said it's so pretty that they kept it up on their mantels!

But as we all know, just this one technique alone is not going to seal the deal. So, I also got these sellers' names, emails, phone numbers, and addresses and put them into our CRM. I used sellers' email addresses to shoot them an email asking if they got their FedEx package. I used their phone numbers to follow up with a text as well. I created "audiences" for Facebook so that I could retarget them with more amazing content that luxury homeowners would love. If you aren't familiar with retargeting, it's like when you go online looking for a great pair of shoes or jeans. Suddenly, you start to see the kind of jeans or shoes you were interested in everywhere! That's marketers retargeting you. They know what you like, so they're giving you more of it. So now the sellers I'm targeting are seeing me on their front porch, in their email, in their text messages, and on social media! Krista's marketing strategies helped me master this.

Krista has video scripts and ideas for every type of niche for her students. My niche is obviously luxury, so I made a luxury video series for buyers and sellers. Through those video scripts, I learned a lot about high-end clients. I learned that sellers of this caliber want to be very discreet. They want to keep their affairs private. They want to protect their families and lifestyle. They value security. They want proof of funds for all buyer showings, and some of them want a private sale. So, the process with my high-end sellers is very different from how I'd been working with other sellers for the past 19 years. Just doing the videos about luxury sellers' pain points made me learn so much about "the other side." I encourage you to do the same because to be a true luxury Realtor®, you need to know these things.

These videos turned out so well! They are simply stunning, and they cover all the pain points and issues that luxury buyers and sellers have. I am running reach ads with them. I also added them to my luxury email campaign.

Beyond Facebook

Facebook and Instagram are great for marketing, but let's not forget about Google and YouTube. I have captured so many buyers and sellers from these platforms, and most often, they come to me organically, which means free. I upload all my videos to YouTube: drone video walkthroughs, the luxury video series, videos about seller tips and buyer tips, market update videos, and videos about what's happening in the community. Then I create playlists for each category. In some of my luxury video ads, I direct them to my luxury playlist on YouTube so they can binge-watch me. In every video, I give them so much value! Once I have the video uploaded onto YouTube, I add an update on my Google My Business page, post the thumbnail and the video description with the link to the YouTube video and—voila!—I'm on another platform.

And then there's LinkedIn. Do you know that this is where high-caliber professionals hang out? For those of us in the luxury market, we need to be there as well. All of my market update videos, luxury videos, and drone property tours get posted on LinkedIn. I target corporate professionals that may be looking for a luxury home in Las Vegas or Henderson or a local homeowner looking to sell theirs. LinkedIn is seen as a more professional platform compared to other social media, so I love this for finding luxury clients. Having a well-maintained profile on LinkedIn with endorsements, recommendations, and a professional network can significantly enhance your credibility and appeal to luxury clientele. You can also message directly to their profile to build rapport.

Educating Them About the Market

All homeowners, and especially high-end homeowners, care about the equity they have in their home and current and future market trends. This is why it is so important to set them up to get a monthly market report with all the stats. It's even better if you do your market updates in a video. In her program, Krista gives you the information you need for these reports. Her eight monthly market reports are so easy for you to recreate in the video! It's a no-brainer and nobody else is presenting updates like this! I plug these market update videos into all my Facebook and Instagram ads, YouTube, emails, LinkedIn, etc.

I not only use my update videos, but I also use automated market reports so I can be in their mailbox too. These are 4-page, good quality, market reports that have a ton of information on them and a smart QR code that notifies me if they scan it. It leads them right to the home valuation page of my luxury website.

Learning From Blowing It

Once I started doing all of this marketing, I started getting sellers responding and wanting to meet with me—yikes! This is where I started to freak out. I love my jeans and boots, but that's not what a high-end client expects. What the heck am I going to wear?!?! I love my Jeep, but I probably should be in a Lamborghini. What the heck am I going to drive?!?! I'm from Oregon, and I talk a little redneck, so what the heck am I going to say?!?!

Let me just tell you, my first $10 million listing appointment was a crap show. I was nervous and didn't feel comfortable in the outfit I was wearing. I know I was too eager to get the listing. I didn't have all my luxury presentation materials together yet, and I stumbled when we got talking about numbers. It was a hot mess, but I learned so much from it! One huge lesson I took away from my first $10M listing appointment was the importance of staging: how it works, how much it costs, which rooms should be staged, and when they take away the furnishings, etc. I learned that you 100% need to have a great relationship with a good stager. I found an amazing one, and she is now a part of my team.

I never thought of not getting that listing as a failure, only as a learning experience to know more and to be better. Like Krista says, when you first started kissing, you weren't good at it. But you were motivated, so you kept doing it and got great at it! That's how it is when you start listing luxury homes!

Selling $300k-$500k homes seemed so much easier! But I just kept thinking that when I sell these luxury homes, I am going to make 3X, 4X, maybe even 5X more than I am right now selling the easy ones. Like Krista says, "Hard now or hard later, you pick!" I still do all the things I've learned for marketing no matter what price range home I'm listing, so the cost is the same. However, it sometimes takes longer to sell higher-end homes, which means more marketing dollars. It's still 100% worth it!

After that first bad experience with a high-end homeowner, I reached out to a Luxury Specialist, and she answered all my questions and calmed me down. She told me to deliver a pre-listing presentation, which is also what Krista had taught me to do. So, I got that ready and delivered it before my next listing appointment. She explained to me that she likes riding a Harley, but she's not going to show up in her Harley gear. She coached me that you have to dress the part.

Krista reminded me that you also have to know your numbers and know the community. She coached me to not act like I absolutely loved the home but to play it cool. And she told me not to walk in like I was desperate for the listing. She reminded me that I have so many amazing marketing materials to show this homeowner that they will be overwhelmed with everything I was going to do for them.

Since then, I have started landing high-end clients, and my sellers are so blown away by my marketing. It truly warms my heart to hear all of their compliments! I always want them to know what's going on, so I send them all the links to the drone video walkthrough of their home, the Facebook ads, the MLS sheet, the personal property website, the 3D tour, and the brochures and postcards via mail. I also email them a syndication report that allows them to see their home online at The Wall Street Journal,

Robb Report, Unique Homes, Mansion Global, UPMKT, Luxury Estate, Barron's, and Market Watch. Along with this report, I show them all the views our ads got and our minutes of watch time. I encourage them to share the links with their friends, families, and business partners for extra exposure. They love to share these links because the videos are so good! Most of the time, my sellers are so impressed that they want to buy their home back from themselves!

A Great Support System

Besides learning to make killer videos and how to get over 400K views from proper marketing, my absolute favorite thing about Krista's program and her eXp organization is the people. Some of the agents I've met have turned into some of my best friends! As a broker/owner for 10 years in Las Vegas, everything has been up to me. I was the one who had to inspire my agents, teach them how to be amazing Realtors®, teach them the latest cool tools, teach them how to think outside the box, etc. It was all on my shoulders. In real estate, other agents never help you with anything because they are in direct competition with you. I finally feel like I have this whole tribe wrapping their arms around me and my team to help us all reach our goals.

I hope this chapter gets you excited about hitting that higher price point and making more money without needing to scramble to sell 100 houses a year. I have been able to take six vacations a year plus take Sundays off to spend more time with my husband. We love to crawl around on rocks in our Jeeps and ride across the country on our Harleys. Making more and selling less has made this possible. If you want more time back and more money and are motivated to do what it takes, you can definitely do what I did!

Takeaways

1. If your goal is to be a luxury home agent, you need to really believe that you have what it takes to be one!

2. To be successful with high-end clients, you need to understand how they think, what they worry about, and what's important to them.

3. One of the best things you can do is to find coaches and mentors who are already successful in the luxury market and who will guide you.

4. Know that you're going to make mistakes at first. Just learn from them and don't let them get you down.

WINDY GOSS

eXp Realty

☎ 702-334-1669

✉ Windy.Goss@eXp.com

⊙ Las Vegas, Nevada

Finding Your Authentic Voice in Video

by Alisha Collins

In this chapter, I'm going to talk about finding your voice. The reason I'm writing about this is because if I hadn't found my voice utilizing Krista's program, I would not be in the position I am today. To me, finding your voice means being able to express who you are authentically in everything you do—especially in the videos you create. But I want to begin with where I stand today before diving into the journey that brought me here.

In June 2023 we took an amazing family vacation. My husband stayed behind to work on some projects at our home in Georgia and I flew back home to Casper, Wyoming. On June 26th, my husband had a severe gallbladder attack and was taken to the emergency room. I had been home less than 48 hours when we found out he was going to need a cholecystectomy to remove his gallbladder. They said it was a common surgery, but something told me to immediately fly back to Georgia to be with him. He would not be able to come back to Casper, Wyoming for several weeks. So, I threw some clothes in a bag, drove to Denver and flew back to Georgia.

On June 30, my husband was diagnosed with metastatic esophageal cancer. We also found out that not only did he have esophageal cancer, but that it had spread to over five different places in his body. We were devastated to say the least. Thankfully, we were "stuck" at our home in Thomasville, Georgia which is right next-door to one of my very favorite people and best friends. My friend, Leslie Bennett, and I met almost six years ago in Krista Mashore's coaching program. We always supported and encouraged each other in the program, and we became best friends. (In 2017, before Leslie joined Krista's program she had only sold 3 homes, one of which was a lot for her parents. In her first year with Krista, which was 2018, she sold 28. Then, as a solo agent, she closed 60 in 2019, 110 in 2020, and 134 in 2021. Then, during years when we had the worst markets we've had for a while, she closed 112 in 2022 and she closed 111 in 2023!) We often pondered the serendipity behind our acquisition of a second home, especially one so close to our friend. But at that moment we understood—the diagnosis was the underlying reason that we had ended up where I could be supported by my best friend.

We finally went back to Casper. Then about a month and a half after the diagnosis, my husband got sick. He spent 2 ½ weeks in the hospital in Denver. Denver is about 4 ½ hours away from our home, so I'd spend the week there then come home on the weekends and list houses. One time I listed four homes in one weekend. All of the listings that weekend came from the videos I had made. Sometimes when I was driving back-and-forth I would cry thinking about where my career was and how grateful I was to not only be able to do what I love but that it was continuing to bless my family. Amidst challenging circumstances, I found myself in a position where I was not only able to provide care and support for my husband but also to maintain and continue my business.

Let me just stop and ask you: If a similar crisis happened in your family, would you be able to say the same? Would you be able to care for a loved one and still keep your business going? Would you have the support of a network of peers who would honestly care about what was happening to you and help you?

By the time of my husband's diagnosis, I was definitely doing business differently than I had done in the past. It's as if the groundwork I laid through my work with Krista has built a safety net, ensuring that when times got tough, I had something to fall back on. This realization has been both surprising and comforting, highlighting the importance of the work we do today in preparing us for the uncertainties of tomorrow.

I've continued to do videos during this time about real estate and about my life (excluding the cancer diagnosis because I haven't gotten to the point that I can talk about it on video yet). Continuing to provide value to my community through videos has been the one normal thing in my life that keeps me sane. My videos are something I can do anywhere at any time. Being able to do that is what has kept the business coming in. People are able to still watch and engage with me even when I wasn't working. "Views While You Snooze."

Where I Started

Let me go back to before meeting Krista and the business I had back then. My real estate partner, who was my mother's age, decided to retire. It was at the end of 2017, and over the year I had watched her become really technologically inept. She could send an email, she couldn't write an electronic offer, and she dang sure couldn't do a video. I didn't want to become that person. I knew that I had so much to learn but didn't know anyone who could teach me. I also felt like I needed to figure something out about lead sources because I was relying a lot on Zillow, and my Zillow bill was just growing and growing and growing.

Then this bubbly, energetic, gorgeous gal popped up in my Facebook feed. The moment I saw her, I thought, *That's me in 10 years. How do I get there faster?* I wanted to be like her, and I couldn't wait to get there! I realized the solution to my problems and the answer to my questions was to hire her as a coach. It was the most money I'd ever spent in my whole entire life and that was scary. When you are down to the wire and you are willing to pay somebody to the point of no return, it's *past* the time when you should have hired help. And that's where I was. I had never been coached before, but I knew that I needed help to get me where I wanted to go. The interesting thing about that is that, even though I never had a coach, I was already selling about a hundred homes a year.

But I wanted more, and I knew to get there, I really had to invest in myself so I could learn what I needed to learn. I had dabbled in social media, but I felt like I wasn't that great at it. If I'm being honest, it wasn't just a *feeling*. I really *wasn't* great at it. I wasn't good at the video part either. (Today, I know that *no one* starts out being good at video!) I booked the call, and I made the decision instantaneously to join Krista's program. It has really changed my life, my career and the life of people around me. I dove into her program wholeheartedly and did everything she told me to do, when she told me to do it. I was an excellent student! But one of the most important things I did was to find my authentic self, my voice, in my videos.

Finding My Voice

In business, especially in real estate, I think it is so important that you find your voice and let yourself be who you really are. When I finally found my voice it opened up so many new doors for me. Like anything else, there were steps that I had to take to find my voice.

For example, about 13 years ago, I was at a health conference in Phoenix, and I ended up getting meningitis. I felt like my head was ready to explode and I honestly thought that I was going to die. I remember telling my husband all the things I wished we would do, like eating around the kitchen table every night. I also told him how much I despised dressing up. When he heard that, he said, "Well, then stop." Well, obviously I didn't die and as soon as I got home, I bought a good-looking pair of jeans, nice boots— and I doubled my sales the next year.

I know it was because I was more confident and felt like I could be myself. I wasn't being who I thought everyone wanted me to be. I was being my true self. Even with my big personality, I was more approachable. I wear jeans and a T-shirt to show houses, and nobody cares. If they do care, I'm probably not their girl. Krista loves dressing up and wearing heels and dresses and I love that for her, but it's just not me. It's tempting to try to be someone else. It might be tempting to try to emulate me or like Krista. But you have to be yourself.

Years later in Krista's program, I learned that one of the pieces of finding your voice is finding your authentic self in video. I want you to know that I started at the bottom. I had no idea what I was doing. I didn't know how I could translate the voice I'd found—jeans, T-shirts, big personality—to videos.

I remember this one specific day. I think I had been in Krista's Coaching program for three or four weeks. I remember Krista saying, "What is something you can do? Is there something that you could do every single week that would keep you on track to do video? What is something you're passionate about? Find something you love doing and use that as your basis." I thought, *Okay, I love dogs so much that I have eight of them and I really wanted to start doing a Pet of the Week.* I had been dreaming about this idea for a while and could not wait to work with my local Humane Society. I was praying to God that they would let me do it. So, I went and talked to them about the idea, and they said "Yes." Next thing you know, Alisha's "Pet of the Week" was born. Krista and

I came up with an amazing tagline, "We not only find homes for people, but we find homes for pets too."

If you've ever seen any of my presentations, you know that the very first Pet of the Week was *horrible*. It was me with a tripod. At first I didn't have a mic, the lighting was bad and the dogs weren't even in the video. You could hear everything around me. But as bad as it was, I knew that I had to keep going. (Nobody's watching your videos at the beginning, anyway. Haha!)

Now I have a mic, the lighting's better and I have someone who videos me. We have a logo, a format and all the things that make a professional-looking video. I don't overthink these videos. I just do them. Pet rescue is definitely near and dear to my heart, and it's something that I don't have to fake. The Humane Society started letting me make videos with their puppies before anybody got to see them. That helped me boost my views. I spend between $30 and $40 a week promoting each Pet of the Week video and people just love it.

Across the country now, there are a lot of people that use my little "Alisha's Pet of the Week" idea. They even use the logo and change the name on it to theirs. Not only have we helped adopt over a hundred pets, but it also keeps me from adding to my pet family, because we all know I don't need any more animals!

I had found "my voice" in other areas and now I was finding my authentic self in video. This project definitely helped me with that because talking about animals is so easy for me. If you don't like dogs, then you shouldn't be doing a pet of the week. You need to find something else. You could do cooking videos, beach videos, or videos on cleaning tips. There are so many endless possibilities of what you could do. Like Krista said, "What is something you're passionate about? Find something you love doing and use that as your basis." Doing that will help you express your authentic self.

Your videos do *not* have to be and *should not* always be about real estate. Mine were about dogs, helping the community, and supporting charitable causes. People will still recall that I'm a Realtor® even though I'm not boasting about my business in these videos. I'm talking about other parts of my life, but they still associate my real estate brand when they see me.

So that's how I started. I also did every single video that Krista said to do, all the scripts in her vault. I did videos on houses and informational videos about real estate. That was almost six years ago. Were these first videos good? No, they were horrible, just like my first Pet of the Week videos. I started out with this guy that is still my videographer. Back then, he didn't have a gimbal to keep the camera from shaking. He didn't have the right lens. Still, I put money behind the videos to place ads on Facebook. I implemented Krista's "Brand Awareness Digital Marketing and Retargeting Facebook Strategy" and placed ads behind every video on Facebook through the Ads Manager. And Krista kept giving me tips on how to get better, so I improved.

But you know what? Even those first horrible videos worked! I'd probably only been doing videos for two weeks when I ran into this gal that I worked with at the Chamber of Commerce. I hadn't seen or talked to her for about 15 years. She called me and said, "Oh my gosh, I saw your videos and my daughter is ready to buy a house. I think you're the one that can show her the ropes, and make sure she understands everything." I ended up selling a house to her daughter. Since then, her daughter has probably given me 11 referrals that became 11 closed transactions—all from a video that her mother saw right when I started! The point is that you just have to start. Your videos don't need to be perfect, and you never know who is watching. I never would have gotten that referral from the gal I knew 15 years prior if she hadn't been watching them because she wouldn't have remembered that I was in real estate. Case in point, videos work!

A second thing happened right after that. In one of Krista's trainings, she told us, "You want to do these specific postcards and you have to do them this specific way." So. I did it. It's another strategy that she teaches, "Digital Location Domination," that combines digital advertising (video and Facebook ads) with an Every Door Direct Campaign using 8 ½" X 11" postcards. It's all about having people see me everywhere. They see my videos, my postcards, and my signs, so they feel like I'm the one to choose in that area. Adding the videos to the postcard campaign is the key to getting people to know, like, and trust me.

Soon after, another past co-worker called me. (It actually scared the crap out of me because I had been in my early twenties when we had worked together and she was always a little scary!) She called because she wanted me to list her house! Then someone else who had seen my videos called and said, "This friend of mine wants to list with somebody else, and I think her price is way too low." I ran right over there. I was so excited because I just started Krista's program, and I knew all of the ways that I could to promote her house on social media. I was going to do it exactly the way Krista had taught me. I'll tell you what, the homeowner signed with me the next day. I ended up selling it myself and listing another house.

Yes, I used to do horrible videos, but they still worked! Recently I was on a coaching call, and someone said, "We don't have it. We don't have the video knack like Alisha." (The gal that said that is never going to live it down.) I stopped her right there, and said, "Wait a second. I have made *thousands* of videos in six years. Of course, I'm going to be better than you are. You think I have some knack but in reality, I've practiced, yes, practiced by making videos a ton of times." You cannot get better if you don't start and you can't get better if you don't keep going. It doesn't matter if your first videos are a hot mess! You *will* get better if you keep at it.

Comparison is the thief of joy. If you start comparing your *beginning* to my *middle*, it isn't fair. Plus, it won't help you grow. If I compare my middle with somebody else's journey that is further along down the road, it will beat me down. Everybody's journey is different. You're different. You have different experiences, and you have the ability to bring those experiences to other people through video.

Now you may look at me and think, *Oh, she's got it all together. Oh, she's lucky.* But it's because I busted my butt, and I did everything Krista told me to do in the beginning. I dove into her program wholeheartedly and did everything she told me to do. (Now, do I currently do every little thing in her program? No. She continues to add more and more all the time and I can't keep up with her now!)

What's Your Voice?

One of the things about "voice" on video is that it isn't just the *sound* of your voice. It's your gestures, too. Sometimes people don't like that I talk with my hands a lot, but it's part of who I am. Not only is it your gestures, it's also the look on your face. It's the confidence you show (or don't show) through your posture. It's also the emotions that whatever you're talking about evokes in you, and the emotion it evokes in the other person. Voice shows passion and it shows energy. It shows people who you truly are.

When people watch your videos where you're being your true self and then meet you, you want them to say, "Oh my gosh, I feel like I know you." You want to be the same

> *Every single one of us has a gift and a uniqueness that people like. We have to find our unique voice and be our true selves.*

person you are on videos that you are when they meet you. **Every single one of us has a gift and a uniqueness that people like. We have to find our unique voice and be our true selves**. I met a guy who replaces sewer lines the other day and I'm like, "Hey buddy, we've never met. It's so nice to meet you." And he said, "Well, I watch all your videos, so I feel like I know you." I said, "That's exactly what I go for." I hear it all the time from clients.

However, I don't usually hear it from contractors, so that was super cool.

Another part of your voice is your niche. If you've watched any of my shorts or seen anything I've talked about on YouTube or Facebook, you will know I love horses. I could go all in on rural properties but in Casper, you can't just focus on rural properties alone. There are just not enough. That said, people know that I'm the rural girl who loves horses. When new clients call me, they actually ask about my horse by name. (When that first happened, I promptly called my accountant and said, "Can I deduct her off my taxes?" I think I should. She's my little marketing star.) One of the first videos that I did with her was for a horse property, and it put me on the map. She did so good! At the beginning of the video, she tipped her nose up a little bit like she wanted to show off for the camera. Sometimes people even ask me to bring my horse when I go to meet them! It's not always possible, so one time, we had fun and made a video with stick horses. Yes, it's totally okay to have fun with these videos too. The point is to just be who you truly are. That's your voice.

My husband, Bob, has all these sayings, and there are a couple of them I really like (and there are a couple of them that I want to choke him when he says them). One of the ones I really love is "You can't say the wrong thing to the right person." The people who call me off my video ads like me already. They aren't turned off by my high energy and that I'm all over the place.

The other day somebody came into my office, and they had seen me on YouTube. They came to me as soon as they had gotten into town. They said, "Oh my gosh, it feels like we're meeting a celebrity. I see you all over Facebook." It still makes me feel a little weird, but I am happy that they love me. I don't have the fear of someone showing up who doesn't like me or relate to me. When you do videos consistently, people develop a relationship with you, and they trust you before they even meet you. People will hug you. They will be your biggest fan without you having to "impress" them. You already have the connection and relationship you want before you ever meet them. But to get there, you have to keep making videos. You can't just make a few. You need to make them consistently, daily if possible. When you do that, the impact compounds. You get more and more people watching and connecting to you.

Be warned, they're going to binge-watch you. I think I now have a little over 10,000 subscribers on YouTube and 60,000 TikTok followers. When you post good videos that are authentic and give people value, they will watch you for hours. They watch every single video they can find and consume information about coming to your area or about the real estate process. The same thing goes with Facebook, especially now that everything is in short-form reels. They just watch you over and over and over. So, you want to have a big catalog of information. Otherwise you will miss opportunities.

One of the videos I have on YouTube has the second-highest number of views among all of mine. I did it at the beginning of COVID. It was 105 degrees outside, which is the hottest it ever gets here, and it only happens a couple of days a year. The video was about 10 minutes, and I had never done one that long. My assistant was holding an iPad with the script on it, scrolling it up with her finger. My assistant and the videographer were both walking backward as I walked forward. I was sweating to death. I didn't have my fake hair in. I looked horrible. I absolutely do *not* like the video!

Guess what? That video has 140,000 views. I've probably closed 80 transactions off of that one video. What if I hadn't posted it? What if I hadn't even thought of the idea? People don't even notice all the problems I saw in it. I still don't like it, but I'm real glad I made it. Real glad.

Making Mistakes to Get Better

One of the things that has taken me decades to realize is that you have to make mistakes to get better. I'm very hard on myself and this was definitely hindering me from finding my voice. Nobody knows this, but I am kind of negative. I have to work to get past the negativity because I know the only way for us to get better is to make the mistake, learn from it, and not make the same mistake again. You also have to practice. You are not going to be great at something instantaneously, and so you have to repeat it over and over and over. I still struggle with things like my lighting (it's too dark in my videos) and the microphone. I used one of those RØDE mics for years and the sound wasn't good. I always thought the problem was just me or the room, but it turns out I had been plugging the microphone into the wrong part of the camera!

> *One of the things that has taken me decades to realize is that you have to make mistakes to get better.*

Things are going to happen. You are going to record ten videos on TikTok and then realize there was no sound. You're going to do a video at a house you've listed and find out later that the camera didn't record it. Stuff is going to happen and you have to embrace it, learn from it, and move on. One of the very first videos I did was a script Krista gave us in the program, and I did it in front of a green screen. It's horrible. I won't be doing that again, but it still worked! That was five years ago. I've gotten better, and technology has gotten so much better as well. But we all have to start somewhere. You have to suck at the beginning to get to the next step. So, if you never start, you never suck, and you never get better.

Like I said, after my first Pet of the Week video, I hired a videographer because, obviously, I was no good at recording myself. The videographer was an agent in another town, and I don't even remember how I found him. He had just started his videographer journey, and our first video of a listing was horrible. The music's too loud, you can hear the traffic, you can hear the dog barking and the video is *literally orange*. But we thought it was the greatest thing since sliced bread. People thought I was a rockstar and they loved this video. We actually sold this house off this video. What I'm saying is that you just have to start.

I had one moment of buyer's remorse when I first started in Krista's program. I was sitting making my first ad, and it was 5 a.m. I was full of doubt and thought, *What in the heck have I done?* I had added all this extra work to myself, and it took me *two hours* to place my first video ad. As soon as I got it done, I felt relieved. And you know what? The next time it took me less time. Today, I can be talking on the phone and place an ad in two minutes while being in a meeting, all because I did one thing, did it well, then added something else.

Thank goodness I didn't give up! With all I have going on in my life right now (my husband being sick, back and forth to doctors' offices, etc.) I can't spend much time sitting in front of the computer. But I still can do my videos on my cell phone and post them. I can do that anywhere. It's kept my business going. Also, it is a way for me to check out and do something that takes my mind off of all that I'm dealing with. Because I did it when it was uncomfortable in the beginning, I now have this skill that I can use anywhere.

I want you to think back to the first time that you showed a house. You were so nervous that you struggled to get the lockbox open, right? You did it anyway because you had to. You did it because you wanted that sale. The point is you got better. You did it anyway, and now you can talk while opening the lockbox and think about what you're going to say to the client when you walk in the front door, right? Making videos is exactly the same thing. You *have* to do it for your business. You have no choice. It is the wave of the future. Just like being a newbie agent, you've got to let yourself be a newbie at making videos too.

Because I was willing to make my mistakes, learn from them and keep going, my team and I have become little local celebrities. It is kind of weird to say, but it's true. We get calls all of the time directly from Facebook, YouTube and other social media outlets. They're not calling anybody else. They're not working with anybody else. I don't have to sell myself. My videos have done the work for me. And, as Krista says, I'm "winning before I arrive." My team is also benefiting because they are doing these videos now too. It's changing how people view them. My really young agents are talking about the real estate market, lending, new construction, remodels and anything else you can think about. They're attracting people to them! It's really cool to see that we are the authority, and we're serving, not selling.

One way to really increase the impact of your videos is to *repurpose* them. Repurposing is something that took me way too long to start utilizing. Now, we turn every video that I make into short-form videos and post them everywhere we possibly can. Agents get worried about posting the same videos on different platforms at the same time. But the truth is nobody looks at every platform every day, and nobody sees your videos on every platform at the same time. Research shows that most people primarily use two different social media platforms. I'm a Facebook and a TikTok girl. Other people are going to watch YouTube and Instagram. You want to be everywhere! Each one brings in different kinds of leads and it's really, really powerful. Repurposing something that I've done over the last year, maybe a year and a half, and it's catapulted my business to new heights.

Removing Excuses

Everybody has excuses when it comes to starting to make videos: I don't like how I look. I don't like how I sound. I am too heavy or I'm too skinny. I don't have all the materials together that

I need for my business. I don't have a website. I don't have this or that. Who cares? You've got to start anyway. There are things that I didn't have pulled together when I started with Krista, but I did everything she said. So, when she told me to make a video, I made the dang video even though I hadn't finished X, Y, or Z yet.

I also made the time to do videos. In 2023 (in a small town with limited inventory and the highest interest rates in over 20 years), my team sold right around 262 homes. With

> *I'm telling you that you always make the time for something that's important to you.*

help from my assistant, transaction coordinator and my son, I sold 200 of those myself. (Before I met Krista, I was selling about 100 homes.) Still, I made all the videos that Krista says to make on Facebook. I made 1000 TikTok videos just last year. If anybody doesn't have time, it's me—and I still did it. I'm not telling you this to brag. **I'm telling you that you always make the time for something that's important to you.** Somebody asked me recently, "How do you have time for all this?" Well, there are pockets of time in your day where you can make a video, talk about something that's happening and post it. It takes like 30 seconds. Time is not a good excuse anymore. Another excuse people have is, "I can't find somebody to record me." Just pick up your iPad or your iPhone, and you record yourself. Don't wait to find someone. That's just an excuse.

In the beginning, I did *all* of the scripts that Krista had given students in her program. (Back then, there weren't very many to choose from, but now there are an absolute ton of them for all different niches, more than you could probably record in an entire year.) This was really great for me because I have learned that I am definitely a script girl. At the beginning of this journey, I *needed* a script. In fact, I still frequently use scripts for my long and factual YouTube videos. But almost everything I do now is off the cuff.

If starting with scripts like the ones Krista offers helps you get started, go for it. You'll start with those scripts and then eventually you'll say, "You know what? I think it would sound better if I changed this part or said this instead." You will start developing a voice of your own.

Don't overthink. Done is better than perfect. I still have to chant this to myself because sometimes it's really hard to press record. I'm a perfectionist for sure, but I'm not afraid to fail. I take massive action. If I were to say, "Hey everybody, what's my superpower?" They're going to say that I "do it now"—right now!—because that is how you get to the gold quickest. I'm willing to invest time and money to do that.

When I don't want to make a video I tell myself: *What if the information, the story, the facts that I'm about to give somebody helps them save money, pick the right real estate agent somewhere else, whatever?* We can use our knowledge and make videos and actually help people. People comment all the time, "I wish I would've known this before I bought a house," and that's how I know I am helping someone else. Take yourself out of it and think, *Okay, I don't want to make the video today, but what if somebody needs to hear this?* If you think about *them*, not yourself, you'll make it.

Videos That Serve Your Community

That's one of the important things about doing these videos. You have to do them with the intent to serve your community, to give them information that they need or that brightens their day and makes their lives easier. For example, at the beginning of COVID, I think all of us were pretty uneasy. I remember getting on our coaching calls as everything was starting to shut down and it was a little more somber than normal. But one thing I love about Krista is that she is the quickest pivoter I've ever met in my life. Something happens, she pivots. So, on that call, Krista said, "Okay, you guys, let's go. Let's get local businesses on Facebook and do Facebook Lives." Krista's idea was that with so many small businesses suffering, we should all try to help each other. Her brilliant idea was to go live with local small businesses and feature them.

I went live on Facebook every single day for a month! I talked with different business owners every day at four o'clock about what they were doing. I did one on telehealth and how you could stay healthy. We did numerous restaurant videos with how you could get takeout. It put me in front of the businesses' viewers, and it really helped with goodwill in the community. I mean if you're being your true self, goodwill comes naturally. It was easy yet it was so helpful for those businesses. In such a trying time, I felt like I was able to make an impact on my community. During COVID, it was really critical to do everything you could to keep your head in the right space. Going live everyday really helped me because I was still able to give back. It gave me something to work on and get excited about. And helped me keep my mind out of the dumpster! This ended up being something that truly helped the small businesses and made me feel so good.

I'm the president of the board of a nonprofit here, the Olivia Caldwell Foundation. The CEO's daughter, Olivia, died when she was 21 months old from brain cancer. Our fundraising gets bigger and bigger every year and a lot of that increase is coming from the addition of videos we've done. The effect that you can have on your community with video is absolutely tremendous and unlike anything you can think of.

Do the Hard Things

Here's what I want you to do. I want you to go make videos. I want you to take massive action even if you're nervous about it. You have to decide to make the change. And I know you can do it. And I think we forget that we can do hard things.

A year and a half ago, Krista asked me to come and talk on stage. I'd never done it before, and I was terrified. I get nervous every time I have to talk in front of somebody. I reminded myself that nerves are good because it means we care. On the way to the event, I remember being so scared, and a friend of mine sent me an inspirational video. As I was watching it tears were running down my face. She also sent me a message that gives me goosebumps every time I repeat it. The message said, *"Alisha, this is the time in your life that you were made for."*

I say it now to you: You are here for a reason. This is the time in your life that you were made for. This is the time that you can take this massive action and change your life for the *best*, not just the better. This is your time, but you have to make the decision to seize it. You have to take massive action and you have to work extra hard. You can't just sit back and think it's going to come to you. This is work. And you want to do one thing at a time. I can't stress this enough.

Even after 20 years in real estate, I know that I need to continue to learn and grow every day, which is why I'm still on all of Krista's trainings. Krista actually reminds me of myself. Like her, I always strive to be better. I'm always asking: "What's the next thing I can do to serve my clients better? What's the next thing I could do to educate myself so that I can promote their properties to the masses? What can I do to keep them coming back?" I'm not afraid to take action; in fact I take action daily.

So, take action. Make the effort to do videos and discover your own unique voice. Time passes anyway. But if you become willing to make mistakes, learn from those mistakes and keep making them, what's going to happen is you're going to end up with a catalog of videos on Facebook, on YouTube and wherever else you decide to post. You'll get to see that even those first horrible videos can have a positive result.

Takeaways

1. When you find your voice and let yourself be who you truly are, you'll feel much more confident and won't have the stress of trying to impress new clients.

2. When you start doing videos, you have to let yourself suck at the beginning to get to the next step. If you never start, you never suck and you never get better.

3. When you're authentic in your videos, you'll attract the people who will like and trust you for who you really are.

4. Using videos for your business is not just a good idea. It is the wave of the future and something you *have* to do for your business.

ALISHA COLLINS

*Alisha Collins Real Estate Team
eXp Realty*

307-247-1806

Alisha@CasperPowerHouse.com

Casper, Wyoming

Lead With Value

by LaToya Latimore

I remember scrolling through Facebook on a normal day and coming across a cheerful, energetic woman who sounded as if she were speaking directly to me! I was on the edge of my seat, leaning in, wanting to hear more. You know that feeling you get when you encounter a good soul, and you just know that it is the start of something meaningful. When you know it is a relationship worth pursuing because everyone before just did not connect with your spirit in a way that was meant. Well, this was me during the Spring of 2019 when I heard this beautiful, energetic woman talking about selling 100+ homes a year. She hooked me from the start! Her energy matched mine and I knew if there was anything more that needed to be learned, I was surely going to learn it from her.

My real estate sales journey started in 2016, shortly after relocating for the second time and still feeling extremely homesick. Leaving our home state of California right after buying our dream home was the hardest thing my family ever had to do. My husband, Donald Latimore, and I, now known as the Latimore Group of eXp Realty, were sick and tired of corporations making decisions about our family's lives. Starting off as dual career agents, working full-time jobs demanding 50+ hour work-weeks, we were determined to make our real estate sales business a success. We knew we had to be efficient and leverage each other during evenings and weekends to make this business work. We wanted to do more than just invest in real estate and work 9 to *faint from exhaustion*!

We went from struggling six-figure W-2 earners to eventually walking away from our jobs and winning the hearts of our clients in Columbia, South Carolina. When we made the decision to leave it all behind, we took our real estate sales business to the next level. When I quit my job in 2018, we tripled our closings in 2019. We went from closing $3 Million in 2018 to $9.5 Million the following year. Even though we were on the verge of greatness, we still knew something was missing.

So, when I read Krista Mashore's book, *Sell 100+ Homes a Year,* in 2019, a fire lit. It burned so deep inside of me, and I wanted more. It wasn't enough for me to just walk away from corporate America. I needed this for my husband too so that we could continue to flip homes, sell homes, and build a legacy for our six daughters. That's right, SIX! Someone had to break the cycle, and I knew it had to be us. I knew we were capable of producing far more than just 43 closings at $9.5 Million a year. Although we were learning so much from other great agents across YouTube and received great training from the brokerage we started with, something was still missing. We knew that cold calling, door-knocking, and open houses were not something we wanted to do for the next 20 years, and there had to be a more sustainable way.

Krista Mashore was popping up every time I scrolled through Facebook and the message was loud and clear. I wanted to pop up everywhere and capture the hearts of current and future South Carolina residents. My eyes were completely opened after reading her book and the real journey began.

Leading with Value

Don and I made it our sole purpose to own and operate a business that "Leads with Value." This is where our tagline "Helping You Build Wealth Through Real Estate™" developed from. Whether we are assisting a first-time home buyer, an investor, a homeowner who is looking to gain every bit of their hard-earned equity, or even someone thinking about getting licensed to sell real estate, it became our mission to provide the best value.

Stay with me over this next chapter while I take you through the journey of how we went from closing 43 homes at $9.5 million to closing 103 homes in a single year at $21 million. And we did this all by taking what we learned from the Mashore Method and by *leading with value*. See, it is not one single thing that you do that leads to success in real estate. It all starts with (1) your vision. From there, (2) you must have the right mindset. This includes surrounding yourself with the right people to ensure you keep the right mindset. Next, (3) get your branding together. Then finally, (4) you must develop sustainable systems that allow you to scale. Treat your business like a business, and it will pay you like one.

I have been working in sales since I was a child. I was ambitious and eager to be the best at everything. Even in high school, I graduated in the top 3% of my class with honors. My first real job during my freshman year at Sacramento State University was at an electronic store selling home theater systems at the Good Guys. I outperformed full-time salespeople, working only part-time while getting myself through college. I could either sell the $300 boombox on the wall or upsell a family to a $10,000 home theater system. I chose to upsell every time just by simply listening to people.

From there, I was hired as an Account Executive for a subprime lender. I helped families get out of debt by offering home loans. I could either sell them a 29% unsecured personal loan or upsell them to a secured mortgage loan that could save them thousands monthly. Again, I chose to listen and upsell. I was a top performer every year. Running in the top 5% consistently in the northwestern region. I don't say all of this to brag. I say all of this to say that *selling is not what makes you successful in real estate*. You can be the best car salesman in the world, but it won't matter in this business. I have seen former schoolteachers and former nurses outperform top salespeople.

When you are dealing with people going through real-life situations, you need to be able to connect and build a genuine relationship. You need to be able to read people and listen to what they are really saying so that you can find the most valuable solution for their needs. When you *"stop selling and start serving,"* it becomes much easier to have meaningful conversations with people. If you can remember this, you will always be leading the pack. When I first heard Krista say the words "stop selling and start serving," it resonated with me because it is who I am. It is what I was training other agents to do, but I never quite put it into those specific words. This is where our brand truly took off.

Using Video to Lead With Value

There are always pivotal moments in your life when the right words trigger the right reaction. You just have to be an action-taker to bring it to fruition. See, when we made the decision to use our real estate license to sell, that was not the original plan. Originally, we were just tired of dealing with real estate agents who didn't know how to run analyses to find us the right properties to flip. So, the idea was to get licensed to have access to the properties and be our own agent. It wasn't until I was nearing the end of real estate school that the right words were spoken to me. I'll never forget it. It still feels like I just heard these words yesterday. I will summarize them for you.

You can be the car dealer who pays hundreds of thousands of dollars for inventory just to sell cars and struggle each month. Or you can pay the few hundred dollars it takes to get licensed—

and the small monthly Multiple Listing Service Fee to have access to billions of dollars of inventory—to make an unlimited amount of money. It was those words that made this business loud and clear for me. Billions of dollars of inventory, small monthly fees, and UNLIMITED income. The light bulb clicked so brightly, and we were ready!

Now let me relate this to our decision to lead with video. We could continue to call expired listings, call FSBOs, door-knock and perform open houses. With cold calling, it's a numbers game. Back in my lending days, I remember making phone calls from 10 a.m. to 7 p.m. just to close 5-10 transactions a month. I was making hundreds of dials to get a small percentage of contacts. Most of those resulted in applications. But more applications were declined than pre-approved. Then it was from the small number of approved applications that I had a chance at getting them in the door for a full consultation. Finally, an even smaller number received final approval and closed.

The same thing is true in real estate. We didn't get licensed to have a small number of prospects each month. Cold calling in real estate results in very few contacts. It is even worse now than it was when I first started. With so many spam calls, most people do not even answer the phone if they do not recognize your phone number. Then there is door-knocking. Go out in the heat or rain and patiently wait for someone to answer the door and pitch to them in hopes of a transaction. Being face-to-face, you do have a greater chance. But it is not ideal. You can only physically knock on so many doors in two to four hours. In the South, people love to talk. So, you are not getting in front of that many doors. Open Houses are another face-to-face opportunity. But again, the numbers are too small, and most are not qualified to purchase until years on out. I know this because I am still converting people years later that I met at open houses within my first three years in the business. You can have the best offer in the world. But if you can only pitch it to a few people at a time, you are not going to close a hundred homes a year.

Where am I going with this? As I mentioned, I can pay a small monthly fee to have access to billions of dollars of inventory and make an UNLIMITED amount of money. Well, in real estate, I can make hundreds of calls, door-knock and conduct open houses just to have a small number of prospects each month (usually less than 50). Or I can record a few videos and get myself in front of an unlimited number of prospective clients each month (Krista teaches the Monetization Multiplier Principle as it relates to this).

Fast forward. I read Krista's book for a second time in August of 2020. It was at that moment when I finally began recording videos and posting them to YouTube. Instead of working with a low number of prospects, it finally resonated with me that video will get us in front of thousands of people in our community at a time. Just like everyone else, my videos from the first year are absolutely horrible! In fact, they are laughable. When I see the thumbnails, I just laugh really loud. But do you know what? I started, and over time, it got much better. If you want to see results, you must be an action-taker. You also must be consistent.

When we started our video journey, we had so many ideas and wanted to do everything. But instead, we created a video system that was efficient and easy to duplicate. Don focused on creating and posting quick raw videos to social media while I focused on long-form content to serve our growing database. He focused on keeping our brand relevant on social media while I focused on nurturing all our opt-ins. We became so seasoned at running ads that we consistently gained 200-400 new opt-ins every month. Many of those videos developed through concepts and marketing techniques learned through Krista's Video Maven. The greatest takeaway was where to find content and how to convey it through video.

We learned the difference between brand awareness and conversion ads. Brand awareness is when you pay for ads to just put yourself in front of people so that they see you over and over in their feeds. Conversion ads are when you want them to opt-in. They are costly and don't work in today's economy. Getting prospects to opt-in is what we're used to. Keeping their focus on your branding is a separate system. Here is how we operate this system: Once leads opt-in, they route to our Customer Relationship Management (CRM) system. Choose your CRM very wisely. The best CRM tool for you is the one that you will *actually use*. Automation, marketing, lead follow up, lead nurture and integration with other apps are the things you should be looking for. We started off with just under 3,000 leads and quickly grew to a database of over 14,000 prospects. It continues to grow every day. I know what you are thinking. This is larger than most real estate agents' following on social media. That is absolutely right. I can get in front of 14,000+ prospects at any given time and deliver a message using video.

Using Marketing Updates to Lead With Value

This is where the real fun begins. Once prospects are in the CRM, they are automatically routed to the appropriate email campaign. These emails go out on scheduled intervals with timely messages. They are a combination of videos and blogs that keep them informed with tips, resources, next steps, lead magnets, etc. Bottom line, these prospects continue to get exposed to our brand and how we serve. And, we are providing valuable information they can actually use. If they are looking for homes, they also receive automated alerts of properties available on the market meeting their criteria. If they are selling, they receive market snaps automatically that we put on a monthly or bi-monthly schedule. All of this is automated. You just have to set it up. And yes, it took time crafting the perfect email campaigns.

We are able to see what properties our prospects are looking at and how often. We are also able to see what emails they are opening and how many times they open it. If you had a system like this, how easy do you think it would be to convert? With this system, we are no longer cold calling, knocking on doors or compelled to hold open houses. I can send property tours directly to prospects based on their home search behavior. We are providing information they want, not being a nuisance—and that's value. Our days on the market for listings is less than our MLS average of 59 days. We average less than 2 weeks on the market due to our ability to market using video and Facebook strategies Krista teaches us. Our calls are not cold because these are warm or hot leads that are engaged with our content. Agents on our team do not fear picking up the phone because they are able to lead the conversation with value (and we are recognized, so it's more of a warm call).

You are probably wondering what specific content is being used for our videos. I will talk about Don's social media strategies in just a bit. For now, I want to focus on database nurturing. One of the key components of our video marketing strategy is building and maintaining a strong database. This includes not only current clients, but also past clients, potential clients, and even industry professionals. The CRM software allows us to keep track of all our contacts and their specific interests or needs.

By having a well-maintained database, we can send targeted and personalized content to each individual. This could include new property listings that match their search criteria, market updates in their desired area, or helpful tips for buying/selling real estate. By tailoring our content specifically to each person's interests and needs, we are able to build trust and establish ourselves as experts in the industry.

Every week, I focus on creating content for residents and homeowners. To keep things simple and manageable, I use hot topics mentioned in Keeping Current Matters. If the topic was worth posting there, I know I can quickly rewrite the content in my own words and recycle the message. I post it in the form of a blog, video, or email copy. All it takes is one good newsletter a week to keep your branding in front of the masses. Our weekly newsletter has a combination of blogs, videos, and property tours of our listings. We speak to every single database member with these newsletters, including the looky-loos who will eventually take action sometime down the road. I do not have to be creative every week. Most of the time, I recycle old videos. It does not hurt to get more views. I have new opt-ins every month. So, repurposing videos is a great way to be efficient with your time. Repurposing videos was another great technique learned through Krista's coaching.

The first year will take most of your effort. After that, it gets much easier. Initially, I spent too much time editing my own videos and could not produce them fast enough. I used software such as TechSmith Camtasia and had a great deal of fun bringing our messaging to life. I edited all my videos for a very long time. Now, there are so many sites, such as Fiverr, that can edit your long-form content for you at a reasonable price. I also learned of this leveraging tool through Krista's coaching. For short-form videos, I prefer editing fast and easily on CapCut and Opus Clip. With Opus Clip, I can take my old long-form videos and create several reels with the click of one button. It is amazing!

We noticed the greatest shift in our business after just one year of being consistent with using video. It was the summer of 2020 when we became intentional with video marketing. The next pivotal moment was moving our real estate team to a more virtual-friendly brokerage. We made the move to join Krista Mashore's organization at eXp in December 2020. Well, 2021 was the first year that we closed over one hundred transactions at just over $21 million. Video had exposed us to so many more prospects than anything we ever did before. I still get referral calls from people I don't even know because we have nurtured so many prospects in our database. Not only did video help us reach a wider audience, but it also helped us stand out from our competitors.

As we evolve with video and content marketing, we continue to look for efficiency tools. One key tool that has helped us in creating more content efficiently is Jasper, a powerful AI tool. With its help, we have been able to produce high-quality content at a faster pace. We believe in leveraging technology to improve our processes and provide better value to our audience.

In today's digital age, content is king. It has become the currency through which businesses connect with their audience. That is why we are constantly striving to create more meaningful and useful content for our customers. This is how you lead with value. Giving people the right message and at the right time. It is no longer about cheesy videos that tell you these are the three steps you take to buy a house. Consumers are looking for experts to which they can relate.

Using Omni Presence to Lead With Value

I mentioned that this is how we manage video marketing in our database. Now let's talk about Don's social media strategies. As a brand, it is important to establish a strong and consistent voice across all platforms. This not only helps build trust with your audience but also makes you more recognizable in a crowded market. We strive really hard to practice the 80/20 rule. *For your social media business page and groups, eighty percent of what you post should be community-focused.* The other twenty percent should be conversion-focused. For your social media personal pages, eighty percent of what you post should be personal. The other twenty percent should be about your real estate business. Do not forget about Google and YouTube. These platforms are still the largest search engines. Long-form content and business stories are great to share on these platforms. Omni presence is another strategy we learned through Krista's coaching. You need to show up everywhere!

As I am writing this chapter, I am thinking about a phone call I had with a homeowner prospect about a month ago. While I was talking with him and scheduling our next meeting, he literally looked me up on social media. He went onto Facebook and entered my name to see if my page matched my wit. He was able to see that I was friends with his wife and quite a few other people he knew in the community. I remembered each person he referenced very vividly, and it gave us something more to talk about.

I mention this story to demonstrate just how relevant you need to be when you are marketing your business. Paid Ad spend will get you in front of far more people than just posting to social media. Yet, you still have to post to social media for people to know who you are personally. Prospects are googling you, searching you on social media and determining what you have in common.

So, you really need to have a healthy mix of running paid ads and showing your personality through social media posts. You'd be surprised at how many agents I enter into Google, and it is crickets. I mean, I often cannot find a single source of information that would inform me that they are the real estate agent I need to call. These are the same agents that express concerns about their business in real estate mastermind groups across social media. You cannot hide from marketing and be successful in real estate. Hiding out and hoping to be found is not a winning formula.

Don has always done a great job of sharing our family and who we are as a hard-working couple through social media. I often speak with ladies who knew me well before our very first conversation because they already connected with who I am as a person through social media. Whether we are at home cooking dinner with the kids, at a school function watching our teen play her saxophone, out celebrating wins with our real estate team, driving around town laughing at how we are as a couple, or just working on one of our latest flip projects, he posts about it everywhere! Who you are outside of real estate is the most important part of your brand. And people want to know about it.

This business is not for private people. No one wants to work with the secret agent they can't connect with. Would you hire a quiet attorney if you were accused of murder? No, you would hunt down the pit bull of attorneys. The same is true when a first-time home buyer gets fed up with losing in bidding wars. They hunt down the agent that appears everywhere they are. I know this because I have prospective buyers in my database who hire my team after they have fired another agent. Our branding speaks so loudly that the choice is obvious. I often have prospective sellers asking us to list their home after they fire their agent. Just because you do not see many likes on your posts does not mean people are not watching. So always post to create brand awareness.

Using Niche Marketing to Lead With Value

The other system we became seasoned with is narrowing down our niche. Krista talks about this extensively through her coaching. You waste a lot of time and money when your audience is too broad. This is why detailing what your brand is about and who it serves is really important. Your brand voice should reflect your niche and speak directly to them.

We have honed in on serving move-up buyers. This means that all of our branding and messaging is tailored towards this specific audience. We use language and visuals that resonate with move-up buyers. We address their unique needs and concerns.

This approach has allowed us to connect with our target market on a deeper level, build trust, and establish ourselves as experts in the field. By speaking directly to our niche through our brand voice, we lead with value and show how we can help them achieve their goals.

But why stop at just one niche? As you continue to grow your business, consider expanding into other niches within the real estate industry. I mentioned that Don and I flip homes. We started holding properties and flipping properties in 2007 when we were married. We really focused on it when we relocated for the first time in 2012. By the time we relocated to South Carolina in 2015, we were experienced investors. Well, we never lost sight of that when we started our real estate sales business. I believe many agents make niching harder than it has to be. If you enjoy something and are passionate about it, then you make it a part of your business. In our case, we really love making homes beautiful.

For Don and me, it is never about making a quick sale. So, we see beyond the norm. 2021 was our best year not only because of video, but also because we focused on what we do best. That is, making homes beautiful. Somewhere between 2020 and 2021, our desire to help others sell for more and maximize their profits really spilled into our videos. Our vendor partners, past clients, friends on social media and prospects in our database talked about what we do heavily. We landed several listings in 2021. Nearly half of them were properties where our investment company poured money into renovating homes on behalf of our clients. As a result, all of these homeowners were able to sell their homes for far more than their neighbors and they gained more of their equity. We did not charge a ridiculous fee to achieve this either. But what we gained was a community of homeowners who sang our praises to anyone who would listen.

Those listings gave us an opportunity to market homes in a light that no other competitor was doing. We focused heavily on staging, photography and videography. Our branding stood out because of it. Homeowners knew that by listing with the Latimore Group of eXp Realty, they were going to get maximum exposure and profit tremendously. So, we attracted more move-up buyers. We named this program or offer "Home Makeover Concierge."

Niching does not have to be hard. Just be intentional about who you serve and how you serve them.

Leading With Value Means I Win Before I Arrive

We pride ourselves on how we truly stand out from our competitors. Taking the time to educate your community and taking the time to create materials that your audience can understand, is more than what most agents will do. Most agents focus on the right now, the immediate fix versus the long-term strategy.

I remember during our first three years of grinding. We always made it a point to leave something of value with every prospective client. Again, this is what our brand is. This really became relevant with running ads and showing up everywhere with video. There is nothing worse than having great content, serving thousands of people, only for them to go with another agent when they are ready. So, taking the time to provide great resources for homeowners is the most important system to focus on. Listings bring more business! Always remember this. Listings get you maximum exposure because they provide more opportunities to market. Simply put, listings provide you with more opportunities to serve.

Another thing that came out of the year of selling more than 100 homes is an efficient listing system. Krista coaches heavily on location domination and the CMA drop-off process. If you have not learned about this, you need to capitalize on this learning opportunity before your competitors do. Krista teaches this so well that even her students don't want other agents in their market learning about it. It truly gives you an unfair advantage.

I adapted a version of this strategy. Between 2020 and 2021, I personally signed 52 listing agreements without ever stepping foot inside a seller's home. Yes, *52*. I did this all by winning before I arrived. I developed a video and packet drop-off system that won homeowners over before I even completed a consultation through Zoom. By the time we met for the Zoom, they were ready to sign.

Think back to everything I have referenced so far in this chapter. Homeowners were seeing us everywhere across multiple platforms on video. Then they were being nurtured in our database with video and valuable content. Then once they raised their hand, we dropped off even more valuable content at their doorstep. By the time we met via Zoom, they already knew what our company was about and how we were going to serve them. The Zoom was there to reiterate what they already knew. The choice was obvious. It did not matter if they were speaking with other agents. They hired the Latimore Group of eXp Realty because they already trusted us and formed a relationship with us over time. This is what Krista means by "Win Before You Arrive." And I never would have put all the pieces together so brilliantly if I did not stumble across her ad during the Spring of 2019.

During those two years, listings accounted for 32% of our total sales. Listings bring you more business. If you have a bad year in real estate, just take a look at how many listings you took on that year and you will see where you fell short. Focus on leading with listings. If you can lead with listings, you can lead with value. Again, you have the opportunity to create content that serves. Not content that sells. People do not want to be pitched. They want a relatable human to provide them with the value they are looking for and at the right time. So, show up everywhere and every time! This is how we sold more than 100 homes in a year. We remain in the top 1% as the direct result of video marketing strategies.

Takeaways

1. Your success is based on how much you *serve*, not how well you *sell*.
2. Leading with value means you give value in everything you do, from the content of your videos to the way you help sellers prepare their homes.
3. You can only serve people if you engage with them and truly listen to what they need and want.
4. To serve more people, you need to expand your reach beyond the old-school tactics of door-knocking, cold calling and open houses. The most effective way to do this is with digital marketing on social media.

LATOYA LATIMORE

The Latimore Group -eXp Realty

803-563-3706

RealEstate@LatimoreGroup.com

Columbia, South Carolina

SCAN ME

**Free Gift: Bonuses
Time To Take Action!**

Information alone is not enough. I've put together this **free expert resources member's hub** to help you get started now. Customize the strategies and tactics from this book to *your* business and marketing plan, with guidance, top producer tools and extra trainings.

KristaMashore.com/TopProducer

Becoming a Community Market Leader©

by Chris Pesek

Prior to having someone as a client that you can wow with your real estate knowledge and processes, how do you create raving fans? How do you get people talking about you in the community as one of the "good ones?" How do you get recognized as Businessperson of the Year? How do you get nominated as a Hometown Hero, an award for someone who goes out of their way to help other people? Yes, that's the ultimate culmination of my becoming a Community Market Leader© and implementing certain ideas over the last four years. I was named Businessperson of the Year and was nominated as a "Hometown Hero" for pouring my knowledge into other people, for spreading the word about local businesses, local nonprofits, and trying to generate a genuine community in the area we live.

In all the lessons I've learned from Krista, focusing on being a Community Market Leader© is something that stood out to me and has allowed me to focus on bringing all of the lessons I've learned in the program to serve my community. I've been able to continue to grow my sphere of influence locally and, because I love doing it, people in the community know that I truly care. They see me giving back to the community, lending my learned skills and talents to help others grow their businesses. This, in turn, has allowed me to grow my business using a stable foundation that I can always rely on if any of my additional marketing efforts start to fail.

In this chapter, I'm going to show you a couple of projects I've done to serve my community. I want you to think of them as examples of what you can do, but it's important that you find what you are passionate about and use that passion to provide service to your community.

What's a Community Market Leader©?

One of the core concepts Krista teaches is to be a Community Market Leader©, which means to "Serve, NOT just SELL." Ultimately the more you serve, the more you will sell, but service always comes first. Doing things for the community and local businesses is one of her core trainings.

To me, the concept of Community Market Leader© was natural. Growing up in a small town gave me a unique perspective on how communities operate together. In our town of roughly 2,000 people, we didn't have a lot of convenient options to shop at large chain stores or eat at large chain restaurants. The nearest Walmart was almost 30 minutes away (it was the time of the 55-mile-a-hour speed limit). Chain fast food was the same distance, and the closest Red Lobster was an hour away. So, all our business was done locally. I knew the owners of the lumberyard and I went to school with their children. The wife of the manager was one of my religion teachers. It was the same for the grocery store and the two restaurants in town, the barber shop and every other business.

But the thing that stood out to me from an early age was that when help was needed, people in the town came together and the community felt like a big family. Dysfunctional at times, plenty of fights, but at the same time, the mutual admiration and love were there as well. You could see it when we had a church picnic, a school fundraiser or the town's 4th of July weekend festivities. Everyone showed up. Everyone helped out. If you needed to know where something was, where somebody was or how to get somewhere, all you had to do was ask. I can remember visitors from out of town needing help and seeing my parents and others assist without thinking twice.

I started my real estate career in Austin, Texas, which is anything but a small town. Even in our small subdivision, I only knew our immediate neighbors and only spent time with two of those families. My wife grew up in Austin, but the early 2000s seemed like a lifetime away from the Austin she grew up in. We could tell the growth was happening quickly so we decided to move to one of the suburbs, Dripping Springs, where we would have a little bit more room around us and get a chance to move into a community that felt a little closer to the town I grew up in. Even though Dripping Springs is only about 20 miles from downtown Austin, in 2016, it was a completely different world, but it's a world I was familiar with.

I started Krista's course in March 2020. Perfect timing, just as a global pandemic was erupting. In hindsight, the timing really *was* absolutely perfect. I specifically remember working on identifying our Ideal Client on one of Krista's coaching calls. I realized my Ideal Client was me. I had already developed an online presence with the help of Krista's program that allowed me to reach an audience that most small business owners have no clue how to reach. It only took a couple of months to realize that small local businesses were hurting more than anyone else. When the world shut down, everyone started shopping online. Local Main Street boutiques and restaurants got devastated.

I started to think back to where and how I grew up and knew that I had to do something to help the community I was living in. But what? I got creative and put some effort into it. And of all the lessons from Krista that I've applied, I know my success in growing my real estate presence in Dripping Springs started with the idea of helping local businesses stay open during the pandemic.

Community Date Night

My wife and I have always made it a priority to continue to date each other weekly since we were married in 2002. Those two ideas seemed to mesh perfectly and the idea of Community Date Night was born. In a nutshell, I wanted to encourage the community to find some way to continue to spend money locally, either at the businesses that people loved or at businesses they had never heard of. With my growing Facebook audience, I was able to get in front of thousands of community members. I was able to reach out and remind them of the importance of continuing to date your loved ones as well as loving on the businesses they'd come to accept as just a normal part of their everyday life. When a local small business shuts down and word of it hits social media, people always leave comments about how it was their favorite boutique or favorite restaurant. They comment that they loved going there with their mom or their dad. And they are just so sad that it's not around anymore! I've done the same thing. A business may be one of my favorite places, but life gets in the way, and it's gone. Then I regret not having visited more.

Here's what I decided to do: Once a month, I would sit down with the owner of a restaurant, or a brewery, or a bar or a bakery—anywhere we thought would make an interesting date. Drawing on the knowledge of video I was gaining through Krista's program, I interviewed the business owners. I'd have them talk about why they were in Dripping Springs and why the community was important to them. I'd ask them why they decided to become entrepreneurs and why they decided to open that restaurant or a brewery. I'd ask how long they had been in the community and what their favorite things about Dripping Springs were. Those videos became the backbone of promoting Community Date Night.

At the time, I was still a little unsure of myself and what we were doing, so I started with the places we had already been on dates and where we were already familiar with the owners. Business had slowed down to a crawl, and those business owners were beyond ecstatic that someone was trying to help them make it through the pandemic. They were on board with anything that could help put more people through their doors and generate revenue. We always promoted some type of special for date night, so the community felt like they were getting a deal. And while, even to this day, not all date nights are huge successes in terms of the number of people that show up on those specific nights, the owners continue to rave about the results. It dramatically increases community awareness of these businesses. The videos not only promote the businesses but, more importantly I think, allow the community to get to know the other community members who are behind these businesses.

When you visit a small business, if you get to know the owners, it puts your view of that business in a completely different light. If you only go to that business once or twice, your odds of getting to meet the owners are slim. These videos I promoted on social media reminded people that businesses are more than the stones, wood and glass that make the building or the location that makes it convenient. The businesses are run by people who live near you, shop in the same places as you, have kids that go to school with yours, and are the people you see on the other side of the church on Sunday. Even if you never actually meet in person, they're your neighbors.

Personally, I'm much more likely to continue to patronize a business if I know the owners, if I recognize them in town and I can tell them "hi" while I'm shopping for groceries. People were already stopping me in the grocery store because they'd seen me on Facebook promoting my listings. Now the business owners I've videoed tell me that people stop them in the grocery store to tell them they watched the interview they did with me. Or that they weren't able to actually make the date night, but they went on a different night and were blown away by the food and the hospitality. They also say that before the video, they really didn't know the business existed. I've had so many stories like that from business owners that it's getting hard to keep track at this point.

We are just starting our fourth year of community date night and at this point, we have been to 27 different locations locally for date night. All of the business owners who have done one are eager to do another. As word spreads and as other business owners see the videos and the response, they're beginning to contact me, wanting us to do a date night at their business. I've gotten to know so many people over the last four years that I never would have been exposed to had I not chosen to start this project. It's not just the people who see me doing the videos and who see my ads on social media. It's the people who come to date night and take the time to stop by our table and thank me for what I'm doing for local businesses. Some of them have become friends and have attended every date night since the first one where they met me. It's become common for groups of 8 to 12 people to get large tables on date night and literally have a community date night.

Twelve Days of Christmas

When it comes to implementation of ideas, I have to be very careful and understand my limitations. I always want to implement everything immediately. Then what typically happens is that I have way too much on my plate. After a couple of months, I have to reevaluate and get rid of things that aren't immediately necessary. To paraphrase what Krista says, implement, refine, perfect and then move on to the next iteration or idea.

Toward the end of the first year of date night, the response had been so good from the business owners and the community alike, I knew I wanted to do more. This time, I wanted to do something for businesses that weren't eating or drinking establishments. In November of that year, I saw a Chamber of Commerce announcement for "Christmas on Mercer." It's a local craft market downtown where artisans from around the community set up booths so people can shop on Small Business Saturday. That's where the idea of the "12 Days of Dripping Springs Christmas" came from.

I knew there were several boutiques, craftspeople and other businesses locally who could use the help around Christmas time. In talking to one of the business owners, I was shocked to find out that over 80% of their yearly revenue was generated between Thanksgiving and Christmas. The question was, "How do I help these community members?"

I had gotten pretty good at interviewing business owners, and I was getting much better at Facebook ads. I was seeing amazing results with retargeting and expanding my social media audiences, so the answer was pretty clear at that point: Find a way to produce more video content specifically on Facebook and produce a larger audience for these businesses. The general layout for the "12 days of Dripping Springs Christmas" is to produce 12 videos with local business owners discussing who they are, when they moved to Dripping Springs, what their business is and why it's a passion for them. Then we make sure to talk about the product they have and any specials they are running for Christmas.

The local businesses I've promoted in this program include wineries, chocolate makers, boutiques, coffee roasters, estheticians and even a woman who sells cute little succulent plantings. In the first year, I thought I'd start December 12th and do the 12 days leading up to Christmas. It worked well for the most part. I did live streams on Facebook, both in person and also virtually, and then I took those live videos and promoted them with Facebook ads.

I learned a couple of lessons that first year. One, I should have started them closer to Thanksgiving. People need time to shop before Christmas and the businesses that were interviewed the last couple of days before business likely didn't get a purchasing bump that year.

The second lesson was doing 12 businesses was not gonna be enough the following year. So, I started again the next fall. The 12 businesses from the prior year all wanted to do a spotlight video again and six new businesses joined in. So, the 12 days of Christmas became 18! I started promoting the videos on December 1st of that year, but again, I felt like I didn't give people enough time to do their shopping locally.

I've learned not to mistake trying to make things better for not getting results. Several business owners were ecstatic about their increase in sales and the increase in the amount of traffic to their Facebook pages. They also got more interaction on their Facebook pages from people leaving comments about the interviews, how much they loved the gifts they had been given from that business the year before or how much the recipients of those gifts appreciated getting something from a local small business that they loved.

As with all other things we've put into place: implement, refine, perfect. While I don't think I will ever get to perfection with any of these ideas, refinement and working *toward* perfection is the goal and, for me, the key. The third year with the 12 days of Christmas led to more changes. First, doing in-person live interviews and trying to set up times to release them daily while navigating multiple schedules became a bit of a headache, especially around the holidays.

Also, in my mind, December 1st still wasn't early enough because it was after Small Business Saturday and Christmas on Mercer where several of the businesses I was highlighting had booths. I knew I could help them generate more customers that day. I decided to move my first videos up to the Monday before Thanksgiving. Knowing I would have to navigate my own travels around the holidays as well as different parties and get-togethers, the idea of doing live videos every day for three weeks straight was quickly losing its appeal.

I solved this issue by letting the businesses know that I would be filming on Thursdays. I could shoot between three and five videos on Thursday that I could quickly edit and schedule to be released as live videos on Facebook on the daily schedule. I still gave business owners the option of filming in person or virtually. It made it exponentially easier on me to just plan shoots on four days.

Again, all of the business owners I had worked with before were eager to do another video, and there were more additions than in previous years. As is the case with anything you do long enough, the third year was by far the best in terms of total views, shares, comments, likes and the businesses letting me know about the number of people letting them know they loved the video and they love their store, restaurant, etc.

Live Here, Give Here

Implement, refine, perfect—then move on to the next idea! Over the course of the first two years of Community Date Night and started doing the 12 Days of Dripping Springs Christmas, my audience had grown. I was doing something I definitely enjoyed. I was filling a niche in the community and promoting other people as opposed to myself. My client list had grown and the number of referrals had grown. But I still felt the need to give back in other ways and to continue to pour myself into the community.

The second year of doing the "12 Days of Dripping Springs Christmas," something occurred to me. Not only do small businesses in this area do the majority of their business during the holidays, I had seen a stat that the vast majority of nonprofit donations come in during that same time frame, between Thanksgiving and Christmas. My ability to give back to nonprofit organizations and people in need has grown as my business has grown, but it's something I learned from a young age. No matter what, there is always someone in greater need than you, and you can help them somehow, some way. I decided to do another video series between Thanksgiving and Christmas highlighting local nonprofits. Large nonprofits like United Way and the Red Cross obviously have a need. But again, I was focused on making a difference in the local community.

I chose five local nonprofits the first year to highlight on Facebook. Because I had gotten so much better at live interviews doing Date Night and 12 Days, it only made sense that I utilized the same format for interviewing nonprofit directors: What is the nonprofit? Why is it important to you as the director? What successes have you seen? Why is the nonprofit important locally? It's easy to generate a 10 to 20-minute video on any of these topics.

No one wants to hear me talk about real estate for 10 minutes except for my clients. But almost everyone wants to hear me interview a local nonprofit that can arrange for them to adopt local families who are in need around Christmas to make sure the children have presents and the parents can cook a Christmas meal. Almost everyone wants to hear about the local boys' shelter that takes last-strike boys out of the foster system, puts them into an environment where they learn discipline and accountability and teaches them a trade. And I want to generate money for those causes!

After the initial feedback on the first five videos I did with the local nonprofits, I knew I wanted to make it a more permanent, year-round content piece. Implement, refine, perfect. That following January I went immediately into converting what I had referred to as **"Live Here, Give Here" for the local nonprofit spotlights into a monthly spotlight.** Through the local Chamber of Commerce, I had gotten to know so many local business owners with brick-and-mortar stores. I went to them and asked them if they would like to be a part of highlighting local nonprofits, period. Of course, because of the rapport I had developed with them, every one of them was on board. So, I went about identifying local nonprofits to highlight. I did a little bit of research online and asked local business owners for the nonprofits they wanted

> *"Live Here, Give Here" for the local nonprofit spotlights into a monthly spotlight.*

to see spotlighted. That gave me a working list of about ten to start with. I went back to the same format: interviewing the director of the nonprofit to talk about the nonprofit and then using what I had learned about Facebook ads to promote that video to the community.

Being able to specifically target the community I live in made this part of the job so much easier, and so much cheaper. For a couple of dollars a day, I can get local businesses and non-profits in front of literally thousands of eyes they would normally not have access to. Even so, I always remember to implement, refine, and perfect. To leverage the business owners with brick-and-mortar storefronts I referenced earlier, I produce a one-page flyer every month for them to display in the store. The flyer has two QR codes on it and directly references the "Dripping Springs Nonprofit of the Month." Those two QR codes direct people to an "About" page on the nonprofit's website and to the donation page. So, while people are out and about in the community, shopping locally, they can scan the QR codes and learn about local non-profits they may have never heard of and donate to them immediately, even if they don't see my videos on social media.

I will never recoup all the time, effort and energy I've poured into other local businesses and nonprofits. I'm OK with that. I operate from the mindset of being a *Go-Giver*. I would never have read that book or known what that term meant without Krista Mashore. And now, knowing that I've directly promoted over 20 local nonprofits and more than 40 local businesses and have asked nothing from them in return gives me an amazing feeling of peace and satisfaction. If I hadn't gotten to know the local businesses through Community Date Night, I would never have gotten to know the other local businesses for my 12 days of Dripping Springs Christmas and also never would have been exposed to most of the local nonprofits. It's just been one singular idea that has continued to spin off other possibilities of growing my audience locally and growing my referral base and growing my sphere of influence.

And again, all of this has been done without me talking about real estate. The only people who want to talk about real estate are the small part of the population that is actively engaged in or considering doing a real estate transaction. Promoting other people has allowed me to stay in front of potential clients who may be considering a real estate transaction at some point in the future. Staying top of mind and continually reminding people how much you care has been a pretty amazing way of generating business for the last four years. When they see me promoting local businesses, Date Night, and local nonprofits, they are also reminded that I am in real estate. It truly is a "win-win."

Digital Marketing Mastermind

Implement, refine, perfect and move on to the next idea, right? So, where do things go from here? What's the next iteration of Community Date Night? In training with Krista, I've come to understand that digital marketing is part of being a smart entrepreneur, a smart business owner and a smart real estate agent. I was discussing social media marketing with a local business owner last year and he mentioned his master's degree in marketing. We went down a huge number of rabbit holes discussing, comparing notes and challenging each other on preconceived notions and potential options for each other's marketing. Something kept popping into my mind as the next idea. Coincidentally,

Krista had a complete training on this: How to Create a Local Business Marketing Class for Small Businesses.

In the future, the business owner I mentioned and I are going to start a social media and online marketing mastermind for the other local small business owners. Most people get so lost working in their business and working in their passion that they don't have the time or the drive to learn how to do their own marketing. Most of them are left trying to hire a marketing company to "post for them on social media" without having any real knowledge of what that looks like, if it's going to work, or why they want to do it in the first place.

Once a month, we are going to host free classes for local business owners to train them from the bottom up. The first class is already planned: "How to build a Facebook business page and an Instagram business page and have them connected to each other." A class this basic seems absurd to me at this point, but I remember the time before I met Krista. Back then, I didn't know anything about Facebook advertising beyond using the "Boost Post" option and thinking I was actually doing some good. Just like the small business owners that I've been promoting, I was considering hiring a "social media account manager" to run things for me.

Starting with this basic idea, each month we will teach local small business owners how to manage their social media accounts, how to advertise on them, how to identify their avatar, how to specifically advertise a niche they fill—essentially everything I've been taught over the last four years by Krista. I get to teach with and learn from a business owner who has a master's degree in marketing and who advertises five separate businesses of his own on YouTube and Google PPC (pay-per-click). Every month, we will take turns teaching the class for 15 or 20 minutes. Then, for the last portion of the hour, answer specific questions and brainstorm ideas within the group to help the other business owners reach a larger audience, increase their online presence, stay top of mind with their consumers and, ultimately, make more money.

Think about a group of 30 to 50 local small business owners who are being taught lessons which will expand their business and generate more income for their families. Then think about all of the people they meet throughout the year. Every month, they'll be with a Realtor® who is not asking them, "Who do you know that needs to buy or sell a home this year?" They will simply be given tools and have knowledge shared with them that is incredibly valuable, for free. Obviously everyone at these masterminds will know I'm a Realtor®. But I'm not talking to them about real estate. I'm taking the knowledge that's been poured into me and pouring it into other people to make their lives better. Will there be business that comes out of this? Absolutely there will be! However, would I be okay with it if I never generate a single bit of business from this course? Also, absolutely!

How Being a Community Market Leader© Impacted My Own Business

I know the burning question is always going to be, "What has it done for your business?" The answer to that question is ever-evolving. Obviously, the owners of the businesses and non-profits are huge fans of mine. In fact, the 4th date night we ever did directly led to a $27,000 closing two months after the date night. I remember the conversation with those owners specifically. "Please don't let anyone know about this transaction. We know several Realtors® locally who are considered good friends, but *they have never done a thing to try and help our business.* In fact, I don't know that they've ever been into our business themselves." I've had at least five referrals from local business owners with that exact same sentiment.

The reason why Community Date Night, 12 Days of Christmas, and Live Here, Give Here work so well is because of the old saying from Theodore Roosevelt: **"People don't care how much**

you know until they know how much you care." At the end of the day, promoting local businesses and nonprofits is more about pouring into other people in the community. In the videos, the only thing I even mention about real estate is at the very beginning when I introduce myself and it's very brief, "I'm a local real estate broker, but I'm here to talk with the owners of..." When people see you over and over promoting local businesses and talking about choosing to spend your money locally, if

> *"People don't care how much you know until they know how much you care."*

they align with that mindset, they will seek you out. And frankly, if they can't align with that mindset, they aren't the people I want to do business with.

Coming from a position of giving more than I receive (Serve, Not Sell) has been critical to see this idea come to life. I'd be lying if I said I didn't hope this would lead directly to real estate business, but I never knew how or how quickly that would happen. I just knew that I wanted to help other people locally and help to create the type of community I wanted to live in.

Growing up, people didn't help because they expected something in return. I often witnessed arguments over whether or not someone would accept payment for the help they provided. I always laugh because even to this day, my dad and I argue over whether or not he's going to pay me for something I do for him. Same with my aunts and uncles, same with my friends. Being a *Go-Giver* isn't just a sneaky way to get more business. If you're implementing any of these ideas strictly in the hope that it will generate business for you, people will see straight through it. To me, being a Community Market Leader©, being the "Digital Mayor" of your community, is about giving without the expectation of anything in return.

I have knowledge and skills now that I can pass on to other people to make their lives better. I see it as my responsibility to share that knowledge and those skills within my community. It's no different than a parent sharing their knowledge of life with a child. Will it pay off in the long run for the parent? Absolutely! But what if that parent chose to simply sit back and let their child experience life without any guidance? What if a parent let their child make all of their own mistakes and try to learn along the way? I think it's pretty obvious most of society would view that parent as a bad parent. Parents want their children to be better off growing up than they were. A way of shortcutting avoidable mistakes in life and getting more out of it in the end.

Why would it be any different for me with the knowledge and skills I've obtained from Krista? Why did she feel the need to share the knowledge she's gained over the years with me? Was there a business aspect to it? Yes, obviously. But I can tell you I have received way more from Krista and her programs than the cost associated with them. It's the reason I still take calls from prospective students and Realtors® who are considering joining her and sing her praises. She is a *Go-Giver* and gives way more than she expects in return. It's one of the lessons I learned early in life that I probably forgot along the way, but Krista reinforced it.

Find Your Own Passion

As a way of wrapping up, I want to drive home the concept of being a Community Market Leader©. And trust me, it's not about Community Date Night, 12 days of Christmas, nonprofit of the month or a social media marketing mastermind. These are things that have worked well for me that may or may not work for you. You may not be led to give back in the same way I do. Think of these projects I've created not as a plug-and-play strategy for business generation but as a catalyst to thinking about things you care about and are important in your life.

Being a Community Market Leader© is not about my business. I love to tell people about great places to eat, my favorite spot to grab a drink, my favorite places to shop, and where I bought the hat I'm wearing. I'm not alone in this—most people enjoy doing it too. It's just that with the knowledge I've gained from Krista's mentorship, it's so much easier to reach a large audience, which will inevitably benefit my business while benefiting others.

That being said, if you choose to work on any of the projects I'm talking about, make sure you are devoted to what you're doing as a passion. If you are doing any of these strictly as a means to expand your business, it will show. People will be able to tell you aren't being genuine. So, if you don't care about local restaurants, find another selection process for what you're promoting.

Maybe you're an animal lover and you want to promote animal shelters like my friend whom I met through Krista's program, Alisha Collins. Maybe you're a wine lover and you want to talk about wine clubs or tasting rooms like another friend and colleague, Kate Fomina. Maybe you love the outdoors, and you want to talk about local outdoor recreation activities. My point is, as long as you're doing something local and promoting other things that are local instead of just promoting yourself, you're going to build your audience and you're going to build your reach and your sphere of influence.

How can you make the things you care about a bigger part of your business? Show people you want to work with how much you care and your business will come. When you decide on the way you're going to give to others and pour into them for their benefit, then begin to implement, refine and perfect. Once that process for that part of your business has become second nature, look for their next logical iteration, something you love, something you're passionate about and then, implement, refine and perfect.

Takeaways

1. Being a Community Market Leader© is based on Serve, Not Sell. This is not just a way to generate business. You need to be sincerely committed to service.
2. Find ways to use your talents, knowledge and skills to serve your community without expecting anything in return.
3. Don't just try something once. Be sure to implement, refine and perfect before you move on to the next idea.
4. And most importantly: People don't care how much you know until they know how much you care.

CHRIS PESEK
Dripping Springs Home Team
Pesek Properties

512-736-1703
Chris@DrippingSpringsHomeTeam.com
Dripping Springs, Texas

Facebook: The New Mega Mall

by Cheryl Fowlkes

I went to Krista's three-day seminar in 2021 and was hooked on her energy and the things she was doing. I was also amazed at the results she was getting. Once I got into the program, I was a little scared in the beginning. There was so much! Plus, Krista emphasizes using video and I was not a person to be on video *at all*. This was one of the biggest hurdles for me to get over. But now, I'm a believer.

I owned a small brokerage and had several agents working with us. We focused on ranches and homes. I was selling between 8-14 places a year and some were high-ticket properties. I wanted more visibility for us but wasn't sure how to do it. Since being a part of the KMC program I have learned and implemented so much into my business that I never even thought about doing in the past. Since implementing several parts of this program, my volume has increased to 15-20 properties a year, plus the dollar volume of the transactions has increased each year. We now often get multimillion-dollar listings when, in the past, I might have had one or two a year. My gross commission has definitely increased from $100,000 a year to over $250,000 a year.

In that first three-day seminar, I saw the things she was doing to gain attraction for herself and her listings through social media. I was not very good at any of the social media platforms. I did have a Facebook account and I'd get on it maybe a couple times a month... maybe. Facebook helped me know when someone had a birthday so I could wish them Happy Birthday. We all use it for that, right?

I knew I needed some change in my business. Doing things the way we have always done them or like everyone else did was not yielding better results. Krista pointed out that we have to do things differently now and that includes digital marketing. Why? Because more than 60% of the buyers and sellers are shopping online whether it's for food, clothes, car or even a home! The internet has become the new Mega Mall of the world.

Facebook: The New Mega Mall

Remember when, as a kid, you could go to the mall and "watch" folks be weird? Come on, you know you did it! You could sit and chat with a friend and comment to each other: "Did you see that outfit? What were they thinking?" or "Did you see what that guy just did? That is so weird!" I have to tell you a story about my husband, and this will date me. During his senior year of high school in the late '70s, he loved Darth Vader from Star Wars. He actually made a Darth Vader papier-mâché mask and got a black cape. He'd take a cigarette to make smoke while he walked through the mall with his buddies. No kidding!! Boy, did folks stop and stare. It was embarrassing and I'm glad I wasn't dating him at the time.

No one really goes to the malls anymore, but they will watch folks do outrageous things on YouTube, Twitter or Facebook! Now they have a massive audience instead of just a few!

I understood that, but one big question I had was, "How do we use this for my business? How do we get more attention than just our friends and family on social media?" As I learned, it is by being a *marketer*, not just an agent. I had to learn what my objective was and then get *attention* to get the results that I needed. I needed to increase my presence in the marketplace as a real estate professional. This is *not* something you can do for free. I have tried. Most agents are doing just what I did a few years ago: I used to put my listings with a blurb about the property and one or two pictures on my Facebook page. Then I'd sit back and *hope* that people would see it. But honestly, how many people ever would see it? This is not what effective digital marketing looks like.

Let me ask you a question: When a seller hires you to sell their home, what is your strategy to actually market their property to reach a broader audience? To reach the masses? Most agents can't answer that question because we did not study how to do this in our real estate classes. We didn't magically figure it out on our own and no one ever taught us this. So, we'd just put our listings in the MLS, stick a sign in the yard, maybe email out an e-flyer to agents, then slap it on our Facebook page. That just doesn't cut it anymore.

The only way to reach a broader audience is through marketing as a digital marketer. You have to think like the Nikes, McDonald's and Burger Kings of the world. How do they get your attention? Yes, I know, you're not a shoe company or a hamburger joint. Still, you *are* trying to get everyone's attention, right? The way to do this is through repetition and awareness using social media. You need to use a *business* Facebook page to reach a broader audience. Most buyers and sellers are *not* right in our backyard. Some are in another state or even a different country. How do you target people who are looking to live or sell a property in the areas we serve? It is by using social media just like those companies that advertise in our Facebook feeds every day.

Remember how you were checking out some hair products the other day using Google and, not 10 minutes later, there was an ad on your Facebook page for that particular product—and it was on sale!?! They do that through Geo Mapping. What is Geo Mapping? Honestly, it is a very technical term and we don't really have to fully understand how it works. However, we get to take advantage of it when we use targeted ads on Facebook to reach or engage with an audience. The thing is that if you want to get beyond just reaching your friends, you have to pay to play in this world.

When I first started, what I thought was advertising on Facebook was just posting my listings on my page with maybe a picture or two with a small description similar to the MLS. Then I'd pray that somehow someone who might want that property would see it. I might "boost" the post. (I wasn't really sure what that did, but, hey, Facebook wanted me to. So, I did it hoping to get more action.) Nope, that didn't work either. Facebook made money, but I wasn't getting any more leads or seeing any more activity on my homes.

Once I started Krista's program, through the help of her and her team, I learned how to create a Meta Business page. This is basically a business Facebook page that is different than my personal page. Facebook then sees me as a business and not just someone chatting with friends. I started running some ads with photos of my listings where I was paying $1 a day. I ran my ads for 3-5 days and was getting my $1's worth of activity, maybe 5-10 people who were liking or commenting. I was unsure about spending money every day on an ad. It just seemed "too expensive." Still, it was working a lot better than just placing what I used to think was an ad on my personal Facebook page, where I would get maybe one thumbs up or a heart in a week, usually from a family member.

I needed to learn more so I went back to my training modules and weekly trainings with Krista. She and her team taught us how to properly set up an ad that stated this was for housing so I didn't go to Facebook jail. (If you're just being a nuisance to people who have no interest in what you're offering, Facebook will put you in jail by restricting what you can do.) I had to make the decision: Do I want to "reach" a lot of people or did I want to "engage" with them? I have to be honest; in the beginning, I didn't really understand the difference. Engaging people (which is what Krista teaches) is about letting them get to know you and trust you by offering them valuable content for free. It's not just running ads to sell them something. It's the difference between tapping someone on the shoulder and saying "hello" to get their attention versus actually forming a relationship with them by giving them something they value. Krista broke it down and helped me understand it, and showed me step-by-step how to set it up in my campaigns. It's the exact same way that she does her own ads. In fact, she does everything she teaches us and continues to use the same techniques and strategies daily in her own businesses because it works.

What I learned was that I first needed to "reach" as many people as possible and the best way to do this was to put a minimum of $3-5 per day per ad. Okay, I am not going to lie, I started to sweat. I thought, *This is going to cost me a fortune. I don't have the money for this.* But I kept hearing that old adage that you have to spend money to make money. So, for the next month I ran the ads for 3-5 days, then off for a few days and back on. The ads were mostly for some of my listings and we focused on "reaching the masses." I'd put at least $3-5 a day behind the ad and target a selected area or a very large area, depending on the property.

Once I started doing this, I started seeing that I was reaching thousands of people, not just a few. I was feeling good. This was getting exciting! Through the business page on Facebook, you can actually see your results, track them and watch them grow. I was finally seeing my numbers climb and could start showing my clients, "Look at how much action your property is getting." I was able to show them a lot more than just the clicks on the virtual tour.

ADs vs Socials

HOURS WATCHED:	220
REACH:	229,458
IMPRESSIONS:	341,903
VIDEO PLAYS:	149,837
ENGAGEMENTS:	42,227
THRUPLAY:	30,793
ZILLOW:	889

521 MILFORD STREET

VS

REACH:	217,250
IMPRESSIONS:	526,547
VIDEO PLAYS:	250,325
ENGAGEMENTS:	54,430
THRUPLAY:	13,402

556 LAKEVIEW DRIVE

ADs vs Socials

HOURS WATCHED:	288
REACH:	102,688
IMPRESSIONS:	341,903
VIDEO PLAYS:	29,837
ENGAGEMENTS:	52,227
THRUPLAY:	20,793

VS

ZILLOW:	313

1975 BONIFACIO STREET APT. 6

HOURS WATCHED:	350
REACH:	567,068
IMPRESSIONS:	441,903
VIDEO PLAYS:	259,837
ENGAGEMENTS:	72,227
THRUPLAY:	40,793

VS

ZILLOW:	115

887 ROMORA BAY COURT

ADs vs Socials

5204 SUNGROVE WAY	
HOURS WATCHED:	559
REACH:	132,000
IMPRESSIONS:	750,000
VIDEO PLAYS:	10,500
ENGAGEMENTS:	41,000
THRUPLAY:	26,710

VS

ZILLOW:	1,509

3005 ELIZABETH LANE	
HOURS WATCHED:	227
REACH:	154,369
IMPRESSIONS:	323,372
VIDEO PLAYS:	25,200
ENGAGEMENTS:	101,000
THRUPLAY:	10,521

VS

ZILLOW:	709

But I still needed to do more. Up to this point I had not done any videos, not personal or professional. To get the results I needed to change from the old-school thinking and get into making videos and using digital marketing.

The Scary Power of Video

This was a rough transition for me. I was not used to doing them or being seen on video. I'm an introvert, and that is definitely *not* in my comfort zone.

Krista kept telling us how powerful videos could be, but it took me over 6 months to do my first video. And I only did it then because I was challenged: If I didn't turn it in, I would have to pay one of my competitors $1,000 and I was *not* doing that! That was a motivator for sure.

I was scared to death to start doing them. I felt I was too old. I didn't like the way I looked or the way I sounded. It would take me *hours* to do one small 3-minute video. And even after all those hours, it wasn't perfect and so I'd think, *I need some better equipment. Yeah, that's what I need. I'll put it off making videos until I have better equipment.* Great excuse to procrastinate, right? One of the top agents in the program, Alisha Collins used to tease me and say, "Yeah, you're just fixing to do it!" Yup, I was just fixing to get some lights or a green screen before I did the videos. Then I figured I needed a teleprompter and maybe I needed a different camera. It finally got through to me what Krista was always telling us: "Done is better than perfect, do it now!!!"

So, I started just doing videos with my cell phone and I got a wireless mic for better sound. That's it. I talked with another agent who told me to just let the video run, even through the bloopers, let the editor edit them out. I thought, "No way," but I tried it. I realized my frustration was in the stopping and starting and trying to do it perfect the first time through. Now, even if I make a mistake, I just let it run and go back and redo that part and let the editor take it out. (It probably makes for some great laughs for the editor!) I have learned a rhythm for doing it and I'm able to get nine videos done in about 30 minutes. It usually takes 2-3 days to get all nine of them back. Then I use rev.com to add the Facebook burned in captions and let the other social media sites put the captions on. I now have a teleprompter and green screen and use them for my monthly videos but do most of my others on my cell phone.

It has taken me well over a year and a half to feel semi-comfortable in front of a camera. I am a lot better than I was, but each time I get a little better than I was the time before. And that's because I am consistently doing them every month. You don't get better if you don't start. I am also doing video text messages to people, and they love them. This is a great way to stay in contact and it doesn't take long to do. I truly believe these videos have changed the way that I present myself to the world and my clients.

I now have folks asking me who is doing my videos—it's me and my cell phone! I get nine videos done in 30 minutes and shoot them to the editor. When I first started it took me an hour or longer for just one! I have also learned not to rewatch my videos after I shoot them. Rewatching only makes me self-critical and then I try too hard to be perfect on the next one. I've only had to reshoot 1 video after the editor processed it because the sound was so bad. (I had forgotten to put on my microphone and the AC was running in my office. The phone picked the AC up instead of me. Lesson learned.)

That was 2 ½ years ago and now I have done over 100 videos. Folks tell me, "I love your videos and the information that you provide." We discuss all sorts of topics in the videos, from things not to do when buying and selling to things to do and what to watch out for as well. I see my videos being watched now on my YouTube channel and I went from 5 subscribers to over 1,000! My ads went from a few clicks to over 5,000 impressions in a couple of days! Having friends tell me, "I watch your videos and like what you are giving us" really makes me feel like I am doing the right thing and no one else in my market really does it.

In Krista's program, every month we're taught to produce monthly updates on the local and national markets. Then I do between seven to nine more videos a month that are put on YouTube and all the social media platforms with ad dollars to attract engagement. All of the data is relevant nationwide, and we just tweak the information to match our specific areas. A lot of the time, sellers will tell me that they have binge watched me on some of these platforms. They actually feel like they know me before I ever arrive at their home.

True story: I had a seller call and ask me out to their property. I felt a bit reserved as they already had a listing agent for the property, but she said she had seen my videos and thought I'd be a good person to talk to. I showed up and provided the seller my marketing plan and seller's guide because she had asked for some more details. We toured the property and, after doing so, she asked if I would consider working with her agent, partnering with them. I thought about it. This woman's property was not standard or typical for residential agents (like the current listing agent was). I agreed to help the agent for a referral fee because they had not sold a property like this before. I thought I could help educate them on the process.

After a few weeks, it was clear that the agent really didn't want to learn much. She called me and said she was giving me the listing but wanted a *very* large referral fee. I waited a couple of days then politely bowed out. I sent the seller a note explaining that I wished them the best, but I would not be working with her agent going forward. The agent terminated the listing agreement with the seller shortly after that.

A few weeks later the seller reached out to me and wanted me to list the property for them and we did. It was a complicated property that took time and patience to handle all of the details. After the transaction was completed, I received a glowing review from the seller stating they could not have sold the property without me. She raved about all the work that I did and my videos. She said that what sold her on hiring me was the seller's guide and marketing plan that I provided that Krista gives us to position ourselves as unique and different. Everyone she spoke to said they had never seen anything like it before.

How My Business Has Changed

I am now spending max $5 per day per ad (I did splurge on one listing and did $10 a day for three days) and I am reaching a much broader audience which is giving me and my listings more visibility in the marketplace. Before, I was nervous about being seen on video, the cost of editing and the cost to do a video for a listing. It seemed a bit much when you look at adding it to the $500 plus I was already paying for the listing photos. I used to gauge what pictures, how many, should I do aerials or Matterport 360-degree photos? It all depended on the listing, right?

Nope. I've learned the value of doing the same thing for every single listing, no matter what the price point. Each of my listings gets:

- Professional photos
- Matterport
- Aerials
- Video (not just a virtual tour)
- Personal walk-through videos (some edited, some not)
- Personal website for each listing
- 4-page color brochure
- And more!

Did you know that videos actually have a bigger reach or engagement than just photos or a virtual tour will ever have? People like to watch videos. They love to scroll through and see all the things that are going on. They love silly ones too! A virtual tour is just photos strung together to create a moving tour of the property. That is *not* a video and it can't capture the feeling of walking through the property.

Without Krista's program, I would have never in my wildest dreams adventured into making personal videos, educational videos, or market update videos. I would have never put them on YouTube or Facebook—no way! This program has given my clients a broader reach in marketing their properties to more buyers than any other agent can provide. I know my business, but her training has given me the opportunity to do more than any other agent is doing in my area. It's given me the confidence to stand out as the authority and have a competitive market advantage!

I now have people telling me they love my videos and the content that I produce. They see them on Facebook and YouTube. I have other agents contacting me asking who is doing my videos. They were shocked to learn that I do them myself with my cell phone and a green screen. I know that since starting Krista's program I have increased my yearly sales volume as well as price points on my listings. I am producing more content than I ever dreamed I would do. I have co-authored 2 books with her for sellers and buyers. When I produced my first book and gave a copy to my husband, he was shocked and happy for me that I am sharing my knowledge with others. People look at you differently when you present them with a book with you as an author. No other agent in my area is doing that either!

Takeaways

1. Slapping photos of your listing up on your personal Facebook page is *not* "advertising on social media." Few people other than your friends will ever see it.

2. To really be effective on social media, you've got to "pay to play" and use paid ads.

3. Creating videos is the most powerful way to get your message out to the masses. Used properly and consistently, video can build trust and give you authority in your community.

4. You don't have to be perfect. You just have to get it done!

CHERYL FOWLKES

Superior Town & Country Group
eXp Realty

📞 512-749-8509

✉ Cheryl@SuperiorTownAndCountry.com

📍 Austin, Texas

SCAN ME

Free Gift: Bonuses
Time To Take Action!

Information alone is not enough. I've put together this **free expert resources member's hub** to help you get started now. Customize the strategies and tactics from this book to *your* business and marketing plan, with guidance, top producer tools and extra trainings.

KristaMashore.com/TopProducer

How to Go From Zero to Being a Top Agent

by Sarah Stone-Francisco

I know you've already read about some great ideas and strategies in the other chapters. And you've seen how top producers use them to get results. But by this point, you may be asking questions like:

Does this program work for brand new agents? YES!

Does it work for agents in small towns? YES!!

Does it work for busy people, including solo parents? YES!!!

How do I know? Because I am living proof. As a widowed, homeschooling mom living in a small rural town, I became a Realtor®, then joined Krista›s coaching program four months later. Within two months, I had my first two listings because I was implementing the strategies I learned directly from the program. And, in *less than three years,* I became the #5 agent in my entire county! (The four ahead of me are legends who have been selling real estate for 30-40 years or more!)

And before you assume that there is anything special about me, any reason why it would be easier for me and, therefore, comparatively harder for you, let me tell you my story.

Almost ten years ago, the love of my life, who was also the father of my child, my husband of 11 years, and my best friend since I was 21 years old, died suddenly and unexpectedly of a seizure in the middle of the night while we were camping far from anyone who could help us.

Our daughter was three at the time and I had gratefully given up my career to stay home and raise her. We had no savings, no property, no life insurance, and I had no income. Luckily our family stood by us and buoyed us tremendously while I focused on healing and being the best mother I could.

It was a long, painful road with many tears, many dark nights, so many deep breaths, and many, many moments asking God for guidance. Throughout the journey, I maintained the intention of practicing gratitude and surrender. The only way through the pain and dark nights is to truly be with all of the feelings. As Osho, the philosopher from India, said, "The branches are only as high as the roots are deep." I know that by embracing and staying present with the gamut of my experience, I now feel more joy than I ever knew possible. It was only by being willing to expand my capacity for discomfort that I was able to concomitantly expand my capacity for joy. But it wasn't easy, and it took work. And whenever I felt lost or unclear about my direction, I would ask for Divine Guidance, which is what led us to a new life.

Four years after he died, we moved to a small town where I only knew one family, and I started rebuilding community. We started homeschooling, and I started hosting a Homeschool Adventure Club. During 2020, both the growing independence of my daughter and the financial needs of our family had me seeking Divine Guidance again. I began to "live in the question," as my spiritual teacher Larry Schultz puts it. It's a process where you open yourself up to guidance instead of grasping for answers, and

I was looking for guidance on my next direction or career. Several opportunities came my way, but none felt like a zinger that electrified me. But once the message to get into real estate came, it felt like a little electric shock had gone straight into the top of my head, and I knew it was the next thing I should pursue.

So, if I could do it with no resources, in a newer town knowing next to no one, raising a child all by myself in the middle of a global pandemic, I know and trust that you can do it, too.

All you have to do is learn how...

People are always asking me how I did it. I often hear from others in the community who say that I "came out of nowhere." Everyone wants to know: What's the *one thing* that made me so successful in such a short time? Truthfully, there isn't one thing. It's all the things you've been reading about in this book. However, besides hard work, the most important strategy for me has, by far and away, been using video.

I have learned to use video in nearly *every* aspect of my business and at every step of the process: from getting in front of my community, to introducing myself to leads, to explaining contracts and disclosures, to staying in touch with my sphere. Video has set me apart from other agents in my community because it has enabled people to get to know me on a massive scale. Instead of waiting to meet each person individually to be known by them, I am popping up on the feeds and in the living rooms of thousands of my community members every day.

Properly distributed video has proven to be the fastest way to massively scale my business. How do I know? Because *within weeks* of posting videos and running ads behind them, as Krista taught me, people started coming up to me at restaurants and saying that they appreciated my videos. Or, stopping me in the grocery store or at the cafe and saying, "Are you that Realtor® on social media?" Why, yes, yes I am. :)

Video is alive and dynamic, so people feel like they know me way before meeting me, much more so than with any other strategy. I know this because I use a myriad of the strategies in this book. But no one has ever come up to me and said, "Hey, are you that Realtor® on those postcards?" Don't get me wrong. Other strategies are important, too, but they are far more effective when they're used with video. My postcards have a QR code that goes to my website or funnel where people will then see videos of me presenting listings and showcasing my community. My videos are why they pick up the phone and call me. Yes, *people reach out to me asking me to represent them*—all the time!

We're about to close on a property where, just two months ago, someone who had been following me on social media called and asked if I would show him some houses. During the first visit, where my buyer's agent showed him several homes, he relayed to her that he had been following me on social media for a while, and there was no doubt that he wanted to work with us and not anyone else. All of this came from video. (Yes, I already have the need for a buyer's agent to help me handle the amount of business that comes to me. I realized this when, one month last year, I had 13 escrows in contract and was losing additional business because I simply didn't have time to call them back, much less serve them.)

My use of video doesn't just help me get more business. It also tremendously helps me sell my clients' homes! People feel like they know the properties because of the HGTV-style walk-throughs I do for each one that I list. I had one person drive *two hours* to an open house and say, "I feel like I already know this house. I can even recite every line from the video." Even though they didn't end up buying that house, the video is what got them through the door.

Another person picked up a property brochure I had at a listing and followed the QR code on the brochure to the property's website. From there, he watched the video and reached out to me to purchase the property. Not only that, he enlisted me to sell an $11.1 million commercial property *over seven other Realtors®*

that he had already interviewed. I told him that his type of commercial property wasn't a niche I was familiar with. He replied, "I can teach any Realtor® about that. What I can't teach them is how to market like you do." (And he's right. But Krista can! And did.)

On a recent listing appointment with a couple that had moved but kept their house and now wanted to sell, I asked how they had heard about me. They said that their neighbor used to be a Realtor®. When the neighbor found out they were selling, she told them, "You have to use Sarah Stone-Francisco. Her marketing is unparalleled." And the main thing I do differently than other agents in my area is consistently use video and distribute them correctly so that they get massive exposure.

Other agents in the community tell me all the time that they love my videos and that they want me to teach them how I do it. They even tell me that I am a marketing wizard! In a county of over 1,000 agents, I went from having zero business to being #5 in the county in less than three years. Yes, I've worked very hard, but I can attribute a huge degree of that success to using the strategy of video.

Video as a Problem Solver

Video helps me solve so many problems. Here are the top eight:

#1 This one-to-many marketing strategy (versus one-on-one) saves me an inordinate amount of time by putting me in front of *thousands* of people every day. (I couldn't give that many hugs a day, even if I tried!)

#2 Running Facebook ads for my listings puts my clients' homes in front of *hundreds of thousands* of people, giving my sellers (and myself) massive exposure and higher offers. This is my unique value proposition that distinguishes me from my competition and helps me beat out competitors.

#3 Educating people through social media positions me as an authority so that people already trust me before they meet me.

#4 Familiarizing people with my personality attracts the people that resonate with me. They already know they want to work with me.

#5 When I create videos to market my properties, my videos are also marketing *me*, which strategically stretches my marketing budget.

#6 Through Facebook video ads, I stay top of mind so that when people are thinking of selling or buying, I'm the one they think of.

#7 I'm educating the community before, during, and after working with them, so they come to the transaction with a wealth of knowledge and that makes the transaction so much smoother.

#8 My strategically targeted videos continue to put me in front of past clients so that they always remember who I am and constantly refer me to other people. It also helps me nurture others in the community.

Get Started Creating Videos

The results I've gotten using video probably sound great to you. But how do you do it? There are two main components to making video work for you:

1. Producing good videos.
2. Distributing them correctly.

Notice I said "good" videos, not "perfect" videos. There is no such thing as a "perfect" video. In fact, your audience doesn't want *perfect*, they want *relatable*. They want authentic. You might think the product you're selling is houses. But clients can choose from a plethora of Realtors®. So, really, when you're marketing, you're selling *yourself*. But, truly, you don't need to *sell* yourself.

You just need to be *you*. **Be authentic because that is what attracts the people you want to work with.**

What if you don't feel comfortable on video? Guess what? No one does at first! But, as Krista says, "You can't show up to an appointment with a bag over your head. This is how you look. This is how you sound." So, if you're worried about how you look or sound, STOP, SNAP, AND SWITCH! (This is a technique that Krista taught us and it's in her book *Stop, Snap, and Switch*. Unlock this training and so much more in your <u>Bonus Resources</u>: **KristaMashore.com/TopProducer**)

> *Be authentic because that is what attracts the people you want to work with.*

Transmute any self-talk that isn't elevating. You are a gift to this world. There is only one of you, and only you can do what you do the way you do it. You are more than enough. You are perfectly imperfect, exactly as you were meant to be. And, if you play small or hide or don't step into your innate power, then you are selfishly keeping your gifts and service from making a positive impact on those around you.

You are here to serve, so take a deep breath, relax, and PRESS RECORD because the key to feeling more comfortable on video is—ta-da!—*making videos*!

Here are three ways you can get started:

1. **Send video texts to your closest family and friends**. They already know what you look and sound like and aren't going to judge you if you come across as awkward or make mistakes. (And if they do judge you, maybe you need new friends—kidding/not kidding.)

2. **Post Facebook Stories**. These are only visible for 24 hours, and they are mostly visible to those with whom you are already Facebook friends. So, if you post something you don't love, there is a much lower risk of someone seeing it and judging you. (However, keep in mind that you eventually actually *do* want

people to see you so that you can be top of mind when they are looking for a Realtor®.)

3. **Post interviews with local people**. It can feel easier at first if you don't have to talk directly to the camera. Instead, have a conversation on camera with someone you're already comfortable with. Like who? Someone that can give your community *value.* It might be a lender, insurance agent, local official or business owner. Another bonus to interviewing someone is that it will give you the attention of those in their sphere too. So, you'll start to be seen by more people. (Remember: You *want* to be seen by *everyone* so that you can serve more people!)

Just get started creating your videos and don't procrastinate! It can be easy to procrastinate on the things that feel hard. But as Krista reminds us, "Do the hard things now so that you can do the easy things later." One of the ways people tend to procrastinate making videos is waiting until they have all of the "right" equipment. Do *not* hide behind the equipment! As a prominent student of Krista's, Alisha Collins always says, "Stop fixin' to do!" Stop waiting until you have all the "right" equipment to make videos!!

In the beginning, all you need is your smartphone. Eventually, maybe you'll want to get a couple of lapel mics and a small tripod for under $100. Eventually, maybe you'll want to get a green screen and some extra lighting. But don't wait!!! **The worst video is the one that never gets made or posted.** So, JUST START! Lean your camera phone up against a stack of books and press record. What's important is what you say, *not* the tools you use to record it.

> *The worst video is the one that never gets made or posted.*

What to Talk About

Okay, so you're all geared up to make some videos and your next question might be, "What do I say?"

I could write an entire book on content you can produce. (Or, you could join Krista's program and have access to a seemingly unlimited and ever-growing vault of ideas and scripts.) The three easiest ways to come up with content that your audience will find valuable are:

1. **Answer questions your clients are already asking.** Once your clients are in contract, do they often ask you, "What happens next?" Then make a video on what happens during the process of escrow. Do sellers ask you for advice on what they should do to improve the marketability of their home? Make a video on the changes that will give them the highest return on their investment or how to go about decluttering and depersonalizing their house. Do people ask you, "How is the market?" Then do a local market update. The point is that people are already asking you questions that you know the answer to. Make videos answering those questions.

2. **Become the neighborhood expert.** If you highlight shops, sites, and activities, or even whole neighborhood tours, you will start to be seen as the expert when it comes to that area. And small business owners love the attention and free marketing! Your efforts are rewarded because those business owners and their audience start giving you their attention. Then when people think of that area, everyone will think of you.

3. **Re-create popular content**. Find agents on social media who have large followings and posts that get a lot of engagement (views, likes, shares, comments). Don't plagiarize them, but re-make the content and put your own spin on it. (Just make sure that when you go looking for content, you set a timer. You don't want to end up down the social media rabbit hole three hours later!)

Don't overthink your videos, and don't re-record. Test your sound before you go out. And if you "mess up," just move on. Edit it out later, or don't, but *definitely do not waste time* trying to perfect the video while you're recording it. There is no such thing as a perfect video, and your ideal clients will appreciate the authentic you, stutters and stumbles and all.

Getting It Out There

You made the video. So, now what? POST IT!

Again, the worst video is the one that doesn't get made or posted. So, no matter what it looks like, post it! Where? Anywhere! Pick your favorite platform and use it consistently.

Facebook tends to be a great place to start because people of home-buying age and means use the platform. It's also a way of connecting with your community through groups and events, which is a little more difficult on Instagram, TikTok, or YouTube. Plus, Facebook feeds to Instagram, so you can maximize your exposure across the two platforms relatively easily.

What to post?

• Short updates as Stories,
• Short vertical videos as reels, and
• Longer horizontal videos as posts.

Once you're feeling a little comfortable with posts on Facebook, now you want to make sure that *everyone* sees it. This is where the magic happens!

When you're posting to your page, some, but not all, of the people who are your Facebook friends will see your content. That's good but don't stop there. To truly take advantage of the one-to-many marketing that is going to amplify your business, you'll want *everyone* to see it. And for that to happen, you need to run ads.

You'll need to create a Facebook Business Page to run ads behind your posts. This is not simply choosing the Facebook run "Boosting" option. It's not really that effective and I never do that. I'm talking about strategically targeting the audience and communities that are most likely to become your clients and/or buy your clients' houses.

Ads are the way that you get noticed by people in the grocery store, park, and café before you've ever met them. Ads are the way you get your listings in front of buyers who have indicated that they are looking for homes. Ads are the way that you can target people moving within your community or who are moving from other areas to your community.

The details of running an ad seem complicated at first, and it's not something I recommend trying to learn on your own. But it's also not rocket science. Through the Krista Mashore Coaching program, I learned how to easily and effectively run targeted ads step-by-step. Over time, it became a simple and streamlined process that now takes me less than five minutes.

It's through this type of strategic marketing that I'm able to:

- Reach people who have expressed interest in real estate through other websites
- Reach people who are living in, or have recently visited, my area
- Retarget all of these people so they keep seeing me over and over
- Put similar campaigns in front of people so I'm giving them more of what they are already interested in
- Reach people in geographic locations that are feeder areas for relocating to my town
- Use this data to show my unique ability to market for my sellers, which gives me a competitive edge and win more listings

All of this is targeting the people who are most likely to need my help, expanding my reach far beyond what I would organically be able to access by solely posting on my Facebook Stories and feed. These are the people who will end up calling you. Yes, *they will call you!* Krista teaches us how to move people along in their readiness so that they go from warming up to us to seeking us out. There are hours of training in her program that easily and clearly lay out how to do it, but I can touch on some of the elements that make this different from any other program or strategy.

Have you ever gotten a lead, and when you call them, they act like you're bothering them? Well, this is the opposite. Through strategic targeting and retargeting your Facebook ads you're creating a parasocial relationship whereby people genuinely think they know you, just like a celebrity's fans feel like they know them. When you show up in their feed over and over, delivering valuable content that solves their problems, they begin to not only feel like they know you and like you, but they also start to *trust* you despite the fact that you've never even met them yet. Now, when they have a real estate need, it is so much more likely that they're going to reach out to you. Not only are you top of mind by staying in their feed with consistent posting, but you've also created the goodwill and trust that makes them want to seek you out above all other Realtors®.

What It Looks Like

Through Krista's program, I learned what types of content to put out, when to put it out, and to whom. For example, one video I made addressed concerns of first-time homebuyers. I posted this widely with advertising dollars behind it that got the video in front of as many people as possible. I did this to capture the attention of enough first-time homebuyers who would stop and listen to me.

> *I'm able to focus my advertising dollars on people who are drawn to me instead of wasting money on people who don't resonate with me.*

Then, I was able to make a second video that addressed another layer of questions or concerns of that same audience. By strategically targeting people who saw me once (who had stopped and watched a little of that first video), **I'm able to focus my advertising dollars on people who are drawn to me instead of wasting**

174

money on people who don't resonate with me. This is called a funnel and moving people along in the funnel is what gets your phone ringing. You no longer have to call leads and talk to people who act like you're bothering them.

I am living proof that the strategies Krista teaches can lead to massive success for any Realtor®. At the heart of Krista's program, one thing that sets this coaching program apart from any other is the way she teaches us how to make and distribute valuable content. This helps people get to know, like, and trust us. Because of this, when they need help with real estate, we're the ones they think of and already feel positively toward before even meeting us.

Anyone can make a video, and anyone can post it, but learning how to strategically do so is what has catapulted my business to the point of garnering the attention of my entire county. Not a day goes by now when someone I've never seen before says they recognize me. It's all because I learned how to post and distribute effectively through Facebook.

Takeaways

1. Even a newbie who is a busy solo parent living in a small rural community can be a top producer!
2. The key to getting comfortable making videos is to *make videos*!
3. The real impact in using videos comes when you learn to use paid ads to distribute them correctly. Learning retargeting campaigns is essential!
4. Rather than chasing down leads, when you create good videos and distribute them correctly, people will be *seeking you out*.
5. Adding video to any other strategy will make that strategy so much more effective.

SARAH STONE-FRANCISCO

Stone Luxury Homes
Century 21 Cornerstone Realty

530-802-0239

Sarah@StoneLuxuryHomes.com

Valley, California

The World Has Changed and So Must You

by Carlos Zapata

In the exciting and dynamic world of real estate, being adaptable is not just another skill. It's an indispensable requirement. I have been immersed in this industry for almost twenty years, living through its ups and downs with the passion and commitment of someone who sees this not just as a job, but as a true vocation. Yet even having that passion, I've faced challenges. My biggest challenge was seeing the market evolve at dizzying speeds so that, over time, my entire marketing strategy became ineffective. The radio advertising that once was my star strategy for attracting clients from 2006 to 2010 eventually stopped shining, plunging me into a sea of doubts about my future in this field.

The idea of leaving real estate, after dedicating the most intense years of my career to it, filled me with sadness and frustration. *"What now?"* became a constant echo in my mind. Looking for new directions or reinventing myself was no longer a choice but a *necessity* if I wanted to move forward. It was 2019 and as I searched for answers, I stumbled upon Krista Mashore's program. It couldn't have been by chance. It was the answer I needed so I could adapt and evolve in a market that no longer responded to traditional tactics.

My journey of transformation and discovery has been enriching. It has also been revealing. In this chapter, I'll share my personal and professional growth. By sharing my experience, I hope you'll see how innovation and the ability to adapt can open doors to new opportunities, even when it seems all routes are closed. I encourage you to move forward without fear of change, to seize the opportunities that the digital era offers for us in real estate. Adaptability is the real key to not just surviving but also thriving.

There was a moment, a critical instant in my career, where everything I had built seemed to fall apart before my eyes. I had used radio advertising for several years. During that time, it was effective and reliable in its ability to attract new clients for me. But suddenly, it wasn't working. The radio waves that once carried my message to thousands of ears now seemed to get lost in the air. This was an incredible blow to my marketing strategy. But it was also a wake-up call that told me I needed to change.

With every radio campaign that fell flat, I started to realize that the world had changed, and with it, the ways people searched for and found their future homes had changed as well. Everything had gone digital. Media like radio that had been fundamental had become obsolete. To survive, I had to rethink *everything* I knew about real estate marketing.

Out of My Comfort Zone and Into the Digital Age

The decision to seek new strategies was not easy. I knew I'd have to leave the comfort of what I'd known for the uncertainty of something totally new. But deep down, I knew this was the only possible path if I wanted to remain in the work I love. Fortunately, I discovered Krista's program. It seemed like a light at the end of the tunnel. I felt that with her help, I could not only learn about digital marketing, but I also had the opportunity to reinvent myself and adapt to the demands of the 21st century.

Krista opened my eyes to the possibilities offered by social media and digital marketing. She also taught me the importance of building a strong personal brand and connecting *authentically* with my audience. Every lesson, every strategy, every tool that Krista has shared, became an important piece in my professional transformation.

It wasn't just a change in marketing strategy. It was a true metamorphosis in my approach to the real estate business. What I learned created a new chapter in my career. I experienced greater reach, deeper connections with my audience, and, most importantly, the opportunity to continue growing and learning. The moment I joined Krista's program, I knew that the failure of radio advertising

> *Krista taught me that every social media post, every video, every article on my blog should be an extension of my commitment to my community, a tool to educate, inspire, and build trust.*

was not the end of my path. It was the beginning of an exciting adventure.

I stepped into the world of digital marketing with a mix of skepticism and curiosity. I had high expectations after hearing all the success stories of her students. I imagined marketing campaigns that went viral overnight, a flood of potential clients knocking on my door, all ready to buy! Well, the reality was more challenging—and enriching—than I expected. Digital marketing was not simply, "Post and wait." It's an art and a science that requires strategy, patience, and above all, *authenticity.*

Through Krista's training, I learned that digital marketing went beyond mere online presence. It was about creating *genuine connections, sharing knowledge,* and *offering value.* **Krista taught**

me that every social media post, every video, every article on my blog should be an extension of my commitment to my community, a tool to educate, inspire, and build trust.

This meant a profound change in my mindset. Where before I saw potential "clients," now I see people with dreams, doubts, and specific needs. Krista helped me understand that my goal should not be simply to sell properties but to be a valuable resource, a reliable guide for people who were on the complex journey of buying or selling a home. This client-centered approach transformed not only my marketing strategy but also the way I related to my work and the people I served.

Discovery and learning in the world of digital marketing involves a lot of trials and errors, successes and lessons. But, with each step forward, I felt more equipped and empowered. Thanks to Krista's influence, my approach evolved from "selling properties" to *creating connections*, from "doing marketing" to *building a community*. This change not only revitalized my career but also reaffirmed my passion for real estate, showing me that even in a field as old as this, there is always room to innovate, learn, and grow.

Being a Latino Professional

As a Latino real estate agent, I faced a unique set of issues that seemed to add to my challenges in the competitive real estate market. One of the most significant barriers was overcoming prejudices and stereotypes. I saw this both within the industry and in the broader market. Plus, it wasn't easy to find appropriate mentorship that matched my cultural and professional experience. I was not just looking for a mentor. I wanted someone who understood the complexities of navigating the real estate market as a Latino professional. I was looking for someone who recognized the richness that our multicultural perspective brings to the business.

Krista's program not only addressed the techniques and strategies of digital marketing but also emphasized the importance of authenticity and personal connection. These principles deeply resonated with me. Through her mentorship, **I learned to see my cultural background not as a hindrance but as a unique asset that could and should be integrated into my personal brand and marketing strategy.**

For example, one of the key teachings of the program is to create content that genuinely reflects who I am and what I value. I began to produce videos and social media posts that not only showcased properties but also shared success stories of my Latino clients.

> *I learned to see my cultural background not as a hindrance but as a unique asset that could and should be integrated into my personal brand and marketing strategy.*

I gave advice on the home-buying process in two languages and discussed how to overcome financial barriers. Doing this allowed me to connect more meaningfully with my audience and showed them that I understood their concerns and aspirations.

Another obstacle I faced was resistance to change within the industry, especially in adopting new technologies and digital strategies. But Krista's training provided me not only with technical knowledge but also with the confidence to innovate. With the tactics I learned, I was able to position myself as a reliable source of information and advice. This eventually helped me build a solid client base that valued my modern and client-centered approach.

Overcoming these challenges was not an overnight process. I had to be patient, persistent, and constantly willing to learn and adapt. Every time I overcame an obstacle, it strengthened my belief in myself. Thanks to the teachings of Krista's program and my determination to overcome specific challenges as a Latino agent, I not only advanced my career, but I also contributed to the growth and diversification of the real estate industry and, by honoring my culture and being authentic, I believe I've shown that having a diversity of perspectives enriches our industry and makes us stronger as a community.

Personal and Professional Transformation

Joining Krista Mashore's program marked the beginning of a professional transformation. I completely redefined my career in the real estate sector. It wasn't just acquiring new skills in digital marketing. It was a complete reinvention of my approach to the business, my clients, and most importantly, myself as a professional. Participation in Krista's program has also been a catalyst for change in my personal life. I've been able to redefine my relationship with work, the community, and my family.

The program encouraged me to transcend my own limitations, challenge the beliefs that held me back, and broaden my vision of what was possible. I learned to value my heritage and unique experience. I was then able to integrate my heritage into my personal brand in a way that resonates authentically with a wider audience. This evolution filled me with renewed confidence in my abilities. It created a deeper connection with my clients, who appreciated the sincerity and passion that now always characterizes my work.

Also on the personal level, the program has taught me the importance of balancing professional life with personal life. I've learned to use digital marketing strategies not just as work tools but as a means to connect more deeply with my community and family. My new ability to communicate and educate allows me to share my knowledge and experiences more effectively with those around me.

Professionally, I learned to use social media not only as platforms to advertise properties but also to educate, inspire, and connect with people meaningfully through the videos, courses, seminars, and content I create. My focus on providing value and knowledge has helped me establish myself as a reliable authority in the real estate market.

I've now expanded my vision of what is possible in the real estate world. Using digital strategies to create a genuine connection with clients has not only boosted my career. It has become my standard for how agents can and should interact with their market in the digital age. I no longer follow traditional and often outdated methods. I've become an innovator and a thought leader within the community. Plus, I've been able to bring much more value to clients, contributing to their success as well as my own.

From Local to International

This value and education-centered approach allowed me to expand my reach beyond my local market, opening doors in new markets that previously seemed inaccessible. I learned to tailor digital strategies to specifically address the unique needs and preferences of new audiences. My new ability to create relevant and attractive content, combined with a well-executed digital marketing strategy, enabled me to capture the attention of potential clients in various locations, both nationally and internationally.

The expansion into new markets was also made possible by my ability to use digital tools for virtual tours and online presentations, thus overcoming the physical/geographical barriers that traditionally limit a real estate agent's reach. This not only increased my client portfolio but also diversified my real estate practice. I'm now able to explore market niches and investment opportunities that I never considered before.

When I look at my journey through Krista's program. I see tangible achievements that have exceeded my initial expectations. I can see clearly *before* and *after* in my career in both geographical expansion and a notable increase in income. Expanding my operations to three different states and various countries was a professional milestone for me. It also symbolized my breaking the physical and mental barriers that had limited me.

Attracting international clients has represented one of the most significant changes in my real estate practice. Having the ability to reach a global audience and connect with people from different cultures and regions has not only diversified my portfolio but also enriched my professional and personal experience. These new clients were attracted by the authentic and valuable content that now characterizes everything I do. I'm living proof that borders are no longer an obstacle in today's real estate world.

Part of my journey has been recognizing the importance of mentorship. I had recognized the need to adapt and evolve and now I see that *continuous learning* is essential in our dynamic industry. In the changing landscape of real estate, adaptability, continuous learning, and the willingness to embrace new strategies are not only key to survival but to thriving. Krista not only provided the necessary tools and knowledge for me to transform my business. She also gave me support and reinforced my belief that I could do what was necessary to make the changes I needed to make.

Impact on My Clients

After implementing strategies learned in Krista Mashore's program, I've had countless client success stories and moving testimonials from clients who have not only found their ideal home but also the right investment to generate passive income for them. To me, this reinforces that a well-executed digital marketing strategy can have a profound impact on people's lives.

One of the most significant stories comes from a family who, after several failed attempts to buy a house, felt discouraged and almost gave up on their dream. One day, they stumbled upon one of my videos on social media where I explained the home-buying process in a clear and accessible manner. This video not only provided them with the information they needed but also restored their hope and confidence. After following several practical tips that I had shared, they got in touch with me, and I was able to help them overcome the financial obstacles that prevented them from moving forward. This family is now the owner of a lovely house they can easily afford and now call home.

Another example is an international investor who was looking for investment opportunities in the local market but faced linguistic and cultural barriers. Through my posts in South America and videos that break down the complexities of the real estate market in the Miami area, this client was able to better understand the available opportunities. This ultimately led them to make several successful investments. In addition to assisting in the purchase of their properties, I was able to connect them with the right lender, accountant, and lawyer—all experts in foreign investments.

These success stories and testimonials from satisfied clients are the clearest evidence of the positive impact that a digital marketing strategy which is centered on value and human connection can have. These success stories have not only redefined my real estate practice but also enriched my professional experience, showing that behind every transaction, there's a human story waiting to be told and shared. These experiences reinforce my commitment to continue exploring and enhancing my approach to digital marketing, always with the goal of providing a service that not only meets but exceeds my clients' expectations.

The lessons learned and the successes achieved are a testament to the transformative impact that a mentor can have on a career. Looking back, it's clear that Krista's program was much more than a series of lessons on digital marketing. It was an invitation to rethink my role as a real estate agent, to challenge the status quo, and to embrace a future where the possibilities are as broad as my willingness to explore them.

Recommendations for New Agents

If you are a newer agent, here are some thoughts I would like you to consider:

As the real estate market continues to evolve, it's essential for new agents, especially those who are Spanish-speaking, to equip themselves with the tools and knowledge needed to excel. Diving into training programs can be transformative, as long as the programs focus on three fundamental pillars: mindset, adaptation, and differentiation in the competitive market.

The first pillar is to adopt a mindset of constant growth. Learning doesn't end once you obtain your real estate license. That's just the beginning. Training programs, like Krista Mashore's, offer an in-depth approach of knowledge and strategies not found in traditional learning. It's crucial to stay open and curious, willing to absorb and implement new ideas and techniques that can boost your career.

The real estate sector is undergoing continuous digital transformation. Agents who quickly adapt to new technologies and digital trends, such as social media marketing, SEO, and the use of customer relationship management (CRM) platforms, are better positioned to capture the attention of modern buyers and sellers. Training that emphasizes digital competence is invaluable, giving you a significant advantage in the market.

Finally, differentiation is key. In a saturated market, finding and communicating your unique value is essential.

> *Finally, differentiation is key. In a saturated market, finding and communicating your unique value is essential.*

Ask yourself: *What makes me different from other agents? How can I use my cultural heritage, personal experiences, and specific knowledge to better serve my community?* Training programs can help you polish your personal brand, ensuring your message resonates with your target audience.

For real estate agents at a crossroads, wondering how to navigate the challenges and opportunities of the current market, my invitation is clear: Embrace continuous learning, adopt new technologies and digital marketing strategies, and don't be afraid to differentiate yourself in this competitive market.

The shift in focus from a product-centered (i.e., listings) marketing strategy to one centered on value and human connection has redefined what it means to be a real estate agent in the digital age. Integrating digital marketing into my daily practice has not only enhanced the effectiveness of my marketing efforts but also deepened my understanding of my clients' needs and desires, allowing me to serve them better.

Looking to the future, I recognize that continuous learning is the cornerstone of longevity and success in the real estate industry. The field is constantly evolving, with new technologies and trends emerging at a rapid pace. Committing to continuous professional development is essential to stay relevant and competitive.

Takeaways

1. In the digital age, traditional geographical boundaries for real estate professionals no longer exist.

2. To survive and thrive in today's real estate world, you must be willing to step out of your comfort zone and adopt new technologies and ways of thinking.

3. Digital marketing is no longer a product-centered marketing strategy but is now one centered on providing value and human connection.

4. You bring the most value to your business, your community, and your clients by embracing who you authentically are.

CARLOS ZAPATA

Pitbull Team Real Estate

786-529-4075

Carlos@PitbullTeam.com

Miami, Florida
Virginia
Maryland

Facebook Ads Done Right

by Betsy Flores

Navigating the rollercoaster of the real estate market is pretty much the job description of every Realtor®. You get the highs (like when houses fly off the market at crazy prices) and then the lows (like when interest rates shoot up and everyone's too jittery to make a move). Over my 24 years in this game, I've ridden all those waves and then some.

Enter 2019, a year that really threw me for a loop—and that's saying something! Backtrack a bit and you'll find that my hubby and I had been killing it in real estate since the early 2000s. We consistently ranked in the top 1% of what was a much less crowded field. Fast forward to 2019, and our market had exploded with competition. Amidst personal challenges, like my mom's battle with breast cancer and my husband dipping his toes into construction, I was the one left to figure out a new playbook for our business.

By the time midsummer hit, my transaction list was a big fat zero. It was clear that my old ways weren't cutting it anymore. After botching what I thought (thanks to a friend's referral) was a guaranteed listing, I was at a crossroads. Then, as if by fate,

Krista Mashore's face kept popping up on my Facebook, speaking right to my struggling soul.

I had a tech background, and I knew I was behind the times and needed a major upgrade—STAT! Krista's relentless online presence was the nudge I needed. It was either shake things up with her help or start dusting off my resume and find a corporate gig. I kept thinking, *What if she could teach me to do what she is doing, constantly showing up in my feed? If she can do it nationally, I'm sure she could teach me to do it locally.*

I went all in with Krista, deciding it was do or die time for my real estate career. She started with teaching us all about mindset which was a game changer for me. Suddenly, I wasn't just some agent "getting left behind." I now knew I had a wealth of experience and was ready to bring my A-game into the digital age.

I zeroed in on perfecting my listing process the way that Krista taught it. It was different than anything I'd seen before, and it was a game changer for me. At the same time, I was also diving deep into strategies Krista teaches for video marketing and social media magic. What she taught wasn't just about slapping some videos up on Facebook. It was about a whole new way of connecting with clients and standing out in a sea of agents. I was learning how to create videos that help my audience build a relationship with me, and how to make sure the videos were actually *seen*. Let's face it: It doesn't matter if you create content or videos when you only get views from your mom. What matters is to expose your videos and content to people who do *not* know you. And that's exactly what I was learning.

My commitment to revamping my approach, especially with Facebook ads and creating engaging content, quickly began to show real results. People started to notice me, sending referrals my way and helping me build momentum even as 2020 threw the world a curveball with the pandemic. Because that crisis meant everything going virtual, our new "digital-first" strategy was exactly what the moment called for. While other agents were struggling and freaking out, trying to figure out how to be effective in the digital world, we were already there and getting even better at it.

When COVID hit, we had a new plan within days. As soon as businesses and the world got shut down, Krista came up with a plan to support local business, which in turn helped me stand out. We used our digital platform to showcase local businesses hit hard by the pandemic, running promos, and rallying the community. It was about being more than just a real estate agent. It was about being a true Community Market Leader©.

Beginning in that pivotal moment in 2019 when I decided to go all in with what Krista was teaching me, the journey wasn't just about salvaging my career. It was about *transforming* it. Thanks to Krista, I learned that adapting, embracing new tech, and **focusing on what clients really need is the key to not just surviving but thriving in real estate.**

Earn the Right to Ask

So let me share with you how I leveraged Facebook, the strategy that has been instrumental in the continuing growth of our business. Krista's "Earn the Right to Ask" Facebook brand awareness campaigns are like no other. They're focused on getting your content to actually be seen so that people get to know, like and trust you. They also position you as the authority. And on top of that, once people reach out to you, the next step in each campaign is to give them valuable resources. This is completely different than the approach most agents use. Integrating Facebook ads into our real estate marketing was a game-changer, especially when we focused on brand awareness.

> *focusing on what clients really need is the key to not just surviving but thriving in real estate.*

A brand awareness campaign using Facebook ads is all about getting your property listings, open house announcements, and your brand as a Realtor® in front of as many eyes as possible. Think of it like casting the widest net across the huge ocean of Facebook users so you can catch those who might be interested in buying or selling a home, even if they›re not ready to take that next step yet.

Here's the deal: There are different objectives on Facebook, and it's critical to determine what your objective is, who your target audience is, and where people are in your funnel or their exposure (for example, are they warm, hot or cold leads?). That will determine the strategy you use in your Facebook campaign. Anyone can boost a post. But *real* power is having a clear strategy and implementing it. In a brand awareness campaign, you're telling Facebook that your main goal is to expose your ad to as *many* people in your target audience as possible. This is perfect for Realtors® because, of course, you want to make sure your listings and services are seen by a broad audience in your specific geographic area, and you want to connect with as many of your "Ideal Clients" as possible.

You start by defining your target audience, your Ideal Client. This could mean people living in your city or region, folks interested in real estate, or even individuals engaged with local community groups. You can get really specific in defining your target audience and tailor your ads to the types of clients you're most interested in attracting.

Once your target audience is set, you opt for a brand awareness objective for your Facebook ad campaign. Facebook will then optimize your ad to be shown to as many people in that audience as possible (within the limits of your budget). It's like telling Facebook, "I've got this awesome listing or open house coming up, and I want as many people in [XYZ] group as possible to know about it—and also to know about me!"

Now, here's the kicker: Because you're focusing on building your brand and you're paying for attention and exposure, you're playing a numbers game. Not everyone who sees your ad will be interested or in the market for a new home. But that's okay! The idea is to increase awareness of your brand and listings. Over time, doing this builds a larger pool of potential clients who think of you when they're ready to make a move. If someone isn't aware of you before they are ready to buy or sell, you've got a problem. They need to know you *well before* they're ready to make a move.

To make the most of your brand awareness-focused ads, you want to pair them with eye-catching images of your listings. You can also use videos for virtual tours to grab attention. The goal is visibility, so make your ads stand out!

It's also so important to keep an eye on your ad performance through Facebook's analytics! You want to track how many people you're reaching so you can adjust your strategy as needed. You might find that targeting a smaller, more specific audience increases engagement, or perhaps broadening your reach brings in more leads over time. Be willing to test and improve to get the results you want.

We also use these analytics (views, watch time, engagements, hours watched, etc.) when we go on a listing appointment. They clearly show how our digital strategy beats out anyone else in getting exposure for our listings. We get hundreds of hours of watch time and thousands of engagements. During listing appointments, I'm not talking about doing open houses and a brokers' tour. Through the analytics, I'm showing them how I kick the pants off any other Realtor©.

When you use Krista's brand awareness strategy and digital retargeting campaigns in your Facebook ads, it's like having a digital billboard in the busiest part of town—only better! It's all about doing it the right way. You're not just broadcasting your message to *everyone*. You're specifically targeting potential clients who are most likely to need your services now or in the future. It's a smart (and necessary!) move for any Realtor® looking to expand their clientele and make their presence known in the competitive real estate market we're in. You'll have all your friends and even people you don't know saying, "I see you everywhere!!"

Facebook Pixel Power

When I talk about the digital toolkit that transformed my real estate business, I can't overlook the magic of the Facebook "pixel." It has supercharged our Facebook ads. A Facebook pixel is like a digital spy. It works invisibly in the background of your website or funnel, gathering valuable insights about the visitors who are interested in your listings or real estate services.

Here's how it works: A Facebook pixel is a small piece of code that you install on your website or funnel. It's like having a basket at the door of an event where people leave their business cards as they enter, but instead of business cards, it collects data. This data helps you understand the actions visitors take on your site, such as viewing a listing, signing up for an open house, or requesting more information about your services. Without the pixel's information, you have no idea what visitors to your website are interested in.

This information is gold! It allows you to create highly targeted ad campaigns that speak *directly* to the needs and interests of your audience. For instance, if someone visits your website and looks at a specific property but doesn't reach out to you, the Facebook pixel can help you "retarget" that visitor with another ad for that very same property when they scroll through Facebook later on.

Better yet, you can use this information to retarget people who previously viewed that property and retarget them with similar properties later. This is important because the average buyer doesn't just wake up one morning and decide to go out and buy a home. They research for 9-12 months prior to taking action. Even before going on the listing appointment, I show sellers how I use this retargeting in the pre-listing marketing video that Krista taught us. This is how you win before you arrive.

There is so much magic in retargeting. In fact, I'd say it's really the gold nugget of these ads. But there's more. The pixel also provides insights into how effective your ads are at driving potential clients to *take action*. This means you can fine-tune your campaigns for maximum impact. You can focus your ad budget on strategies that work and tweak (or drop) those that don't.

For example, say you've got a listing for a charming bungalow that's perfect for first-time homebuyers. You've posted about it on your website with a virtual tour and detailed information. With the Facebook pixel installed, you can track how many people show interest by viewing the page of this listing. Later, you can create a Facebook ad that targets these interested visitors with a compelling call to action, like an invitation to an exclusive open house event for the bungalow. It's a direct, personalized approach and it makes potential buyers feel seen and that you understand what they need and want.

Also, the pixel helps you understand the broader behaviors of visitors to your site. You can identify trends, like the most popular types of properties or the information visitors search for most often. With that knowledge, you can tailor your website content and your ads and build content in your funnels to match what people want. This not only improves the effectiveness of your ads but having this kind of information also can also help you improve your overall marketing strategy.

It's no longer just guesswork. Incorporating the Facebook pixel allows you to make *data-driven* decisions. It's like having a behind-the-scenes consultant who gives you the insight you need to constantly optimize your online presence and ad campaigns so you can connect with your target audience more effectively. For Realtors® looking to compete in this digital age, mastering the Facebook pixel (in conjunction with a brand awareness and retargeting strategy) is not just helpful—it's a necessity.

Retargeting

When Krista taught us the strategy of retargeting audiences with Facebook ads, it turned my real estate marketing on its head and could do the same for you. Picture this: You're hosting an open house. A potential buyer walks through the door, takes a look around, but then leaves without giving you their contact information. What can you do? Well, if this was a visitor to your website who looked at a particular listing or bit of information, you can "invite them back" by retargeting them. But this time, you invite them back through their Facebook feed.

Even better if you have a funnel for the neighborhood set up, you can have a QR code that drives the buyers and sellers to that funnel and pixel them that way. They'll also see tons of relevant neighborhood-specific information that adds value, educates and positions you as the authority.

Retargeting works by focusing on people who have already shown interest in your services or listings. Whether they visited your website, clicked on a previous ad, or engaged with your content on Facebook, these are people who are already warmed up to your brand. They just haven't taken the final step of reaching out to you.

Let's say some of the people who visit the listing page for a house on your website don't schedule a viewing. If you've set up retargeting through Facebook ads (and you've got the Facebook pixel doing its data collection magic), you can create an ad campaign that is specifically targeted at these visitors. This retargeting ad could highlight a virtual tour of the house, a call to action to schedule a private showing, or even showcase a glowing testimonial from a recent happy buyer to build trust in you and your services.

Retargeting is effective because it keeps your properties and services top-of-mind for people who are already part way through the decision-making process. It's a gentle nudge, reminding them of what caught their eye on your site or ad and encouraging them to take the next step.

This strategy is invaluable. It allows you to build a series of touchpoints with potential clients to connect them to your brand and your listings. The beauty of retargeting is that it is precise and efficient. Instead of casting a wide net with your ads, you can focus your efforts (and your budget) on people who have already shown an interest. And these are the people who are more likely to convert into clients.

Implementing retargeting in your Facebook ad campaigns is straightforward, especially with the help of the Facebook pixel. You can divide the audiences you want to target based on specific actions they've taken on your website, like visiting a particular property's page, searching for homes in a certain area, or even how much time they've spent on your site. Knowing this level of detail allows you to tailor your ad content to match their interests which makes your marketing more personalized and much more compelling.

Retargeting does more than just increase your chances of converting site visitors into clients. It also increases the overall effectiveness of your digital marketing efforts. It ensures that you're investing in ads that target people who are genuinely interested in buying or selling property. For any Realtor® who wants to maximize their online presence and lead generation, using retargeting is not just beneficial—it's essential.

Adding a Sales Funnel

When you integrate a "sales funnel" with your Facebook ads, you end up with a seamless journey that guides your leads (aka people) from their initial curiosity to the final action of buying or selling a home with you. Using a funnel with Facebook ads doesn't just capture leads. It also *nurtures* those leads by directing them to the engaging and informative content you create.

Imagine you're running a Facebook ad promoting a free virtual workshop on the "Top 5 Secrets to Selling Your Home for Top Dollar in Today's Market." Someone scrolling through their Facebook feed sees your ad, feels intrigued, and clicks on it. This click takes them to a landing page created in your funnels app (I use the CRM that Krista developed called The Mashore Method that has funnels within it) which is specifically designed to give them more details about the workshop and capture their contact information in exchange for registration.

This is where the nurturing starts. Once they've registered, your sales funnel kicks into high gear. The funnel allows you to design a series of follow-up emails that keep the registrant engaged and excited about the upcoming webinar. These emails can include tips, testimonials, and sneak peeks of what they'll learn, building anticipation and establishing your authority as a real estate expert.

But the funnel journey doesn't end when the workshop is over. After attending, participants are moved further down the funnel. They receive more targeted follow-ups, perhaps offering them a free home valuation or a one-on-one consultation to discuss their real estate needs. Each step of the funnel is designed to add value, educate, and gently guide the potential client towards choosing you as their Realtor®. Each phase also positions you as the expert and promotes a parasocial relationship with these people.

The beauty of using the funnel alongside Facebook ads is that it is automated so that good leads don't fall through the cracks. It also has the ability to be highly personalized. You can create different funnels for different types of clients (sellers, buyers, first-time homebuyers, etc.) and then use Facebook ads to drive traffic to these funnels. This way, you always know that the right message gets to the right people at the right time.

For a Realtor®, this system is incredibly efficient because it not only helps *generate* leads, but it also *qualifies* them. By the time a potential client reaches out to you directly, they've already received a wealth of information through your funnel. Plus, they're much further along in their decision-making process. They're not just cold leads anymore. They're informed prospects who are more likely to convert into clients. And through the information you've given them all along the way, they will already *know you*, *like you* and *trust you*!! They see you as the expert and you have differentiated yourself.

Integrating funnels with Facebook ads also provides valuable insight into which parts of your funnel are working well and which need tweaking. You can see where prospects drop off, which emails have the highest open rates, and which calls to action are most effective. This information allows you to continuously optimize your funnel for better results.

Incorporating funnels into your Facebook ad strategy is like giving your real estate business a 24/7 sales team that works tirelessly to convert leads into clients. It makes the most of every click your ad receives and every visit to your website. It turns initial interest into action. The pieces you create that prospects see on their journey through your funnel (emails, videos, etc.) will educate, nurture, and convert them. If you are serious about leveraging digital marketing to its fullest potential, mastering the art of sales funnels and Facebook ads is not a "nice to have." It's essential for success in today's competitive market. Krista, the "Queen of Digital Marketing," taught me everything I know about how to create great funnels and ad campaigns.

We've all seen that the world of real estate is rapidly evolving. You can leverage the power of Facebook ads to expand your brand awareness, connect with potential clients, and drive growth in your business. When you use targeted campaigns, retargeting strategies, and integrate advanced tools like the Facebook pixel and sales funnels, you are able to not only attract leads but nurture them through the entire sales cycle.

By diving into Krista's program and applying these strategies that she taught, we've gone from having zero transactions in 2019 to 30 in 2020, 51 in 2021, 62 in 2022 and 57 in 2023 (one of the toughest markets in my career). We no longer have to guess about what ads or campaigns we should do. We now have the data to know what works. Yes, it did take some effort at the beginning to learn and implement our Facebook ad system. But don't be intimidated! Once it's in place, you'll find that it's much easier to maintain than the traditional non-digital methods of marketing.

Takeaways

1. Brand awareness campaigns are designed to help you connect with thousands of the types of people you want to attract.
2. By using Facebook pixels, you can get all the data you need to tweak your ads and campaigns to get you optimal results.
3. Retargeting allows you to capitalize on someone's initial interest by approaching them again with information they care about.
4. Funnels allow you to take a "cold lead" on a nurturing journey that turns them into a client. It also positions you as the authority, showcasing the value you add. You can win their business even before you meet them!

BETSY FLORES

Harvest Real Estate Group
eXp Realty

📞 210-889-7495

✉️ Betsy@HarvestAgents.com

📍 San Antonio, Texas

SCAN ME

Free Gift: Bonuses
Time To Take Action!

Information alone is not enough. I've put together this **free expert resources member's hub** to help you get started now. Customize the strategies and tactics from this book to *your* business and marketing plan, with guidance, top producer tools and extra trainings.

KristaMashore.com/TopProducer

How to Get Your Time— and Your Life!—Back

by Alex Mayer

I don't think any of us become real estate agents with the idea that we want to work 50-60 hours a week. Whether you are new to real estate or a seasoned professional, it becomes apparent quickly that the traditional styles of doing real estate almost *require* you to work that many hours if you want to be successful. The vast majority of brokerages are teaching these outdated methods, and the licensing process certainly doesn't give you any real perspective on what it takes day-to-day to be profitable. After working really hard in the business for a couple of years, I knew there had to be a better way. Fortunately, I found it through Krista Mashore's program.

A little background on me. I got licensed in real estate in November of 2016. I was lucky enough to be recruited into the top real estate team in my territory (Rochester, Minnesota) after a successful two years as a top salesperson at the best local car dealership. My first broker and team taught me the process for leading a prospect from online lead registration to appointment, to contract, and finally closing. That team disbanded in June of 2018, and I went independent.

After years of being on a split with my first broker, I was lucky to find a brokerage in my area that only required a small desk fee, so I was a 100% commission agent. But I always treated my business like I was still on a split—putting 30% of my income back into the business of generating leads online. And I was profitable at it as well!

But here's the problem: It was a hamster wheel. If I stopped making the phone calls for a week—or even one day!—that was going to hurt my pipeline a few months down the road. I had to constantly make those phone calls 2-3 hours per day to keep business coming in. And every time I got on the line with a prospect, I had to prove that I was an agent worth talking to. I was working 50-60 hours every week following up with prospects, going on appointments, showing houses, and handling negotiations. It was a grind. I remember days laying on my office floor at 8:30 p.m., resting while waiting for some confirmation from a client or another agent. I knew I needed a different way to run my business.

I first found Krista in October of 2018. As a reader, it was her book *Sell 100+ Homes a Year* that caught my attention. I have that book sitting on the top shelf of my office to this day and have even bought a few extras to gift to other agents over the years. Of course, like any of you reading this book, then Krista's marketing started following me everywhere. I couldn't open up my Facebook or Instagram feeds without seeing her image or videos. The question in my mind was, *How does she do that?* And more importantly, *How can I do that in my market?*

In January 2019, I made the life-changing decision to hire Krista Mashore Coaching. It was thousands of dollars, but it has been the best money I've spent in my real estate career. Krista is an amazing coach. She's organized, has a staff of people hired to help agents adapt quickly to her strategy, and she thrives in motivating the agents who hire her to succeed.

For me, the truly advantageous thing was how organized her coaching model was. Because I was already working 50-60 hours per week, I wanted to use my time efficiently and get the most I could out of the program. On Day One of hiring Krista, I had access to 6 months of modules (it's over 12 months for new agents today), a weekly group coaching call with Krista, access to office hours with her staff to answer my questions, and a step-by-step process for implementing her digital marketing strategy. Krista has always had a deep passion for overdelivering on her offers.

Krista's modules are broken up so that each student knows exactly what they need to do each week with a day-by-day plan. For me, that was incredibly helpful. In real estate there are a lot of shiny objects and Krista's program is like drinking from a firehose. But the way the program is set up, I knew that if I committed one hour a day to working through the program, I was going to be just fine.

Within the first few weeks of hiring Krista, I remember walking my dog around my neighborhood thinking, *I'm going to be like the first man on the moon in my city after hiring Krista.* I'd done my research and there was no agent in my market doing anything like the advanced digital marketing strategies that Krista was teaching.

In 2019, the year I hired Krista, I was the top commission-grossing agent at my brokerage, and I remained as such until I left in 2023 to join eXp Realty with Krista as one of my sponsors.

I was working 50-60 hours a week in 2018 prior to hiring Krista. In 2019, that dropped to 30 hours a week because I was still prospecting new clients daily. In 2020, that dropped to 20 hours a week as I had better systems in place. In early 2021, I started a team and passed the online lead registrations off to my agents. I was busy enough with the clients being referred to me or who were interested in working with me because of the systems Krista taught us where we attract clients rather than chase them. So, in 2021, I was working less than 15 hours a week in my business AND I was nominated for Best Real Estate Agent in Rochester, Minnesota. I got Runner-Up.

In 2022, I was nominated again. And I won!

So, what got me from the grind of 50-60 hours per week to 15 hours per week? It's the many systems and strategies Krista teaches. I can't tell you about all of them, but I'll tell you about some that made the most difference for me.

Differentiating Yourself

One of the reasons agents end up putting in 50-60 hours per week is that they haven't differentiated themselves from the pack. And because they haven't shown how they are different, they spend hours on the phone (like I did) to continually bring in new clients. Then they have to spend even more hours trying to explain to these prospective clients why they should hire them. Differentiation matters. If you're the same as everyone else at your brokerage, why should a prospective client hire you over the person to your left or right? You have to ask yourself, *What differentiates me from the person next to me?* This can be a scary thought for an agent—but you're better off asking yourself this today, than having a prospective client ask you during your interview.

Many agents will use buzzwords like "expert," "negotiator," or "marketing," but in my experience, there's not really a lot backing that up. I've seen newly licensed agents use those phrases. Every agent claims to be an expert, but are they really?

Krista emphasizes that if you want to use those words, you must have the ability to SHOW your clients that those things are true. *Show, not tell.* And when you're prepared to show, not tell, you don't have to spend hours trying to convince a client that you're worthy.

When I talk to prospective clients about marketing, I can *show* them my hundreds of videos with hundreds of hours of watch time that reach tens of thousands of people in a weekend. When I say I am an expert, I can *show* them hundreds of 5-star reviews from local clients. I can discuss upcoming changes in the local market and give a "feet in the street" perspective on what's happening in my market today. When discussing negotiations, I can *show* multiple credentials, awards, and ongoing transactions that I'm working on a daily basis. I can *show* someone why they should work with me and that I can deliver a superior client experience.

> *And, because of the system I've learned through Krista's program, I can show them all of this even before I meet them. I don't have to spend time convincing them in person.*

And, because of the system I've learned through Krista's program, *I can show them all of this even before I meet them.* I don't have to spend time convincing them in person. I've sent them through my funnel where they've seen my videos and my statistics. They've already convinced themselves by the time I show up.

Be a Marketer, Not Just a Salesperson

But if no one knows who you are, trying to differentiate yourself isn't going to matter. If Krista's program taught me one thing, it would be this: How to be a marketer. And if you want to be a top producer, you need to learn to be a top marketer!

Within only the first few weeks after running the Facebook advertising campaigns such as the ones Krista's program gives to her students, I started getting messages and calls from my "alumni" clients that they were "seeing me everywhere." I was only six weeks into Krista's program as a whole and I could tell it was working.

In the first two weeks of running ads, I started to notice people looking at me differently. It was a double take here (someone looking at me a little longer) or a "Hey, do I know you?" People recognized me. I remember at around five weeks a person stopped me saying, "Hey! You're the number 1 agent in Rochester!" It wasn't true at that point, but perception is reality.

In those first four weeks of following Krista's strategy, my referrals jumped by 4X what they were. My "alumni" (clients, friends, family, and others in my sphere of influence) saw my videos all over their feeds and they started to refer clients to me regularly. These clients trusted me from the get-go and they were my Ideal Clients—something Krista's program teaches regularly.

Today, in my city, I cannot go out without someone recognizing me. The first couple times it happens, it's a little unnerving. Someone will start talking to you about real estate randomly. You'll have to awkwardly ask them their name. But that's how you know her program is working!

I never fully abandoned my online lead registration phone prospecting. I was brought up into the industry as such and I happen to be really good on the phone. Within months of joining Krista's program, I started getting prospects on the phone who would say, "Hey! You're the guy showing up on my Facebook feed every day. I see your commercials!" It made converting easier and definitely faster as I could just share a video or a funnel. Prior to hiring Krista, I would have to prove my work (and my worth) to a client every time I connected with them. After a few months in her program, I had plenty of videos I could share with prospects to establish my credibility. Today, I have at least four video ads running at a time.

I'm a highly routine person in the morning. I break my days into my offense and my defense. My offense is before 11 a.m. That is when I'm recording my videos, making my calls, and educating myself on ways to better my business. These are the activities that are set to move my business forward. I do make exceptions for closings. I like to close deals at 8 a.m. so I can start the day with a win and get back to my office by 9 a.m. Defense is in the hours after 11 a.m. This is when I go on appointments, schedule showings, inspections, and do the day-to-day activities of client service.

I know that if I get my offensive work done before 11 a.m.—the work needed to move the needle on my business—then that day is mine if I have nothing else left to do that day. Because of my early morning work, that doesn't happen often because I have so much business coming in!

Prior to hiring Krista, my offensive period was set around making those phone calls. Within a few short months of joining the program, I was finding more efficient ways to spend my time as both a salesperson and as a marketer.

It was a lot of work right in the beginning, managing my current business while also implementing the advanced strategies Krista's program teaches. But the investment of time and money was totally worth it, and the payoff came in sooner than I thought. I just kept doing the work, day by day.

Because I've focused on being a marketer, not just a salesperson, I don't have to spend time every day chasing business. Today I'm able to *attract* business. In 2023, I traveled 14 weeks of the year, mostly road-tripping around the U.S. with my dogs. But because my videos were constantly running back home, I still had ready and able buyers/sellers reaching out to me. They were happy to wait for me to return or tour with one of my agents while I was away. And they were all the ideal types of clients I enjoyed working with.

Imagine getting text messages from people asking you if you would *please* be their agent. That is a reality for me and many of the other agents in Krista's community of agents. There are agents in the group selling hundreds of houses a year. Many agents have won "best agent" in their markets—myself included. And it's all because we have become master marketers.

Time Management

Part of getting my time and my life back has been due to some of the time management hacks that Krista has taught us. The Daily Sheets she has us use have been a huge blessing to me. On the sheets, you plan out your next day the night before and write down the six most important things you need to accomplish (hit list). It made what I needed to get done simple and it made me take time to appreciate my wins at the same time. To this day—five years later—I still practice with the daily sheets. I know that when I make my list of six items in the morning, if I can only accomplish those big dominos then the rest of the day will go smoothly.

Krista's Success Sprint (the Pomodoro Technique plus THRIVE©) taught me that the work will condense itself to the amount of time that I allot for it. If I give myself 30 minutes to bullet point two scripts, I know that I can get that accomplished. If I give myself 30 minutes to record two videos, I'll get that done too. Perhaps the best thing about the Success Sprint is sometimes I'll get into a roll and just keep going for a few hours. Once you put your "butt in the seat," it's easy to get into what you are working on.

The THRIVE© part of the process that Krista added keeps me not only focused but feeling good as I get work done. It's simple and takes only a minute or two. *T* stands for give thanks and show gratitude. *H* is for happy, so you just laugh out loud! *R* is to remind yourself that you have all the resources you need and that you are resilient! The *I* means to take immediate action, "Do it NOW!" *V* is to visualize the results you want as *already accomplished*. And *E* means to expect it, and be enthusiastic about it, and have energy around it. (For a training on THRIVE©, and even *more* bonus resources go to: **KristaMashore.com/TopPro-ducer**.)

How Videos Save Time

As running 2-3 video ads a week became more common for me, I started to notice that I was getting between 60-100 hours of video watch time a week with an audience of 40,000-60,000 area locals engaging with it. These were only 90-second videos. I thought back to the days of phone prospecting 2-3 hours a day and how running the video ads allowed me to prospect to a larger audience with my best content even while I slept!

Whenever I hear someone say, "I don't have time to record videos," I laugh. It will take me 15 minutes to bullet point a script. Maybe 7 minutes to record a few clips for that video. And another 15 minutes to trim up the video. And with artificial intelligence today I can often get the description, caption, and B-Roll back within another 10 minutes. After that, setting the ad to run on Meta will take me less than 10 minutes to run both a video view and a reach ad. Total time invested: 57 Minutes. Total video watch time: 40 hours over the two weeks of running the video. Talk about efficiency!

Early in the program I would "batch record," meaning I'd take 6-8 video scripts from the program or take scripts I'd de-signed on my own (I like to create my own scripts) and I would knock out recording all 6-8 in an hour or two hour time period. I would record these in front of a green screen. When I was done, I would trim them up and email them off to a video editor who would take it from there.

Today, I don't use video editors so much. I've found that my more off-the-cuff content gets a lot more engagement. People just find it more authentic. But if hiring a video editor is something you are into, here's my advice: Create a contest on Freelancer spec-ifying exactly what you are looking for. You can create a contest for $100 that will get you plenty of options. When I created mine,

I would explain that I would pick three editors based on their understanding of what I was looking for. Each of them would get one video recorded with a green screen. I would pay each of them the $100 to edit the video, but I would only hire the first and second place winners for future work. Typically, I would pay $40 for a finished video.

If you batch record 5 videos in an hour, trim it up in another half hour then email it to a video editor for final production, your time invested will be around 90 minutes and your cost will be $200. You may have another 15 minutes of edits for your editor once you get the videos back. If you do 10 videos a month, your total cost is only $400 for a video editor.

But the amount of time you've just saved yourself is huge. *The amount of watch time you will get will be 50X the amount of time you put in.*

Again, today I've found video editors to be less important. People prefer the authentic and real life you. I used to be a big believer in script writing as well, but that's also changed. It's much easier to show emotion and authenticity when you just press record on the cell phone and talk to your people. In my experience, it's about 4X the level of engagement.

Once you figure out how to systematize the video ads your life becomes much easier. In my opinion, there is no reason why you cannot batch record 8-10 videos in a week and be done for the month. In fact, I personally believe that if you do nothing else but record a minimum of 2 videos a week, distribute them correctly and run ads behind them, you will see success.

Support of Great Colleagues

One thing I didn't realize when I joined Krista's program was all the benefits of being part of the community and having relationships with other top students within this organization. Krista Mashore knows the types of students she wants in her program. Her students—the ones who implement what she teaches—are all stand-out agents in their communities. They are Community Market Leaders©. Krista built Krista Mashore Coaching the same way she trains her students to build their real estate business: through attraction-based marketing.

Attraction-based marketing means knowing the ins and outs of your Ideal Client—how they think, what they are searching for, their struggles, their strengths and what really drives them. Because Krista understands her own Ideal Client or "client avatar" (that's me and you) and consistently speaks to that type of person, she attracts those ideal students to join her coaching.

Krista's students are committed to personal growth. They are community-focused, and they are innovators in the profession of real estate. They don't do real estate the old traditional way. They stand out in their markets because they are committed to continually growing, implementing, and finding ways to become better for their clients, their community, and their families.

Krista marketed to that group, and it spoke to me, it drew me in. That's who I am. The same can be said of other students actively in the program. You've met several of them in these chapters. And perhaps you are that person too, and that's why you are reading this today. Krista Mashore is a force to reckon with. She's got a master's degree in curriculum instruction. She knows how to build an organization that supports her strengths while also hiring to fill in for her weaknesses. She is constantly over-delivering on her offers. She eats her own dog food. She invests in her own personal education. (Right now she herself has six coaches coaching her. Crazy right?) Then she works to translate as much as she can from what she's learning for her students.

Krista is the catalyst of this organization, but I believe that bringing in so many like-minded people together gives her program the greatest value (though of course her program has a long list of value). We "Mashorians" are a different breed of real estate professional. We are Community Market Leaders©.

How does this network of colleagues help me get my time and my life back? The professionals in this community are often willing to pull back the curtains on everything they are doing to be successful in their markets. I don't have to bang my head against a wall trying to reinvent the wheel. Unlike other agents I've known, they are willing to reveal their "secret sauce." They are also willing to share their struggles—yes, even the top performers have problems—and help others through theirs. If they have solutions, they're willing to share them. I'm not in this alone, trying to figure it out all by myself. We are committed to our drive to be Community Market Leaders© *together*. It's real. It's human. And it is reassuring to know that we have others working through the same things.

We all have different goals, and you can structure your business the way you want. For me, I wanted to be more efficient and effective with my time. I wanted my time back and I wanted to travel and see the world. Krista's program and the community of other agents through the program have all helped me to achieve that lifestyle today.

Takeaways

1. If you are doing real estate the traditional way and you want to succeed, you almost *have* to work 50-60 hours every week. But there's a better way.
2. If you don't differentiate yourself from the pack, you'll waste a lot of your time trying to convince prospective clients that you're worthy. If you *show* them you are different, they convince themselves.
3. Focusing on being a marketer rather than a salesperson means you will start attracting clients rather than spending hours chasing them.
4. When you do videos, distribute them correctly and follow them with ads, you can get watch time that is 50 times more than the time you spent on them.

5. A few simple time management hacks can give you hours back in your day and help you get more done.

ALEX MAYER

Rochester Area Homes By Alex Mayer
eXp Realty

507-696-7510

Alex@HomesByAlexMayer.com

Rochester, Minnesota

The Secret is in the Systems

by Jenn Sells

I've got to admit that when I heard my phone dinging the other day with a direct message from Krista Mashore (not her organization) asking me to contribute to this book project, I was a little surprised. Yes, I'm one of the original OGs (one of her early students). I've survived in this business for 24 years somehow, and yes, I am a top producer. (Minus maybe 2023, but then a lot of agents had a little wobble that year, LOL! And my wobble would have been much worse without the tools I learned from Krista!) I think you'll find my value lies more in my bluntness regarding this business, my self-awareness, and the reality I bring to the table. I'm not super great at sugar-coating real estate as a career. As a matter of fact, I'm more of the type to tell you the brutal facts. I think of myself as kind of an industry advocate and definitely a survivor.

Look, I am just like you. We all get inundated with emails, company meetings, and social feeds that talk about other agents' success. Very rarely does someone stand up and tell you the truth, the cold, hard nitty-gritty about the road they traveled to achieve the success you see streaming across your cyberspace daily. It's even more rare for them to share their secret, the magic sauce, the road map of ups, downs and stumbles it took for them to get where they are. No, you just see the end product of their work, the wins (or the lies they tell).

For many of you reading this, you may already feel defeated. So many of us in the industry feel a version of this emotion at some point in our career. It is literally the driving force behind the constant *"grass is greener"* moves and perpetual seeking of the *magic pill* of success. You know what I mean. How often do you see an agent jump from here to there and there to here, thinking the *next* company is the key to their success? Here's the bitter pill I hate to make them swallow: They're only about 10% right. Your company does make a difference, but it only takes you so far. The rest is up to you. (Want to know more? Stick with me, babe.)

Welcome to the $h!+ show called real estate, where the odds seem like they are never in your favor. Since this is my chapter to write, I'm going to tell you the absolute #1 most critical part of any high-producing agent: It's all in the systems. I know that doesn't sound very sexy but if you build your business on a strong foundation of systems, you'll reduce 90% of the stress while increasing your production tenfold.

(Alright, if you've truly got a well-oiled real estate machine with all the systems in place, you can skip forward and do your thing. But if you're like the other 98% of agents, it's okay. What I'm going to show you in this chapter may seem overwhelming, especially if you're a newbie. Just remember this: Tackle it one step at a time.)

Starting in a Nightmare

In December 2018, I was standing on the edge of a cliff and in front of me was a bottomless canyon. I literally could not see the bottom. It was filled with clouds and darkness. Sure, my mind contemplated that I could stand there forever and be perfectly safe and secure... maybe. The questions kept rolling through my mind: Could I live with just safe? Am I satisfied with this? The answer was undeniably "no." My feet edged forward, and I stepped off into the unknown. *Whoosh!* Then, like many nights before, I suddenly jolted awake, sweat running down my temples. I snapped out of that damn recurring dream *again*. It was time to make some decisions.

I was just coming out of a brutal two-year divorce after an 18-year relationship. I was down 40 pounds, my ex got to keep our established real estate business of 17 years, and I was facing starting completely over at 44 years old with not one single client, no farm, no systems. To make matters worse, the judge gave me 11 months to refinance our house into my name. *Now what was I going to do?* I literally was on my knees. How in the heck am I supposed to put this house in my name in 11 months? I couldn't qualify for it with the measly maintenance amount I had been awarded, and I definitely didn't make enough the previous year to qualify for the loan. I was living in Denver, one of the most expensive places to reside, a single mom with two teenage girls.

That year I felt like I was stepping back in time, all the way to 1999, when I was originally licensed. They might as well have stamped "greenhorn" on my forehead. I had no brand, no clients, and no idea where to start. I really didn't know how to do anything else career-wise. I've been in or around real estate since I was a small child. But considering I only had 11 months to keep my house, establishing a new farm really wasn't an option. Based on my prior experience, I figured it took a minimum of two years and a ton of money to get that going. I didn't have that long. So, I prayed: "Jesus take the wheel."

Right around the time of my step off the cliff and nightmares, *Whoosh!* enter Krista Mashore front and center. Here was this loud, highly energetic, overly positive woman inundating my Facebook feed and Messenger. (How was she even doing that?) "Be the Community Market Leader©!" I swear, every time I picked up my phone or sat down at the computer, there she was just daring me to succeed. The only thought that I remember going through my mind was, *"I don't have the energy for this $h!+!"* Oh, and let's be honest, my next thought was, *It costs how much?!?* And quite frankly she was almost too positive and bubbly for me. I was feeling doom and gloom. Could she be for real?!?

I jumped on some of her free coaching calls and watched some of the trainings. Then one day, something just got to me. It was that little inner voice saying *Hey, did you see that? You can take over an area digitally in merely months.* My inner voice was constant. *No local agent is doing that kind of stuff, Jenn. You can set yourself apart.* My internal battle continued with the back and forth of whether to jump in or stay on the same path that was manifesting itself in my nightmares. After a good cry, well, you know which choice I made because I am here writing this chapter.

I bit the bullet. I was going to win. I went all in!!!

Do or Don't Do. There is No Try

There's a big lie holding you back and you know who's telling it? Yourself. You are lying to yourself. How many times have you told yourself after a training that you are going to do whatever it was that you just learned? Did you do it? No? See? You're lying to yourself.

Guess what? I've been guilty of that, too. We all do it. Now is the time for you to just stop it. I knew what I was missing was the coaching, accountability and the support! And that's what you're missing too!

I'm going to admit that there's a huge—no, *massive*—difference between those who don't succeed and the top 2% of industry dominators. The difference is so simple to explain that it's mind-blowing. But it's also unbelievable that something so *simple* is also so *hard* to implement. Here's the massive difference: The top 2% *do*. You know what I mean? (BTW, did you know that any given training less than 2% of the people ever implement? Could that 2% be in the top producers. Hmmm...)

But the top 2% get up and they follow the program. They set their pride and all the stuff they think they know aside, and they *do the work*. They lay the foundations, build the systems, take the roadmap that is given to them and implement. They are *consistent* and unwavering. **They do the basic mundane foundational business-building tasks daily until their real estate machine is as Krista says, "unstoppable."** And they adopt the philosophy of "belief," believing that it is going to work for them, so their mind helps them get there faster.

Okay, you say you're ready. You tell yourself you know how to lay good foundations or you're going to implement it soon. Maybe tomorrow. Then you get sucked into an advanced training on something like how to do funnels and you realize

> *They do the basic mundane foundational business-building tasks daily until their real estate machine is as Krista says, "unstoppable."*

that you can't do them because you don't have your CRM, Facebook page, pixel set up, or ad account in place. Let's not even talk about text follow up or any chat systems. Many of us jump right in anyway and start the lead generation activities. We suddenly start to get appointments and "Oh, snap!" The next thing you know you have a listing appointment and then realize you don't have a listing presentation built out, a marketing plan, or anything to differentiate you from all the other agents out there or anything else. Panic! (Yes, we've all been there.)

Again, recognize the lie that your foundation is "good enough" or that you will implement your foundation "tomorrow" and overcome it. It's one thing to have good confidence-boosting self-talk with yourself. It's quite another to tell yourself that you're ready to handle tons of business when in reality you're flailing with the business—or lack thereof that you have now. All the time, money, and energy you spent on generating that lead might as well have been flushed down the toilet because you weren't prepared to actually convert that lead. Am I saying don't go out and seek business before you have everything in place? Heck no! Go forth and get the business, but for heaven's sake, start implementing the systems for everything (seller guides/book, buyer guides/book, marketing plans, seller systems, marketing pre-listing video, lead systems, funnels and follow up, on and on). You need systems in place.

I will be the first to admit that I have lied to myself too, but the only one that ever hurt is myself. It's kind of painful to see people who started at the same time and place as you, yet they succeed at such a high level and open their own brokerages, create mega teams, etc. All the while you know they had the same number of hours in the day, in the same time period.

The top 2% who are succeeding at that high-level "implement and follow" systems. They emulate and follow a system and process that has been proven to work for new and experienced agents alike in all sorts of cities and towns across the country. They model a system rather than trying to reinvent the wheel. They have a great foundation in place. It's also important to remember that the best in the business are always *improving* or adding to their foundation.

Before I really get into talking about the foundation you need, just about any top-producing agent you ever interview is going to tell you that you need to spend your time on *money-making activities,* and no matter what you do, you have to be consistent. I do not disagree. My mom and stepdad owned a small real estate company when I was a little girl. I remember early on in my career my stepdad used to always tell me, "You aren't in business if you don't have something on the shelf." I don't care if you're building a real estate career, a house, your spirituality, or pick any other subject you can think of. If you just jump in and start building (i.e., raking in the clients) but you don't have a way to organize the project/clients with *follow up* and *follow through,* you're building on a loose foundation. All your efforts will likely come crumbling down. Sure, you can have a high production year that way, but there's a high probability your repeat referral business will be low if you get any at all. *However, if you build on a solid foundation (imagine a rock), your efforts are going to pay off a lot faster.*

Real estate is the easiest hard job (and vice versa, the hardest easy job) in the world. You can literally morph your business into just about any niche you can imagine, from being a local community leader and/or location domination expert to building a mega team through lead generation. No matter what you want to build, no matter what your vision is, you've got to have the foundation and the fundamentals in place. Without them, it will feel like all your efforts are constantly getting away from you like water through the sand. It's all about systems, baby, systems.

Back to 2018. My divorce was over, and I started my business. I had to rebuild everything from scratch, but it had to be better. It was time to figure it all out and set my systems up *fast*. Enter overwhelm, the progress paralyzer. Where do you begin? Is it a website, CRM, the brand, seller systems, buyer systems, transaction emails, lead follow-up, all of the above? Yes, no, yes. The key to building a great foundation is to remember, "One thing at a time."

Start with Your CRM

A good Client Relationship Management (CRM) system will:
√ Organize and manage client information
√ Automate follow-up processes and communication
√ Have workflows in place for follow-up and nurture
√ Track client interactions and preferences
√ Nurture sphere of influence, communications
√ Help you build and maintain relationships
√ Leverage technology for communication
√ Provide value to your sphere

Of all the things that must be done for the foundation of any real estate business, the CRM is definitely the go-to starting point. It is quite literally the beginning of what you need to communicate and stay in touch with your sphere of influence. You need it to capture new leads and all their contact information to initiate follow up. Your CRM needs to be able to connect it to Facebook and your website too.

The most basic "must-have" for your business is a CRM, and I thank my lucky stars that Krista had everything set up. Over the years, Krista's CRM, The Mashore Method, has just gotten more robust. The reason it is so good is because she put all of the different systems and platforms that she used to sell over 2,300 homes into one system based upon her experience with what did or did not work. It's literally the ultimate real estate-based system for us, and it was built by a seasoned real estate agent. You are literally running in the dark without a CRM. Get one, learn it and use it. Do not pass "Go" without it. (If you want to learn more about it, take her 3-day free virtual seminar: **KristaMashore. com/Masterclass**.)

A CRM helps you stay top of mind with people in your market and that's *so* important. Why? Because people hire people who are in their *"now,"* not people from their past. (Oh, and for the newbies in the crowd, here's where the harsh reality of a real estate career sets in.)

I remember back in 2012 just after the bail-out, I was driving down the back of the Meadows in Castle Rock, a neighborhood we farmed for years and had 19% market share in. I passed a house I knew to be a client's home we sold a few years prior. We had literally just helped that client avoid a short sale/foreclosure, reducing their payments $650 a month allowing them to keep their house. There was a For Sale sign in the yard—and it was *not* ours! I felt shocked, floored. No, let's be honest, I was mad. To be clear, these weren't just one-off clients. They were lifers. We had helped them buy and sell numerous times. So, we reached out to them to understand where we had gone wrong. Come to find out, some newly licensed agent at their church gave them her card and they wanted to "give her a fighting chance." That's what I mean by the *now. If you aren't staying in your clients' view as "now," don't think for a minute you deserve the business.*

If I give you nothing else, know that.

I recently ran into an agent who sold $21 million with only 20 transactions. She was boasting about it all over social media. Wow! That's pretty incredible, especially in 2023. Not to take anything away from this outstanding success because it was just that, outstanding. But when I asked her what CRM she was using, her response was she wasn't using one yet. I wonder what volume she could have achieved if she had implemented a CRM and had the systems in place to stay in contact with all of her clients. The NAR says that for every client, you could get 6-7 referrals, but that can't happen if you don't have a good CRM in place. So, say she had a CRM but was only able to get four more $1 million transactions from each of her prior 20 clients. That's still *80 new transactions.* And even if she only made 2% commission on those, we're looking at an additional $1.6 million she could have made!

On the flipside, I have a friend and fellow agent who consistently tops the production lists here in Denver. Every Sunday he sits down at his desk with his CRM and handwrites all the birthday cards for his clients for the following week. He is consistent and his communication with his clients keeps him top of mind. He consistently gets referrals and repeat business for listing homes.

Okay, so how many CRMs have you tried? How many times have you uploaded, re-uploaded, and lost critical information? It's so frustrating especially if you move brokerages that offer different platforms. Some CRMs are great at lead generation, some are good for client communication, another will send out transaction communications—but dang it if *none* of them have all three! So, you end up with two different systems and pray you aren't sending too much to your people or that you aren't sending anything at all because you don't know which CRM is doing what.

Pretty frustrating right? I know exactly how you feel. It's like, sure, one does that one thing really well, but inevitably, it doesn't do the other. Then some dumb punk salesman on the other end of a sales call tells you that you need to buy *another* system and reload all your clients into it so that you can achieve the other tasks you want to do. Making it even more painful they tell you that the CRM you are using may or may not sync with Skyslope, and it does not allow you to show the transaction volume year to date, what is coming down the pipeline, or under contract. They may even tell you that you're really nuts to want it all, and let's not talk about wanting it for a team's production. How dare you even think such a thing! Ever feel like sticking your head in the car door and slamming it? Because, hey, I think it would be a lot less painful than navigating the CRM hot mess.

I've personally tried just about every CRM out there. I don't know about you, but the amount of time and endless amounts of money I've spent on them is downright embarrassing. Shoot, some of them almost require a master's degree to even understand. Literally, I've failed, failed again, and, yes, failed again. I've uploaded and re-uploaded my clients into CRMs so many times it's cringe-worthy. And it's a shame too, because so much data is lost when you have to redo everything. In the end, they almost always come up short.

Enter The Mashore Method, built by Krista, who actually produced at a high level. It has everything you want built in, plug-and-play, life-changing, solid foundation stuff, client management, production, transaction management, lead generation, pre-built funnels, client follow-up texts and emails, etc. It is a life-changing real estate retention system that is your rock.

Hey, listen, Rome wasn't built in a day. Take one thing at a time, and work on it just a little bit every day. I promise your CRM is by far the most important part of your business.

Here's the kicker guys! You can spend hours setting up your CRM and you can have it set up for the follow-up all the way to follow through. You can have the birthdays set up and home anniversaries, but it won't do you any good unless you really get in and *automate the systems*. That is the difference between an average agent, a failing agent, and the top-producing agents. Top producers have *automated* a system for everything and very little falls through the cracks.

Here are a few things I suggest you implement and automate in your CRM ASAP:

A. Organize and manage client information:
 1. Names, addresses, #'s, social media links, phone numbers, birthdays, anniversaries (home, wedding), kids' names, favorite restaurants
 2. Home facts
 3. Notes: For example, when was the last time you sent a note or Comparative Market Analysis?
 4. Automate To-dos

B. Automate follow-up processes and communication:
 1. Lead capture and follow-up
    a. long term buyer campaigns
    b. long term credit repair campaigns
    c. long term seller campaigns
    d. pre-listing campaign
    e. after-listing appointment campaign
 2. Tracking client interactions and preferences
 3. Tracking lead conversion and source

C. Nurturing sphere of influence communications
 1. Building and Maintaining Relationships
    a. Birthdays
    b. Home Anniversaries
    c. Newsletters
 2. Long term after sale communication (stay in their *now*)

D. Providing Value to Your Sphere
    1. Seamless updates during a transaction
    2. Home value updates
E. Transactional emails
F. YTD Production

Keeping Your Transactions On Track

The next systems, contract and transaction management (CMT), that are crucial to the success and foundation of your business are pretty self-explanatory. As a matter of fact, I bet most brokerages have these systems set up for their agents. My brokerage uses Skyslope and CTM eContracts. If you are lucky enough to have a CRM that communicates with your contract and transaction system, count your lucky stars. Unfortunately, most do not. Your Contract and Transaction Management system should:

√ Manage contracts, paperwork, and legal documents
   efficiently
√ Coordinate with other parties involved in transactions
   (e.g., lenders, inspectors)
√ Ensure compliance with regulations and deadlines
√ Track transactions and production numbers

Come up with a way to track your active, under contract, and sold homes, especially the year to date volume. I have two Google sheets that talk to a Trello board. The first one is titled Team Sells Transaction Tracker. It has 4 sections (Active, Coming Soon, Under Contract, and Recently Sold). This helps keep the team and me visually connected to the business and helps predict the next 30-90 days of closings.

The second Google sheet is a detailed YTD closed transaction sheet. I can track my production year to date, paid splits, team production, team agent's production, list-to-sell ratios, source of the sale (so I know where to spend or cut next year), paid referral fees, and so much more. This sheet is by far the most important piece in the arsenal to me. If you don't know your numbers, you don't know your business.

It is my dream to have a CRM that actually does it all. Wouldn't it be great to have your contract dates automatically update into your CRM to trigger transactional automated messages and track YTD volume? If nothing else, see if you can get a CTM system that can talk to your CRM.

Systems to Keep on Top of Your Finances

Ask anyone who has been in the business—*anyone.* They'll all have a story about themselves or another agent who came near to financial ruin. I can't tell you how many agents get caught owing more taxes than they have the money to pay. I have to admit I was really good at this section of my business for a while and I never understood how agents could fall so fast—until I too fell behind. It's *really* easy to do. I could probably devote 100 pages talking about agent financial failures, their stories, and things to implement regarding the financial systems we need to have in place. This is critical to your success! The financial systems you need to have in place should help you with:

√ Budgeting and financial planning

√ Tracking expenses, income, and commissions

√ Tax planning and accounting processes

Financial competence is quite literally the most painful part of our business. If I'm being brutally honest, I wonder who in their right mind thought it was a good idea to allow real estate agents to be in charge of saving money, setting aside for taxes, etc. We are literally the most irresponsible, ADHD, Human Resource moving violations (impossible to manage and hard to control), crazy group of non-employable people on the planet. ("Non-employable" people is just a joke. But is it? Ask yourself if you could work 9 to 5 as an employee after selling real estate. See? I'm kinda right. Please don't make me spell out the HR violation part.) We love to spend, and we like nice things. Don't even try to argue with me about this.

I'm not a financial planner and honestly I'm not qualified to give financial advice, but I can tell you some basic stuff you need to implement.

√ Get a CPA.

√ Talk to an estate planner.

√ Set up business accounts, one for business expenses and the other for taxes and payroll.

√ Get a bookkeeper.

√ Have 1 business credit card.

√ Set up QuickBooks.

√ Track your spends and get a mileage tracker.

√ Talk to your CPA about buying your vehicle in the business name.

√ Bottom line: you've got to treat your business like a business!!

As for your commission checks, religiously split them as they come in for taxes, retirement, and life. It'll catch up with you one day if you don't. TRUST ME! If you remember the market in the fall of 2022, you'll remember when interest rates skyrocketed. The real estate world came to a grinding halt, at least that is what it felt like. Buyer purchasing power dropped by $50k-$100k overnight. Sellers grew restless and frustrated as many needed to relocate for work. Buyers reduced offers to 60% of value. Buyers thought it was a glitch and rates would return to 4%, and Sellers could not understand the basic reality that when rates go up, prices come down.

Now, imagine you are an agent in a typical market carrying ten listings with $1500-$2500+ worth of marketing expenses (pictures, videos, print, mailers, social media ads) on each one. At a minimum, that was $15,000 of floating expenses (probably closer to $20k), not including MLS fees, brokerage fees, contract systems, hosting, etc.—and all of a sudden, the real estate market idles. This actually happened to me. Of course, I eventually sold most of them, but not all. You can try to protect yourself with marketing expense clauses in your listing contract, but if the listing expires, you're pretty much hosed.

Moral of the story: Set aside money for the slow times. Have *at least* six months in reserves, but shoot for a year's worth. Also, set more away for taxes and payroll than you think you'll need.

BTW, I want to shout out to my brokerage as I opted in for the 5% of every check to go toward the stock options they offered. What that is worth today is mind-blowing. There used to be a meme running around the internet that showed a homeless person holding a sign that said, "Retired Real Estate Agent." You have to admit it's kind of funny but also terrifyingly true. How many 70+-year-old agents do you know who are still selling real estate? I'm not saying this is the situation for all of them but, please, let's work toward the end goal of actually being able to retire when we want to. And, how many agent retirement parties have you gone to? Lots of funerals but not many retirement parties!

Branding and Marketing Systems

Many agents I've known don't take branding very seriously. They're happy just to fall under the brand of their brokerage. But a great brand and a system that knows how to use it means that you can stand out from the competition and get noticed by your Ideal Clients. Developing a consistent brand identity helps you customize marketing strategies for lead generation. It also helps you utilize social media, email marketing, and other channels more effectively.

One of the most freeing concepts is learning that you can actually be yourself, and people will want to work with you. Oh man, I think that was the hardest thing to get through my thick head when I first jumped into Krista's coaching program. "Know, Like, Trust" is the most basic foundational concept Krista employs in her program. Of course, a lot of that revolves around showing up in videos. I can hear Krista's voice now: "Stop making perfect videos! Your audience can't relate to you!" "You're wasting time redoing the videos, your videos are too long, your videos are too produced." "Who is your client?" Your brand of "know, like, and trust" isn't just in videos you make but in your print, social media, and everything else. Your brand can make or break you. It is just as important as your other systems.

The point is once you realize your brand is *truly who you are* and what you put out into the world, you'll realize those are the people that will want to work with you. Take a minute and really look at the agents across the country that are producing large transaction numbers. I promise you they aren't shiny images of perfection. No, they are just like you and me. They're reflections of the members of their community.

When I found myself having to rebuild everything, I also wanted to be the perfect ideal real estate agent that everyone would just hire based on my looks, my brand and all that junk. I finally realized that people want to work with me when I'm *authentically* me. I'm a little louder than some. I have opinions about things. I wear my Freebirds and love turquoise. People find things in you to relate to. Lean in and be authentically you, that's all I can tell you. Every time I've ever had an appointment backfire, I can pretty much trace it to going on that appointment when I was not feeling or looking like myself.

Case in point: I had a scheduled listing appointment last year in Boulder, Colorado. The home was valued at approximately $1.3 million and located in a well-known area called Chautauqua. I woke up that morning and all I wanted to do was throw on my jeans and my big turquoise rings and be comfortable. (You could say my inner voice was telling me to be my authentic self.) Instead, I let the value of the house get in the way and I opted to wear my blazer jacket and my higher-end look, diamond rings, etc. When I arrived at the potential listing, there was a woman wearing full turquoise, undyed hair—the stereotypical Boulderite—and I looked ridiculous. I lost that listing because I'm almost positive she could not relate to me looking the way I did. That's what I get for not being authentically me.

Your brand secretly tells the world if you know what you are doing or if you don't. Your brand exudes your confidence or your insecurities. So, choose well. It's not just your colors and fonts. It's your Ideal Client and more. Your brand will constantly build and morph into something better as long as the foundation is right. Trying to be something you are not can break you. Don't be a poser.

Can I ask you to just be honest with yourself for two seconds and identify who you are and what clientele you really want to work with? Please, I'm begging you to stop telling the world you are something you are not. An easy example (and definitely not limited to this subject) is that in our industry, the word "luxury" is a highly overused word. Hello?! If you're going to try to fake it until you make it, I don't suggest you do it in any arena you aren't really living in. I'm not saying you can't break into luxury. But that clientele is going to know if you've never walked in that world.

Seriously, I saw a local agent the other day with a social media header that said, "Luxury agent"/"Top Producer." The banner was an image of him in a loaner luxury vehicle in front of a mansion that would *never* exist in Colorado. Maybe Miami, but not here. I had never heard of him, and curiosity got the better of me. I found out that he had sold a total of three homes in two years with an average sale price of $375k. Can't you suddenly hear that commercial "They're gonna know"?

I recently had a close friend compare it to someone who has watched NASCAR for their entire life and then tried to apply every-thing from NASCAR to Formula 1. It's not the same. The money's not the same. The track's not the same. The car is not the same.

If you try to talk about racing to people who are into Formula 1 the same way you do to people who love NASCAR, they're going to look at you a little cross-eyed. If you're not in the luxury arena, stop saying you are a "luxury agent." They see right through you.

Why is it that everybody wants to sell luxury? Do you really want to wear 5-inch Jimmy Choo stilettos and drive a $125,000+ car? I'm not saying you can't break into the market. Of course you can, but are there even luxury homes in your market? Do you hang out in those places? Do you know what they expect? Are you going to have to rent a luxury car or a driver every time you get an appointment? Do you have the right apparel and the right listing presentations? Furthermore, what if you got a multimillion-dollar listing? Do you have the luxury business foundation in place and the budget to market it or would you have to take a small HELOC loan out on your house to afford to do all the things required to market it correctly?

See what I mean? Now apply it to anything and take out the word "luxury." Replace it with something else like mountain properties, or lake properties, or suburban properties. Is it where *you* live? Are these the people who you talk to and relate to, and do you know all the things that are important about it?

That being said, we've all heard the phrase that *"perception is reality"* and it sure is true in real estate sales. My first job at 15 years old was at Southlake Mall in Morrow, GA. I had recently started a new school and was feeling a bit like a fish out of water. I wasn't from the South. I didn't really understand the culture, and if I am being completely honest, the spiral perm trend wasn't really my friend. The captain of the cheer team, Alicia, talked me into competing in the Miss Georgia Teen pageant. After reviewing the expenses, my mother sent me to the mall to acquire sponsorships. Long story short, that experience shaped my self-awareness and helped me identify who I was. It helped me learn to work and how to ask like a salesperson.

At 17, I was promoted to assistant manager at a little mall store called Gadzooks. By 18, I had my own store in Tallahassee, FL. By 19, I was a Travelling Store Manager out of North Atlanta. And by 21, I was a Regional Trainer traveling to 42 stores around GA, AL, SC, TN, FL and to the corporate office in Dallas, TX. I learned some very important lessons at that company that I still use today. *#1 Dress for the job you want, NOT for the job you have.* I guess what I am trying to relay is *you* are your brand. Your clients will hire you based on the perception you put out there.

Once you figure out who you are and who your Ideal Client is, your entire real estate career will be significantly better. When you figure it out, show the world and be consistent. I remember in much of Krista's foundational coaching, she would constantly remind us that being authentically you will literally save gas, time, money, and energy. Lean in and show the world who you are even if it's in Lululemon leggings or Freebird boots.

Marketing Systems

Of course, we have to do money-making activities to survive and keep the pipeline full. You're probably familiar with and already do many forms of marketing. Whatever you do, you need a system for it so you can be consistent. Some of the ways agents market include:

√ Newsletters
√ Monthly Market updates (email, messenger, social media)
√ Mailers
√ Holiday posts
√ Listing announcements
√ Buyer and Listing presentations
√ and … and… and…

But like I mentioned earlier, let's say your marketing pays off and you get a lead. Now what? What are you going to do if you schedule an appointment for tomorrow and you don't have a system in place for that appointment? I'll tell you exactly what you are going to do. You're going to panic. Then you are going to spend time creating what you can remember you should take. You'll be lucky if you remember it all. Now imagine a different world where your system is in place.

Let's say your appointment is for a potential listing. You grab your seller intake forms and you refer to your pre-listing system checklist. Then you gather all the materials that you *already have ready*. For example:

√ Seller Guide

√ Seller Book

√ Marketing Guide

√ Public record printout

√ CMA

√ Folder

√ Town statics - List Reports

√ Active Buyer sheets

√ Copies of Just Listed and Just Sold similar to the property you're going on the appointment with

√ Etc. etc., etc.

Your level of confidence just went up 1000%, and you are *not* panicking. And the majority of this you drop off *before* you get there, a strategy Krista calls "Winning before you arrive." Congratulations! You just won the client. Everything we do today is going to pay off in 30-90 days (depending on if it's a buyer or a seller). Whether it's a pre-listing meeting with a seller, a buyer consultation, or an after-listing campaign, if you take the time to build out the materials and resources you need, your production will naturally increase.

Time Management Systems

Remember a few pages back I jokingly said that many of us real estate agents are ADHD, irresponsible, and unemployable?

Well, I stick to that belief. Many of us are walking disasters. Don't ask an agent to be regimented. We love our freedom! Alright, I won't *ask* you to implement time management. I'll *tell* you, *do it now*! Do what the elite producers do. Once again, I get to tell you that I'm not perfect. (I know, hard to believe, right? LOL) I too struggle with this foundational business subject. It took me basically 20 years to open up my ears and eyes and listen to the people who do this well. I'm still working on this aspect of my systems, but I have to say that productivity and results skyrocket when you know what you're doing each day. Having a time management system in place helps you:

√ Prioritize tasks and activities effectively.

√ Schedule appointments and showings efficiently.

√ Balance work-life commitments and personal time.

√ Continue your education and skill development.

√ Stay updated on industry trends, regulations, and best practices.

√ Participate in training programs, workshops, and seminars.

√ Invest in personal and professional growth opportunities.

√ Have a life!!

The top producers in our industry literally *live by their calendars*. Schedule your tasks. Schedule catch-up time. Schedule lead generation, classes, and available times when you'll show property. Schedule the times you list homes. Schedule free time and family time, when you pay the bills and when you file. Then, *live by your calendar*. Throw out the sticky notes. Throw out the to-do lists. Stop letting the business control you. Just stop! Instead, take control and put every ounce of tasks and appointments into your calendar. Do it.

You may have heard the saying before that "the secret is in the systems." Well, it's true. The secret to success is having strong systems in place. Plain and simple. Every other aspect of this business, from building your online presence to lead generation, relies on the foundation your systems are built on. If you don't have this part of your business in place you might as well take your $100 bills and go flush them down the toilet. Essentially that is what an agent is already doing by generating a lead that doesn't have the system to win the transaction and relationship.

Consistency is the key. Take it one step at a time, but keep at it until your foundation of systems is in place. If you do nothing else in this business, you have to build your systems. Focus on it. Move forward, trudge if you have to. If you're going to survive and *thrive* in this business, get your foundation, your systems in place. Just do it!

Takeaways

1. Top producers know that having great systems in place for all aspects of your business is the key to success.
2. Keep doing your money-making activities, but make sure you get systems in place so you can convert the leads you generate.
3. Your first priority needs to be a really good CRM.
4. As painful as it may be, get systems in place to keep your financial house in order.
5. Don't get overwhelmed by trying to do everything at once. Take it one step at a time.

JENN SELLS
Team Sells Colorado
eXp Realty

303-877-2908
Jenn@TeamSells.com
Denver, Colorado

Daily Sheet Magic

by Lani Belcher

Let me start by telling you that I have seven children, so time is very precious to me. Every minute needs to be utilized since I have so many other obligations that are required of me by my family. Real estate is one of the greatest careers that you can have to be able to schedule around family time and the demands of having a large family. You get to be your own boss! However, being your own boss and not going into an office can be very distracting. There is no one to see if you are not getting the work done for your business. And it seems like there is always something that needs to be done around the house or an errand to be run.

I have been with Krista Mashore's coaching program for almost three years. There is so much that I haven't fully implemented yet. She gives us so much in the program, so we are always continuing to learn and grow. As a result of following her program, I have tripled my business. I can't even begin to imagine the results if I was able to implement everything! Even as I'm working to implement other parts of the program, I have fully implemented one thing Krista taught me that has been key to my success: the Daily Sheet.

I once got some advice from my Grandma, and ironically Krista has the same advice too. She said, "Get up early, exercise outside if you can, and get cleaned up for the day! No better way to start your day." So, when Krista introduced the Daily Sheet, I knew it would help me lay out my day as a map for success.

I absolutely love the Daily Sheet! It keeps you on task. The Daily Sheet is a sheet of actions you need to take every day to help keep you on task, help accomplish your goals, and, most importantly, make you money! This sheet is free and simple to do. Yet, if you do it every single day, it will generate more business and repeat clientele than you can imagine.

Start with Your Vision

The Daily Sheet starts off by having us visualize the day ahead. By doing this, we see ourselves accomplishing the tasks we have set before us. This list of the tasks was one we created at the end of the prior day, the things that are most important to accomplish. Visualizing completing these tasks has helped me greatly. I am not the most tech-savvy person, but visualizing myself accomplishing things that are difficult for me has made it easier. Believe it or not, I have accomplished some of my difficult tasks much faster than I thought possible.

Second, we read the Manifesto that Krista has created for us. This reminds me who I am and that I am unstoppable! I SERVE, I do not just sell! I have an Abundance Mindset, and I know I am the only one responsible for creating the life that I Deserve... And I AM! I am a Community Market Leader©. That is just a small portion of what the full manifesto is. Krista also gave us an audible version of a manifesto called the Millionaire Mindset. I never dreamed or longed to be a millionaire and was content with any effort I put out there. However, listening to audio and telling myself I *can* do it has made me want to accomplish more than I once thought possible. Most importantly, I know that each year I get closer to this vision becoming reality.

Accountability

The third action of the Daily Sheet is to attend Skin in the Game, Monday-Friday. This is a 15-minute call that I look forward to every day. This group of people on the call (some regulars and some new ones) are now part of my family. We each come up with two things that we want to accomplish each day, then share our goals for the day. I have never in my life met such a helpful, inspiring group of people. Multiple people will jump in and give suggestions on how to do a task if someone is struggling or looking for ways to accomplish that task. I have exchanged phone numbers for further discussion since each group is only allotted 15 minutes.

The next day, we state if we accomplished the two tasks that we stated the day before. One time, our group stated that we hadn't completed our tasks. Our Skin in the Game leader said, "Why not? We are on this call to grow and get our tasks done." She got to the bottom of what was keeping us from doing the tasks, which helped us all to be better at getting them accomplished. Having to state our tasks out loud and be responsible is such a genius idea because we don't want to fail. As importantly, we have a whole group encouraging and helping us and cheering us on. We've even shed some tears together about the trials individuals have been going through personally. Prayers are offered on behalf of individuals needing help that was beyond their control. I think everyone could use such a supportive family and daily routine!

Gratitude

The fourth activity on the Daily Sheet is to list five things you are grateful for each day. This may seem easy. But some days, coming up with different things to be grateful for seems hard to do. I've found that reflecting on the simple things that really make you happy helps, even if they are things you take for granted. It is impossible to be angry when you are choosing to be grateful for something. Doing this daily has made me not dwell on the negative because there is so much in this world to be grateful for. Health is most important to me and that makes my gratitude list more than once a week!

Tasks

The fifth thing you do is write out your tasks to accomplish. These can be small or large tasks. As Krista says, "Always eat the frog first!" meaning you should tackle the tasks that seem the hardest first. The days I do this, I notice the days go much better and more is accomplished. I recently accomplished a challenge called 75 Hard. It is a series of things you do each day for 75 days straight. If you miss doing something one day, you start over the next day. I thought it would be fun to make a Real Estate 75 Hard challenge for myself with certain tasks and I included these on my to-dos in this category.

My Real Estate 75 Hard tasks all came from Krista's program, so I thought I would include them here:

1. Exercise and Healthy Eating. Yes, I include that on Daily Sheet tasks because it is SO important to be healthy and feel good about myself. It doesn't matter what the scale says but exercising and eating well always makes you feel better. If you don't feel good, it's hard to do this job. We don't always win at everything we try, but at least we can feel satisfied with accomplishing a simple workout or making a good choice with food.

2. Spiritual time/meditation. Whether it's 2 mins or 30 mins, I think it is important to focus and remember your purpose and your why.

3. 10 video texts. This is simply one of the easiest, most affordable things you can do to keep in front of people and to show them you care. I remember on my birthday I got a video

text from another Realtor®, and this is not a Realtor® I see very often. He sent me a video text and I actually laughed out loud. It really makes you feel important. Every day I send 10 video texts to different people. I find it super easy when you send it on someone's birthday, or special events. You can also check Facebook and look for things going on in their lives to chat about. You can video text potential clients just introducing yourself as a real person. Nearly every time you get a great response and, ironically enough, it actually makes you feel so good when you get the replies. Definitely a game changer. I don't use video texts asking for business or referrals. I just say something nice to them and always say their name and try to make it personal.

4. Get a review. I put this on my task list so I can get my number of reviews up. I don't always get one every day, but I keep it on my Daily Sheet because I know it's important for growing my business. I get so many phone calls saying they read my reviews and liked them. Some of my reviews were Google reviews and some were even Zillow reviews. None of us buy anything without reading the reviews, so why would it be any different when choosing an agent? I have noticed that most people who read my reviews are agents from other states looking for a referral agent in my town. You never know who is going to read them.

5. Post on Google My Business. I want to do this daily because Google is the #1 search engine. I'm still working on this one.

6. One hour of prospecting calls. This does not include transactions you are working on. The idea is to call people who have filled out forms on your ads and people who are checking your websites. You can also call people who have opened your emails, asked for home evaluations, and checked Homebot. You can call your sphere of influence, past clients and people who live around your listings.

7. Two different tasks toward a bigger project. These are tasks that will help me accomplish something that will take longer

than a day to complete, but that will draw me closer to the end goal that I have for the week or month.

8. Attend a Zoom or a class. I want to learn something each day that will help me and my business. I thought the older I got it would be harder to learn. But I am so surprised at how fast I can learn new things when I am truly focused. Don't be afraid to learn because it is so important to be innovative in real estate. Always try new things that can help you be faster and smarter in what you are doing. If you don't know how to do something, ask! Sometimes it is quicker to ask *who*, not *how,* meaning not *"How* can I do this?" but *"Who* can help me figure this out?"

9. Comment on social media. I dedicate 30 mins if needed to comment on potential clients' sphere of influence posts on Facebook and Instagram. This helps my algorithm and helps me stay top of mind. Whenever you can help someone out with something (answer a question, give them a good resource, etc.), it shows them that you are an expert.

10. 5 CMAs (comparative market analysis). I do 5 a day to total 25 for the week. Sounds easy, but depending on the depth you do on your CMAs it can get quite lengthy. The goal is to at least try and send 5 by email to past or prospective clients, updating them on their home value. If you have time, even delivering these to doorsteps will lead to great rewards and a potential conversation with someone. It's so important for people to realize the equity they have in their homes. If they choose to sell, you will be the one they will most likely use. If they choose to refinance, you will have done them a great service by letting them know how much equity they have to work with. They won't forget you.

11. Do one post. I always try and post once a day. It's always easiest if you take one platform first and master it. I was having a hard time posting daily and getting my content out there. This is a main reason why I joined Krista's program because I saw the real estate market was going digital. I needed to be in everyone's face but didn't know how. She is the master of being omnipresent

and getting in all of our faces. This year, I alone had more than 21 referrals from my friends, who remembered that I was an agent from all my posts.

To accomplish all of these tasks, I use the Pomodoro Technique. Krista teaches something similar called Success Sprints with THRIVE©. Basically, you take a certain amount of time and complete a specific task without any interruptions. No phone calls, no emails, just simply focusing on a task. You will be so surprised at what you can complete when you have dedicated time with no interruptions. They sell Pomodoro cubes on Amazon or there are apps and timers you can use on your phone.

Pay It Forward

Pay it Forward is the next section on the Daily Sheet. The idea is to try and do something nice for someone. I know we serve people each day, but I think it really helps to think of something small to do for someone to help brighten their day.

Acknowledge Your Wins and Successes

At the end of every day, write down your successes and wins! Sometimes we don't feel like we get a lot done. But if we can write down at least three wins, we will be surprised at what we really did accomplish. All these little wins will lead to closings, but, more importantly, they lead to happiness. We are happiest when we are most productive. Here you recognize what you are doing well, not wrong. Krista always says, "Success brings success, and what gets celebrated gets replicated."

Calendar Your Day

To close out the day on our Daily Sheet, we calendar out our day for tomorrow. It saves so much time if the day ahead of us is outlined ahead of time. We can mentally prepare for the day and are able to visualize it in the morning and get right into completing our tasks on the daily sheet.

Doing this Daily Sheet has propelled my business forward and keeps me on task daily. If I get sidetracked or go on vacation or simply take a day off, I know that I can fill out this sheet when I get back. I can use my Daily Sheet to set up my whole day, so I know exactly where to start again. Mindset and routine affect how productive (and ultimately, how successful) we are. Each task required on the Daily Sheet helps keep us focused and keeps us thinking of our clients.

I wish I'd had a Daily Sheet when I first started doing real estate. These last three years being in Krista's program have helped me to stay more focused, be more confident, and complete my goals regularly. I now focus on doing money-making tasks, bringing in business, and being innovative. The program has also given me a whole new set of like-minded friends who can talk strategy and motivation. Like I said at the beginning, I have 3X'd my business since joining with Krista. Can't wait to see what next year will bring!

Takeaways

1. Using the Daily Sheet each day becomes a roadmap for success.
2. Visualizing the successful completion of your tasks each morning can actually help you accomplish them.
3. Starting your day with gratitude sets the tone for your whole day. It's impossible to feel angry or discouraged when you're feeling grateful.
4. It's easy to feel like you're not accomplishing much. But focusing on your wins reminds you that you're moving forward.

LANI BELCHER

eXp Realty

📞 702-327-8892

✉ Lani.Belcher@eXpRealty.com

📍 Las Vegas, Nevada

Habits That Set You Up for Success

by Pamela Terry

I am writing this chapter on New Year's Eve, and I'm feeling both humbled and grateful for those who have made such a huge impact on my life. As I think about this, of course, I think about Krista and all she has taught me over the past five years. She taught me plenty of tactics and strategies. But what has probably been most important to me and my business are all the success habits I learned from her. Those habits are what I'm going to share with you.

But let me start from the beginning. I have been in the real estate industry for over 20 years. The first 20 years, I worked for a small brokerage that was locally owned. During that time, we had approximately 5-7 agents in the office. We conducted our business the same way agents had done it for years. I guess you could say everything was done the "old school" way. Now, I'm certainly not saying that it was the wrong way of doing things. But I kept feeling that there had to be a much better way to conduct business, a better way to market myself and grow my business in the real estate industry. Bottom line, I felt the old-school methods would not allow me to grow into my potential as I knew I could.

In 2018, I was scrolling through Facebook and saw an ad for Krista Mashore's coaching program. Well, I called and paid for the 1-year course just like that. I was super excited! The course was all about becoming a Community Market Leader© and I was going to become one! The first year in Krista's coaching program, I doubled my sales. I'm happy to say that my sales volume and the number of homes I have sold have increased each year since then. Yes, I've implemented the strategies and tactics I learned through Krista. But I'd say that it's the habits she taught us that have made the most impact.

Habit #1: Manifesto

One of the first things Krista had us do in the course was to commit to reading our manifesto out loud every day. When I first read it, you can imagine my surprise! This was everything I had been thinking of and wanting to be. I had tapped into a group where I could grow into my potential, and I knew I had made the right decision! The idea of the manifesto is that you are training your brain and stepping into your potential and a new identity. It didn't happen overnight, but by reading the manifesto, I really started to believe in myself as a Community Market Leader©. Here's what the manifesto says:

MANIFESTO

M

I am a **Community Market Leader©.**
I am not just a real estate agent.
I am an **UNSTOPPABLE** visionary!
I am **REVOLUTIONIZING**
the real estate industry and
CONTRADICTING the old school
teaching method and approach.
I am a **LIFE LONG LEARNER**

A

I **SERVE**, I do not just **SELL**!
I strive for excellence for myself and
my clients. I am changing the way
real estate is being done and how
agents are looked at. I don't rely on
traditional measures of getting
clients and generating leads.
I focus on the **FUTURE** !

N

I

I continue to push because I know that
nothing happens overnight. I
appreciate overwhelm because it
means that I am **GROWING**. I push and
GIVE MY ALL and I will **NEVER GIVE UP**.
I choose to be positive because I know
my **THOUGHTS** turn into my
ACTIONS, which make up my life. Once
a goal is declared I act as if I have
already achieved it.

F

E

S

I have an **ABUNDANCE** mindset! I
know that I am the ONLY one
responsible for **CREATING** the life
that I **DESERVE**... and I **AM**!

T

O

Krista
Mashore
COACHING

I AM:
a
M
marketer
A
abundant
S
successful
H
helpful
O
original
R
resourceful
an
E
educator

My name is: _____
and I am a **Community Market Leader©!**

Reading this out loud every morning feels great! I'm not just facing another day of same old, same old. I'm going on an adventure!

Habit #2: Preplan Your Day

Krista has us use a Daily Sheet that helps you plan and prioritize the next day. Every night, I fill out my daily sheet of everything that needs to be done the following day. I prioritize them by importance. Then I timeblock what I need to do by filling out my calendar with the tasks at hand along with how long I plan to devote to each task. It is important to take time in all areas of life, such as your mental, emotional, physical and spiritual health. You must have a healthy balance! For example, every day I schedule a minimum of 30 minutes to 1 hour to devote to my education. It might mean doing a course in Krista's program module, or deepening my understanding in the AI world, or sharpening my skills in negotiating deals with my buyers and sellers. You get the idea. I also schedule in rest, exercise and healthy eating habits so that I can give each day my very best.

Habit #3: Pomodoro Technique

The Pomodoro Technique has helped me immensely! It's a time management method that was developed by Francesco Cirillo in the late 1980s and it is a great way to enhance productivity. It helps you gauge your progress and maintain motivation. You can purchase a Pomodoro cube on Amazon. (The one Cirillo used was shaped like a tomato, and "pomodoro" is the Italian word for tomato.) Krista teaches this technique with a slight modification. When you do it right, the Pomodoro Technique eliminates distractions, improves your mental clarity, and provides you with a short break to mitigate burnout and maintain productivity. Here is how it works:

You begin by time-blocking your work into fixed, manageable time intervals (Pomodoros), like 15 minutes or 20 minutes (Krista teaches us to use 30-minute segments). During that pomodoro, you focus on just *one task*. Everyone thinks they are great at multitasking, but that's not true. When you focus on one thing at a time, you get so much more done! When you finish each Pomodoro, you take a break for a few minutes. Get up, walk around, read your goals, look at your vision board. Krista emphasizes that you should do at least 60 seconds to THRIVE© during your break so that you're training your brain to stay positive and focused on your vision. Then you do the next Pomodoro. It might be a different task, or you can continue with the one you've been working on, depending on how you time-blocked it.

For example, set your timer for 25 minutes and focus on one specific task. When the timer rings, stop working immediately, even if you're in the middle of that task! This is the most important part of the technique because it enforces the idea of focused work within a set time frame. Take a 5-minute break. Stretch. Relax. This gives your mind time to rest. Once your break is over, you repeat the cycle. After completing four Pomodoros, take a more extended break (15-20 minutes). Use this time to recharge. Continue using the Pomodoro Technique throughout your workday. You will be surprised at how much you will accomplish in these short spurts of focus.

To make this work, you have to use it correctly. Put your phone away! Close the door! Focus and avoid distractions! Be accountable to yourself and complete what you started!

Habit #4: Stick to Your Strengths and Your Niche

We all have our strengths and weaknesses working in the real estate industry. Who do you work with the most? Is it the first-time home buyer? Is it working with investors? Is it working with relocation companies, or is it working with REO (lender-owned) properties? You can't be everything to everybody if you want to succeed. Focus on your strengths. Target those people that you most want to work with. Build ads and create videos that educate the people you're targeting. Give them value and a reason why they should choose you as their Realtor®. And you can›t just target them and give value once. You need to be consistent and do it as a habit.

Video is one of the best ways to reach your audience! The hard work I put into my videos and brand speaks for itself. People now tell me they see me everywhere! Now, I know many people procrastinate when it comes to doing videos. It could be they think they look too fat, too short, too tall, the lighting is not good—the excuses go on and on. What I learned from Krista is just do it! I still get nervous! But I don't let that stop me. If you wait until those things (your body, your script, the lighting, etc.) are perfect, it will never happen. I know that most of us are our own worst critic. But no one is perfect so just do it! One of my favorite quotes is from Emma Norris: "Perfectionism is the mountain that has no peak."

Habit #5: Get Good at Social Media

Before joining Krista's program, I had no idea how social media would skyrocket my career! Going through the program, I have learned how to run Facebook ads and effectively target the audience I want to reach. The biggest difference I've witnessed since joining Krista's program is that I'm reaching the masses! Personally, in my area, I do a ton of reach ads while targeting different cities. Again, I don't just do it every once in a while. It's built in as a habit. Each day, I calculate how much I want to spend, how many people I will reach and then set an end date. I typically run a reach ad for at least 14 days. Next I do a brand awareness ad so that the community gets to know me. There's a whole strategy around doing these Facebook ads, which is worth learning to do because it gets you massive attention—and attention is currency!

Of course, I wasn't really sure what I was doing when I started. But I learned as I was implementing. This is why my business has grown each year. Am I perfect using social media? Absolutely not. But I will continue to learn and grow. I encourage you to start a YouTube channel, start a Facebook business page, make an Instagram account, and make sure you show up on Google. You want to consistently post your videos on all social media platforms. I understand that this might take you out of your comfort zone (as it did for me!), but social media is the best way to be seen, heard and get connected to potential clients.

Habit #6: Share Your Knowledge

Another way to add value is to give market updates to your community and to do that, you have to stay current with the market yourself. Let them know what is going on in the real estate world. Talk about the number of homes that have sold, interest rates, and predictions for the market. There are resources out there to help you with these updates. For example: Keeping Current Matters (https://www.keepingcurrentmatters.com), the National Association of Realtors® or your MLS database all have information you can use. Do your homework, then share your findings and become the go-to agent for all real estate news. Again, this isn't something that you do just once or twice a year. You need to schedule doing updates into your monthly routine.

Habit #7: Keep Building Your Business

It's easy to get all caught up in the day-to-day business of real estate and forget to set ourselves up for the future. But you're building your business for the long run so you have to think about that and make it a habit to put some focus there consistently.

One great way to do this is to pick a neighborhood and dominate it. Be the agent that sends out postcards of recent sales and what is currently for sale. Talk about the average home price or drop off a letter with a request to do a complimentary CMA (comparative market analysis). This is a great way to pick up a buyer or a seller. You could do a video of the statistics in that neighborhood. The more the consumer sees your face and hears your name, the more likely they will be to call you for their real estate needs. The key is consistency. Be consistent!

I have created a CMA drop-off box for people who contact me. Inside the box, I have a letter, my seller's guide, an overview of what has been sold in the area, and what is currently for sale. I also include a small gift for them. I have all my contact information on the box along with testimonials from other clients, my tagline, etc. I can tell you that no one else in my area is doing this type of marketing. It will set you apart from the competition. You want to be different!

Habit #8: Find Your Tribe

I got all these great ideas from Krista and other agents within the Krista Mashore organization as well as my eXp family. I now have such an amazing network of other Realtors® across the United States and throughout the world. It's shown me how important it is to surround yourself with like-minded people. Pick your tribe. Learn and grow together. The decision I made a few years ago changed my life both personally and professionally. I can't thank Krista enough for all the value she has instilled in me. The support her staff has shown to me has been amazing. They are 100% the real deal!

Joining eXp Realty has also opened so many doors of opportunity. I am very grateful for the amazing team of brokers who continually provide me with so much support and positive encouragement. Anytime I've needed them, they are there. I'm not sure many agents can say that about other agents in their office. Often we're competing with each other so other agents don't necessarily give each other encouragement or share their knowledge.

But I've discovered that the support of people around you is so critical if you really want to build an outstanding business.

Habit #9: Strengthen Your Mindset

Of the many things that I have learned from Krista, the one thing that really stands out is having the right mindset. It will determine your outcome no matter what you are trying to achieve. Before you do anything, you need to make sure you have a good mindset. Why? Because you get what you think!

Krista taught me that if a negative thought comes to mind, stop and replace that thought with a positive thought before you move forward. (She wrote a book called *Stop, Snap, and Switch* that talks about this and a lot of other techniques to help with mindset. Unlock your own copy of the book and other amazing bonus resources: **KristaMashore.com/TopProducer**.) It's really important to be consistent in changing your old way of thinking if you want more from your life than you have so far. Change requires us to do things we are not always comfortable doing. And sure, you may not always get it right as you're trying new things. But the end result will be rewarding! Remember, it's better to try and fail rather than doing nothing at all. FAIL only means it's your First Attempt In Learning. When you get into the habit of being aware of your mindset and always strengthening it, you'll be able to keep going and growing no matter what life throws at you.

Do you want to know a secret? I still get nervous and scared when I implement something new. I tend to always compare myself to others. As Theodore Roosevelt said, "Comparison is the thief of joy." As soon as I start comparing myself to others, I get depressed, negative self-talk gets in my head, then I'm in a downward spiral. This is where having a strong mindset comes in.

When you hit a fear or a bump in the road, you need to "shake it off"! Remember that what you think influences what you do. Get your head out of the sand, and do another video, add value and help someone. Get a stretch bracelet and put it on your wrist. If a negative thought comes to mind, *stop*, *snap* the bracelet on your wrist so you feel a little sting, then *switch* the bracelet to the other arm as you turn the negative thought into a positive thought. Say it out loud.

Takeaways

1. Train yourself to have habits that will help you keep your mindset strong, like reading the manifesto each morning or using the stop, snap and switch technique to shift from negative thinking.

2. Getting into the habit of time blocking and preplanning your day the night before will help you create balance in all areas of your life.

3. Using the Pomodoro Technique, you'll find that short intervals of focusing on just one task will help you get so much more accomplished.

4. Surround yourself with like-minded people who work *with* you, not against you. Shoot for the stars!

5. Don't be afraid to try something new to stand out from your competitors. Learn, implement, grow! Remember, FAIL only means it's your First Attempt In Learning.

PAMELA TERRY

Homes By Pamela Terry
eXp Realty

📞 301-697-1442

✉ PamTerry1971@Gmail.com

📍 Fulton, Maryland

SCAN ME

Free Gift: Bonuses
Time To Take Action!

<u>Information alone is not enough</u>. I've put together this **free expert resources member's hub** to help you get started now. Customize the strategies and tactics from this book to *your* business and marketing plan, with guidance, top producer tools and extra trainings.

KristaMashore.com/TopProducer

Big and Small Things Lead to Success

by Heather Jones

Ever wonder what it would be like to have random people recognize you and know who you are, but you don't know them? Do you wonder what it would be like to get calls from local area homeowners that you don't know (yet) who want you to represent them in selling their home because they see you everywhere, get your CMA (comparative market analysis) reports, participate in your contests, or see your videos? That's what it's like when you dominate a location in your area.

You may think that only a chosen few can have the kind of business where you don't have to chase after clients and they seek you out. But that's not true. It takes time, hard work, persistence, and definitely consistency, but I'm here to tell you that it *is* possible for you no matter where you're starting out. It's possible to double, maybe even triple, your transactions and income in a year's time. It's possible to make an impact on a small part of your community with your authentic brand. It's possible to be the Community Market Leader© in your area, and it's possible for you to create such a name for yourself so that when homeowners think *real estate*, they think of *you*.

As I write this, it's early 2024 and I've been in real estate for just about six years. I will say that, hands down, my first three years weren't easy. It took me a whole year from my anniversary date to close my first transaction! I was stuck in an old-school mentality of how to do business and I was struggling. But fast forward to today, after three years in the Krista Mashore Coaching program and two years in Krista's eXp organization, I have doubled my business, exponentially changed my mindset and mentality for the better, grown my confidence levels tremendously, and continuously make an impact on my community and the clients I serve each and every day. I do this through consistency, hard work, effort, daily routines and mindset work. I am excited to share that 2023 was one of the best years of my career, not only because of my ending transaction count and gross commission income, but also because of my growth in knowledge, confidence, brand recognition, and so much more. And yes, this was the same 2023 you were in where we had the highest interest rates in like 30 years, no inventory, fear of a recession, and buyers and sellers sitting on the fence!

In this chapter, I want to share some of the things that helped me grow my business and achieve my best year ever. Some of these things may surprise you. They may not seem like they would make a significant difference in your business. But I can tell you from my own experience, they make a huge impact.

Friendships

The relationships I've built in the Krista Mashore community have been such a blessing to my life and to my career. I can't even begin to explain how the community has made an incredible impact on me, but I will try. The friendships I have built are unmatched by any working relationship I have ever built with anyone. Some of the people in this organization have truly become some of my absolute closest friends, and I now call them my family. We are truly here to support and encourage one another. Can you say that about the people in your brokerage or organization? Do you have a group of colleagues that root for you to succeed? I'm happy to say that I do now through being in Krista's program.

For example, my morning ritual of attending the Skin in the Game call every morning at 7 a.m. has had tremendous impact on my life, my mindset, and my focus on work. Being able to wake up and jump on this call every morning with the same like-minded, supportive agents across the nation has been pivotal to my success. When I am down, they are there to support me and lift me up, when I am winning, they are right there to celebrate alongside me.

The friendships I have created and grown over the last three years have helped me increase my confidence, not only in myself, but how I run my business and present myself as a local Realtor®. The support I have received and offered and continue to receive has helped me double my business in the last year and hit milestone goals that I never thought I'd get through. I give as much as I can to my Skin in the Game family, not because I have to, but because I truly enjoy being able to celebrate my fellow Mashorians. And yes, we actually call ourselves that and we are proud of that name! It's such an amazing feeling to have this type of community that wants to support you, that welcomes you no matter what, that helps you along the way through struggles, and that are right there alongside you, celebrating your success.

Routine

The daily routines I have adopted have helped me in so many ways to be more organized, more productive on a regular basis, more connected, more educated, and more present with my work/family balance. I think many agents don't really have a routine. They show up to the office, grab a cup of coffee, check their emails, then try to figure out what to do for the day. Through

Krista's coaching, I have my routine engrained so far deep in my core that when I miss for whatever reason (maybe I'm sick or on vacation), I feel like my day is missing something massive.

Part of my daily routine is to learn something every day. When I started with Krista, I dove deep into the program, into the lessons and modules, into the coaching calls and into the community. I think the best thing that I ever did was to learn everything that was put in front of me and utilize the best things for me at the time. Something Krista taught me was to "learn, implement, master, and repeat." Like she always says, "Mastery is repetition." The idea is to learn it over and over and over again, and when you think you can't learn anymore, Krista throws something new at you to improve and make it ten times more effective.

Digital Location Domination

One of the big strategies that I learned and implemented was what Krista calls Digital Location Domination. I started an old-school version Location Domination back with the traditional method of real estate "farming." With my prior brokerage, I had already had a "farm," but then I joined Krista Mashore Coaching and learned how to put farming on steroids!!! I learned how to plan out in advance, schedule and send Every Door Direct Mail post-cards regularly. I learned how to set up my QR Codes and create my community-dedicated funnels for my neighborhood, Mountain Gate. I learned how to build my custom CMA packets and create videos for both the local area, real estate market updates and community-centered topics and events. Plus, I learned how to use social media for my community coloring contests. With all of this, I have been setting the Heather Jones Homes footprint into the South Corona community. I am confident that one day, not too far in the distant future, I will be the number one agent in my neighborhood. I understand that it takes time, but I also know I can do it.

So how has this affected me so far? I currently have home-owners who live in the area reaching out on a consistent basis, asking me to come see their home for an analysis and to advise them on the selling process. In fact, I just signed a new $800,000 listing from that exact experience. I have built up the paraso-cial relationship with these homeowners before even meeting them face-to-face through my marketing efforts, video content, and community contests. All of these things together meant that they liked me, trusted me, and felt like they knew me before even meeting me.

So how does it all work and come together? First off, you need to select your farm area in your community that you want to target. Once you have a good and deep understanding of who you are going to target and market to, you just need to get out of your own head and *go for it* using all of the techniques and strategies you're learning through this book. Yes, there will be other Realtors® and agents marketing to the same homes, but that doesn't mean that you can't. You can still stand out as a "disruptive digital marketer" to all of these homeowners over your competition. When you follow the strategy Krista teaches, none of your competition can say that they are doing *all* of the things that you are doing. They won't have Every Door Direct Mail Postcards with QR Codes leading to dedicated funnels for your neighbor-hood. They won't have local community videos highlighting small businesses, and regular real estate market updates, and the entire retargeting digital strategy that Krista Mashore teaches. They haven't co-authored a buyer and seller book designed to specifically showcase the kind of expertise Krista's students have that contradicts what most agents do and talk about. But unlike those other agents, if you have done all these things, you can po-sition yourself as a true expert in the area you want to dominate.

Getting Started

Once you pick your farm and you make the commitment and the decision to just go for it—and go for it consistently—the sky's the limit on what you can achieve. I started with a year of planned Every Door Direct Mail Postcards. I committed to sending one a week for six to eight weeks and then shifted to a monthly campaign. The best advice I can offer is to not commit unless you have the budget to *consistently* run the postcards month after month after month. It's a marathon, not a sprint. Once you have begun to put your name out in the community with your Every Door Direct Postcards, you can target the area in additional ways, like sending CMA packages to homeowners in your farm. You can offer them value by making videos or printed materials that highlight local businesses, the best parks, schools, events, etc. Trust me, they will appreciate it. No one else is doing it because it takes time and effort and most other Realtors® are not willing to put that kind of time and effort into really cultivating their farm.

Google Photos

Another way to dominate your location and become the Community Market Leader© is by using Google. By utilizing Google Photos, I have been able to increase my Google presence from zero to over 5.2 million views in less than one year. Where else are you going to be able to increase your audience base that quickly and that strongly? Here's how I do it: Whenever I am anywhere in my Corona community (whether shopping, dining out, at sports events, at the local parks with the kids, or wherever else), I am intentionally and diligently taking digital photos of these businesses along with video footage and content. Later on, I can post this footage and photos to my Google profile, where I can become a Google Reviewer for these businesses and build relationships through this platform. Google Photos has created so much more exposure for me in so many ways and I honestly would not have learned this outside of Krista's program.

I post photos and videos on Google regularly, as well as review the local businesses where I am. So now I am giving back to the community, these small business owners, while building my exposure and showcasing my area expertise all at the same time. This is also a great tool when I am speaking to community business owners about advertising their businesses. Not only am I promoting their business for free through video footage, but I am also promoting them on Google. This type of marketing is something that small business owners sometimes lack awareness and knowledge about. Using my marketing experience to help promote them in the community offers nothing but pure value and service. This type of service pays off tenfold in real estate where referrals are pure gold.

Coloring Contests

Another way that I have made my mark in the community is through my community coloring contests. I know what you might be thinking: *A coloring contest??* When your Ideal Clients are young families with children—first-time sellers and move-up buyers—this coloring contest is the *jam*! I have been doing my coloring contest since I was licensed in real estate. But ever since I joined Krista, I have been able to continue my contest and reach the masses by promoting it through digital video marketing, Facebook ads, Every Door Direct Postcards, and video text messages to my past participants and clients or prospects who fit the mold. The program has also helped me build and put a system in place where this contest runs smoothly and effortlessly every time! This allows me to also create an affordable community event that kids can participate in—and gets my own children involved in Mom's work too!

Parent homeowners rave about how their kids love participating in the contest. It is just so simple to put together and brings so many people joy. To do the coloring contest, you choose an event, a holiday, some special time of year. I personally do an annual Easter Egg Coloring Contest and an annual Halloween Pumpkin Coloring Contest. I do this by offering a blank Easter Egg or Pumpkin on a flyer. Then I run a video ad with rules and instructions on how to participate. I make it available for all children under the age of 12 living in the neighborhood and the city I am marketing to. Parents submit their children's masterpieces to me, and I promote all of the participants on social media for public voting for the winners. The winners receive Target Gift Cards.

All of the participants receive a special goodie bag or a treat of some sort upon entering the contest. I personally deliver these goodie bags with my own kids. It allows me the chance to get face-to-face and start building relationships with the parents/homeowners. Remember, real estate is a relationship-driven business. The coloring contest is a fantastic way to build engagement on social media outlets, get involved with your community, and build relationships with homeowners across your town and/or neighborhood. It's based on the concept Krista says over and over, "Serve, Not Sell." The more you serve your community and give them value for free, the more you will sell.

This contest is an inexpensive way to add more value and engagement into your community through location domination at minimal cost and just some of your time. It helps increase your database in the process as well. After six years of having these contests, I have homeowners calling me to help represent them in selling their homes because they see me everywhere and their kids participated in my coloring contest. In fact, in 2023, I sold and closed an $850,000 home directly from a mom who told me she loved that I offered this contest for her daughter. Already in early 2024, I am working with another family who wants to hire me to sell their house because they see me everywhere and their kids participated in my last contest in the community.

You might be feeling overwhelmed with everything I am mentioning that you can do. Don't worry. Krista always says, "Appreciate overwhelm because it means that you are growing." You're either growing or dying and, wow, have I grown! Once you combine all of these tactics and strategies into your everyday marketing plan, you will, over time, become the true area expert for your town, neighborhood, or area.

Community Funnel

A community funnel is the best way to showcase your expertise and truly make an impact on those you share it with. A community funnel includes everything from local market updates to community business videos, to school information, to neighborhood information. This funnel will allow you to update your audience every month with relevant market information about their area so that you can stay top of mind. This funnel will be used for your local ads and can be linked through a QR Code. When someone scans your postcard or the sign at your open house (should you hold one), they can learn more about the neighborhood that they are shopping in. Because you provided this information, they will begin to use you as their real estate resource. Sharing your knowledge through this funnel will help you win more listings, make more money in commissions, and increase your client base every single time. You will win before you arrive, just like me!

As I build relationships with homeowners in my neighborhood, the process is always the same. I send video messages regularly throughout the year. I add them to a Facebook Ad Audience and begin retargeting to them through video ads. I add them to my Homebot platform, and I add them to my CRM. This allows me to brand myself and constantly be top of mind with each one in some form or fashion. Overall, I am always providing value and serving my community rather than selling.

I will be the first to tell you it wasn't always this "easy." I had to work hard and remain consistent and focused. I had to overcome my fear of video to the point where *done* is better than *perfect*. Krista always talks about GETMO: Good Enough To Move On. The more I do, the more I learn, and the more I do, the better I can become. I learned to accept the fact that people want to see the real me, even if that means I am posting or sending a video with no makeup on or with mess ups. Be authentic and you will shine to the right audience. Someone once told me, "You can never say the wrong thing to the right person." And, man, is that so true in this business!

Stay the course, trust the process and keep dominating. This business is a marathon, a hard one with all sorts of obstacles in your way sometimes. But when you combine this business with your heart and drive and the right tools in place to help you achieve your goals, you will be amazed at how much you can accomplish. I have been able to do things that I only dreamed of doing and I am still a work in progress, striving to reach one new goal each and every day, week, month and year.

Takeaways

1. Finding an organization where your colleagues support you and cheer you on can make a huge difference to your business and your life.
2. If you really want to dominate your farm, use Digital Location Domination strategies, do things other agents don't bother to do, and stay consistent.
3. To really make a bigger impact, take things you might already be doing (contests, postcards, open houses, etc.) and put them on steroids using social media and digital marketing techniques like QR codes and funnels.
4. See overwhelm as a positive. If you're overwhelmed, you're growing.

HEATHER JONES

Heather Jones Homes
Brokered by eXp Realty

📞 661-607-6832

✉ Heather@HeatherJonesHomes.com

📍 Southern California

What's Your Retirement Strategy?

by Jesse Zagorsky

Have you ever been to an agent's retirement party? Really stop and think about it for a minute. It's an interesting profession that we've all signed up for. There is no "last day" and no "pot of gold" at the end of the rainbow. Every year the clock strikes midnight on December 31—and our sales reset back to zero. Then we start the hustle all over again.

I've seen Krista demonstrating the best kind of hustle for years! Long before she was the amazing coach KRISTA MASHORE, she was my friend Krista. We met in 2009 when we were both hustling as REO agents looking to navigate a changing market. Even back then, Krista had a stronger work ethic than almost anyone I've ever met. It's probably why we became friends and still are to this day!

I have so much respect for the growth I've seen Krista go through as she transitioned from REO agent (aka Foreclosure Queen) to top producer in a more traditional market, then becoming a top coach and thought leader in our industry. She has always invested in herself in the form of education, and she pours that knowledge into everyone around her. She leads with her heart and takes more action in a single day than most agents take in weeks!

Even though we've been friends for years, Krista and I became business partners in 2020 when she shut her brokerage down and I referred her to join eXp Realty. I mention that only because it ties into some of the concepts we're going to cover in this chapter on retirement, leverage and compound growth of your earnings over time.

I once heard someone say as a joke, "Realtors don't retire. They expire!" It's a terrible joke, but close enough to the truth, right? I've been personally selling homes for over 20 years, and I have sold well over 1000+ homes. I still LOVE what I do! But that doesn't mean I want to do it until my last day on earth. Fun fact about me: For my entire real estate career, my business partner has been my *mother*. Yes, I'm a certified Mama's Boy. My mom is a total rockstar and is still out showing homes at 77 years old!

On the one hand, she's working as an agent because she enjoys it, and it's a job you *can* do in your 80s. But the other reason she's still out there hustling is because my mom and dad (who has also been a broker since 1976) never quite planned enough for retirement. That's a painful realization for an only child like me to have. Like most kids, I love my parents and would do *anything* for them. Over the years, I watched them invest in rental properties—only to sell those same rental properties off when the real estate cycle took downturns. Their sales business slowed down with the market, and they needed cash to live. Most agents I knew during the recession (2009 - 2012) went through something similar.

That's obviously a problem. You can't keep raiding your retirement fund or investments when the market turns sour. Now as you read, many of Krista's Top Producers made their businesses more bullet-proof by implementing the strategies she teaches. They were able to weather tough markets or family crises. Stuff happens, and if you haven't set up your business to get through rough patches, you need some kind of safety net that leaves you with something when you no longer want to work—or you no longer can.

Agents' Typical Retirement Plans

In the world of real estate, there are 2 main strategies I've seen agents use to plan for retirement:

1. Buying Rental Properties (common)
2. Saving money (less common)

I've also seen some entrepreneurial agents start sales teams or brokerages in the hopes of selling those businesses someday, and that's their retirement plan. Sadly, I can count on one hand all the people I know who successfully sold a brokerage and even fewer who were able to sell a sales team.

As a solo agent, it *is* possible to sell your book of business and create some cash flow while creating a graceful exit. Usually, this involves some type of upfront payment from the person you're selling it to. Then you bring in your new "partner" for a certain period of time. You introduce this agent to your existing clients, and after co-branding together for a while, you get to moonwalk into the sunset and hopefully continue to make overrides on your new "partner's" sales for a few more years. The word "partner" helps during the transition as the handoff is happening, but in truth, this "partner" has actually bought your business.

Sounds complicated, right? It is, and there are not many agents that successfully manage to navigate and sell an existing book of business or sell their personal brand in the world of real estate. If you are considering transitioning a brokerage, a sales team, or even a solo agent's existing book of business to a new owner, there are certain cloud-based brokerage models like eXp Realty that could make this transition easier. That is, if I haven't already talked you out of trying to sell your sales team someday!

So, if all of the retirement options we're used to are a little tough and unpredictable, what is the answer? Here's the good news: there is no one-size-fits-all answer, and there are some pretty good options!

You Need Leverage

The book *Cashflow Quadrant* by Robert Kiyosaki is all about leverage. **If you have a goal to someday retire or just want the freedom to do the things you want to do with the people you want to do them with, whenever you want to do them, then creating income streams where you earn money in a leveraged way will be important.** Adding in a passive and recurring component to your income is going to be even more important if you want to truly step off the transaction treadmill.

> *If you have a goal to someday retire or just want the freedom to do the things you want to do with the people you want to do them with, whenever you want to do them, then creating income streams where you earn money in a leveraged way will be important.*

The *Cashflow Quadrant* breaks down earning money into four categories:

Cashflow Quadrant

4 Ways to Produce Income

Employee
They get paid according to the length of their working hours.
- No Leverage
- Work For Money

They have a job.

Business Owner
They get paid from their business revenue.
- Leverage
- People work for them

They own a SYSTEM.

Self-Employed
They get paid according to their work value.
- No Leverage
- Work For Money

They have a job.

Investor
They get paid from their investments and revenue.
- Leverage
- Money works for them

They own INVESTMENTS.

Krista
Mashore
COACHING

www.KristaMashore.com

In the image, the categories on the left-hand side have *no leverage*. You can be an employee with the benefit of a guaranteed paycheck, but you're trading your time for money. No leverage there. It's an even trade and if you stop putting your hours in, you stop getting that paycheck.

Being self-employed, you still trade your time for money, but now you wake up every day "unemployed" as you hunt for your next client, fee, assignment, or commission check. As real estate agents, the vast majority of us are self-employed. Congratulations! You have fired your boss and now work for a crazy person! (If you didn't get that joke, don't worry, you'll probably wake up at 3 a.m.—hopefully laughing!)

The biggest benefit of being self-employed is that the more we hustle, the more money we can make. As every previous chapter in this book described, there are great strategies that can help you to become a top producer in real estate. Some ways even include fantastic forms of leverage, like running social media ads so you are seen by thousands of people, not just a few. Still, very few have passive, recurring or residual components to the way you make money.

The solution is to look for ways to make money on the right-hand side of the image above, either as a business owner or as an investor. As a business owner, the people who work for you—the time and effort they put into your business—are your leverage to make money. The best business models are ones that involve some combination of leverage, residual income and compound growth. Historically, any agent in the world of real estate who wanted to be a business owner would have to open a brokerage or start a sales team. Unfortunately, both of these have high expenses and lots of liability.

There are some cloud-based brokerages, like eXp Realty, that allow every agent to make money like a broker does, *without* needing a broker's license and *without* the expenses or liability of running a brokerage. They typically call this type of income "revenue share." By contributing to the growth of their brokerage, agents earn revenue share, which is a portion of the gross revenue from that brokerage. Over time, the potential for your income to see compounding growth is a big positive for most revenue share models at cloud-based brokerages. By the way, this is one of the paths Krista and I have chosen to take to create residual, ongoing income.

Another way you could become a business owner is by selling various services to real estate agents or starting a real estate technology company. Since most agents have had years of personal experience with the pains and challenges of being an agent, the logical next step is to start a

> *"If you don't find a way to make money while you sleep, you will work until you die."*

business that *solves* these challenges for other agents. If you are a serial entrepreneur, or just love starting new businesses, going in this direction can have the potential to make money in a leveraged and residual way. Typically, the downside is that it comes with high overhead, high startup costs, and years without much income before you reach a place of profitability.

The 4th quadrant of that image is earning income as an investor, where the money you invest is the leverage to give you residual and ongoing income. To quote Warren Buffett, **"If you don't find a way to make money while you sleep, you will work until you die."** Since you've read this far into a chapter that is all about retirement, clearly you have some interest in figuring out how to stop working before you die—preferably *long* before you die!

There are many ways you can be an investor. You could own real estate, stocks, bonds, gold, silver... the list goes on and on. Mr. Buffett always recommends that you "invest in what you know." Some investment categories layer nicely on top of activities you do as a real estate agent, like investing in REITs (real estate investment trusts) or investing in publicly traded business-es that are related to real estate. And some brokerages even offer you stock awards in the brokerage for doing things you would do anyway, like working with buyers, working with sellers and talking to other agents.

No matter which category of retirement strategy you dive into, one of the most important pieces of advice I can give is to *start planning early.* There's a classic Chinese proverb that says, **"The best time to plant a tree is 20 years ago. The 2nd best time is *now*."** When you combine ways of earning

> *"The best time to plant a tree is 20 years ago. The 2nd best time is now."*

income from the right-hand side of the Cashflow Quadrant (as a business owner or as an investor) and allow time to compound your earnings, this can create a true path to retirement for any real estate agent. But if you haven't started early? Don't just resign yourself to working until you drop dead. You can still put some strategies in place.

There are only three qualities you need for success at any stage of your real estate career. You need to be:
- Coachable
- Willing
- Hungry

When you combine all 3 of these qualities, you can make amazing things happen! Those are the qualities you need to succeed in real estate and those are also the qualities you need to create a great retirement plan for yourself—a plan that has re-sidual income on an ongoing basis. You need to be *coachable* and listen to people who have found a way to set themselves up with ongoing residual income. You need to be *willing* to change how you're operating and find ways to make your business more bul-letproof. You may need to change the structure of your business to give you leverage. And you need to be *hungry* enough about creating a great retirement strategy that you start making it a priority, something you *must* have versus something that would be "nice to have" if you ever get around to it.

Because you're reading a book like this, I know you're smart, open, and eager to be successful. You may not know exactly how, but you're bright enough to go to experts for the help and support you need. I believe in you, maybe more than you believe in yourself. So, borrow some of mine for now. Borrow my belief until you can clearly see the path ahead of you. It's the path you're already on, though you may not know it. You just need to think beyond the way most real estate agents think about retirement and find the strategy that's best for you.

Takeaways

1. If you haven't done much to plan for retirement, the time to do it is *now.*
2. You need *leverage* of some kind to create ongoing, residual income.
3. Use some of the strategies in this book to make your business more bullet-proof so you can weather tough markets and personal crises.
4. Create some kind of safety net so you don't end up having to sell off any investments you've made for retirement.

JESSE ZAGORSKY

Live. Love. San Diego Homes
eXp Realty

📞 858-525-2991

✉ LearnWhyItsTime.com

📍 San Diego, California

If you call Jesse, be sure to mention that you found him from Top Producer Secrets.

The Decision That Can Change Everything

by Lenka Doyle

B y this point in the book, you will have already read from so many of my fellow students, peers, and colleagues. Many of them have become my friends, mentors, and people I look up to. They are all incredibly inspiring and hard-working humans, and I am so proud to share the journey with them. Being able to collaborate with like-minded, driven people multiple times every week in this crazy industry of real estate, marketing, and entrepreneurship has been life-changing.

I want to share my journey with you with the hope it will help you along the way to achieve whatever your goals are. I'm going to share with you the most important decisions I made along the way that got me to where I am today. The fact you are here reading this book means you are looking for more. You already know in your core that you can achieve more, and you are ready to learn and try to figure out your next move.

In this book, we are all here sharing things that work for us, the strategies that elevated our business, the *Aha!* moments that took us to the next level. So, how do you do it all? Which of the strategies should you use for your business? What is that one right thing, and how do you know it's for you? And if it's as simple as doing the ideas in this book, why isn't everyone doing it and succeeding? I was asking the same questions myself about five years ago. But my story starts long before that.

I was born and raised in Prague, Czech Republic, and came to the United States in 1998 with my husband and our son, who was three years old at the time. We moved to Cape Coral, Florida, and we have been here ever since. We absolutely love the laid-back atmosphere, the water, and the weather living here despite all the craziness we endured in 2022 (which I'll get into later). We purchased our home in 2000 and started getting family members to relocate to Florida, which meant many referrals for our real estate agent.

One day, my husband said, "You would be good at this. You should get a real estate license." The problem was that my English was not fluent enough and don't get me started on reading and writing! Remember the tricky questions on your real estate state exam? For me, they were almost impossible to understand. But I decided to do it anyway because we were raising our son and wanted everything possible for him so he could be the best he could be at everything he wanted, just like every parent wants their child to be successful.

Before I Made the Decision

Fast forward to 2018, I'd been in the real estate industry since 2008. I became friends with the agent who sold us our home, and hanging my license with her company seemed natural. I started to learn by dealing with landlords and tenants. Then I transitioned to sales and started to earn a small income. Later I was assigned a mentor (who later became my team leader and eventually my broker) who taught me the ropes of the industry.

For whatever reason, I couldn't break that ceiling of over $100k a year in income. I would make $45,000 one year. Another year, I would climb to $55,000 and then go back to a lower amount. Just a total yoyo effect. It's as if in real estate there was a big secret that no one wanted to share or maybe they were afraid to. I just really didn't know what I didn't know, if that makes sense. I did what was asked of me and more. But I knew I needed something more. I know it was capable of more, but how?

That's when I started to search and browse the World Wide Web for real estate courses and books to read. One day, this real estate coach, Krista Mashore, who kept showing up in front of me on Facebook, offered a free 3-Day Challenge for real estate agents to help them elevate their business. Ok, now we are talking! If it's free, it's for me! (Unfortunately, I didn't know how much my "freebie" thinking would cost me!)

I started to take all of her free courses. Now, of course, if you want to learn more after the three days, you must commit to the program and pay. Well, that is where they lost me. I was not about to pay someone. I felt it was absurd and that I could figure it out on my own. (I can see now how absurd that idea was!) I continued to take all the free and cheap courses I possibly could. I probably did six of Krista's challenges and worked them all the way through.

I always learned something new to implement in my business, and in that first year alone, I generated over $75,000 in income within just a few months of implementing what I had learned for free. Interesting... And then, the following year, I finally did it! I made over $100,000!

The Decision to Invest in Myself

At that time, I was signed up for one of Krista's free courses and I honestly can't remember what we were discussing. But right there, Krista called me out in front of all the people in the Zoom class. "Lenka, how are you, honey? When are you going to join the program? I know you will do so good." I was floored. How did she even know me by name or even remember me? I was surprised, but I realized that this lady was really seeing and paying attention to her students. I am not just a face on the screen. She actually cares. I have to say it really took forever for me to commit. I took another course, which took me almost three years to make the commitment. Yes, three years! Finally, in one of the classes, we talked about being resourceful. So, I became resourceful, made a business plan and a decision, and I joined the Krista Mashore Coaching Program. (Now, I can see that waiting three years to make this decision cost me hundreds of thousands of dollars.)

I was getting pushback from people around me when I talked about the coaching program and the investment. It was one of the biggest obstacles I had to overcome. My broker at the time didn't think I needed any of the coaching and thought it was a waste of money. But to me, the proof was that I was getting better at everything I was doing in such a short period of time by doing the things Krista taught. I was starting to get noticed and stand out by doing things differently. For example, I learned how to do video text messages in one of her free courses, so I started to implement it. I started with old clients, just to follow up and practice—and I got a listing! Sounds so simple, right? That was it. I was getting the confidence to listen to my own gut, and I knew what I had to do, no matter what others thought.

I realized I had to invest in myself, my career, and my business. We hear it all the time that you need to invest in yourself, but we get so immune to it. We invest in our kids. We pay for tutors to help them in school. We hire sports coaches or trainers to elevate our child's game or strength coaches or piano teachers. You name it, we do it! But it's as if there is some sort of off button when it comes to ourselves. We stop investing in self-improvement for ourselves. We think we are supposed to handle it alone now because we are now adults. Well, that's at least what

I thought. I forgot what it really meant to invest in myself until I found the coach, until I found Krista Mashore Coaching.

I set a budget for the money I needed to start the program, set a time frame, and opened a credit card. I also started to set funds aside from my closings in advance, so I had funds to make the payments moving forward and keep going. The credit card I opened earned points and miles. And I did it! I actually made the commitment. Looking back, it was a commitment to myself, for myself, and for my family and future. Part of my business plan and my goals was to gain financial freedom and being able to spend more time with my family. I wanted to be able to fly and spend a long weekend once a month with my son and daughter-in-law, now granddaughter, who had moved out of state.

Results from Deciding and *Committing*

Everything changed so much for me after making that commitment. I joined the program, and it was truly like drinking from a firehose. It was (and still can be) sometimes overwhelming. There is just so much to learn, and you see all the possibilities you had been missing out on. But as Krista always says, "Appreciate overwhelm because it means you are growing." You learn, and you grow, and things get easier. The game slows down, you can see the plays and moves you need to make, and it all starts falling into place. (We are a sports family, and our son played basketball in college on a full-ride scholarship, so the sports analogies make sense to me, and hopefully you can relate also.)

Shortly after starting the program, we had the CMA Challenge. I was all over it. I created a template and started sending CMA packets out regularly. It paid off. I had seven deals going in a very short period of time. I realized I had to keep it simple because I was new in the program and did not have all the marketing materials in place like other agents who had been in the program longer. What was so amazing was collaborating with the others in the program on everything we did. For instance, in the

CMA Challenge, we learned how to do it, and then we discussed how to make the CMA process work for us in our markets. People would share templates and ideas of what worked for them. Being part of a community that was willing to share was so refreshing from what you normally get in the industry.

I started to earn over $165,000 the first year in the program. I remember telling Krista in one of our coaching goal-setting calls that I would like to be able to break the ceiling of $250,000 that year. It was late in the summer, beginning of the fall, and Krista was telling me how doable it was. I was thinking, *Okay, let's do it!* Sure enough, that year, I finished with over that amount! And my business kept growing every year after that with amazing results. Every year, my goal was to do better than the year before, and I did. My next goal is $1,000,000 and I know it is reachable!

Making the decision and overcoming the fear of commitment and getting into a coaching program was the best thing I did. The only regret I have is not doing it sooner. It is actually funny now because Krista calls me out on how slow I was to commit and then has me share it with other students. When I look back to where I was compared to where I am now and measure how much I've grown in my personal life and business aspect, it is really crazy. But to have that growth, I had to do the work and commit.

In September of 2022, I was approached by Andrew Regenhard, owner and publisher of SWFL (Southwest Florida) Real Producers. Andrew is an inspiring person and he informed me I ranked in the top 500 agents in the area. They wanted to do a story so I could share a little about myself. I was so proud to be recognized. I didn't even know that I was ranked in the top 500. I was too busy working Krista's program and real estate to notice.

How My Decision Saw Me Through Hard Times

One month later, in October of 2022, we got hit by Hurricane Ian, a Category 5 hurricane. Things just got crazy. If you have never been through something like this, it is hard to explain.

The whole city and area were just devastated. At one point, we had our dog in a life jacket, and we released the garage door and put floating pool mats on the top of the car in the garage so we had an escape from the water surge. We also put important items in the attic, and I thought we were going to die. Simply, we were lucky. I feel guilty to even bring it up because we did better than others. Yes, we were also worse than some, but at the end, we survived, and lots of people did not. Our thoughts and prayers are still with them and their families—always will be. We had to leave our house right after the storm and stayed for a little time with our son and daughter-in-law in Atlanta.

Fast forward, we came back and fixed what was damaged over time and are still working on it. But how do you work real estate after an event like this? How do I come back from total devastation? Some areas were without power and internet for several months. Our power was out for four weeks and our internet was down for months. The months of November and December seemed impossible to work in real estate, but believe it or not, from the coaching program, I knew I could still work through it. I remembered to be resourceful and learned to "Serve, Not Sell," as Krista is always talking about. I reached out to my clients and asked how and what I could help with. Helping where we could was just so rewarding. I jumped on the coaching calls as soon as I was able so I could keep my mind on a positive track. The response from everyone in the program was also amazing.

In 2023, I received an invitation from Cathy Mann-Seiple and Julie Scott, the hosts of the event Inspired, to be one of the three guest speakers. The speakers were all top-producing female real estate agents who were to share a little about their journeys to success to inspire others. I was in a panic and reached out to Krista. To speak on stage in front of other people was terrifying. As an agent, we are more comfortable in a one-on-one setting. Krista said, "Just be yourself and share your story of who you are." Speaking on stage in front of other people was terrifying and so uncomfortable, but I knew I had to do it. I would regret it if I didn't. So, I asked for help, got support, and did it. It was empowering knowing I can help and inspire others!

In July 2023, my broker Jay Richter informed me I was ranked 45th in Cape Coral, and he told me what a fantastic job I was doing. I wrapped up 2023 with an email from SWFL Real Producers that I was ranked in the top 250 agents in the area and the top 44 in Cape Coral. Having a coach like Krista was the missing piece of a puzzle for me and is the glue that even now keeps it all together.

Do You Need a Coach?

Sure, you can try to take a free course and try to figure out how to do funnels or the CMA process or figure out how to post on social media platforms correctly on your own. But the truth is you will only get so far and at a much slower pace. Have you heard the expression, "Money likes speed!"? Took me a while to get it!

The great thing about having a coach is that you start to change. You notice and recognize things that you have not noticed before. For example, I hear agents being fearful of the current market or economy. A local agent recently told me that he is considering getting a second job. What I know now is that if that is where your mindset is going, that is what you will end up doing. At one time, I would have had that same mindset. Now, I see that I have set myself apart from that kind of mindset that is so common to other real estate agents. I can see opportunities where I didn't before. A changing economy does not scare me because I know how to adapt, what to do, and how to inform my clients. I have become an authority.

I also noticed that the more successful the agents are, the less fear they have about sharing how they did it or what worked for them. I have also noticed (through our collaboration and sharing and working through strategies on market and marketing materials on our coaching calls) how brokers and teams respond to solo agents who get into a coaching program. How they respond is important. You want to be with the ones who support you and push you to do better and want you to succeed! Be around people who truly want you to be successful and not people who want you to be successful only as long as you are not more successful than they are!

The same goes for people and friends you surround yourself with. Through good coaching, you will start to eliminate distractions and negative things in your life. And, yes, it may be some of your friends or people close to you. Coming to this conclusion was one of the hardest obstacles I had to overcome. Actually making the changes I needed to make and acting on them was even harder. But the rewards at the end are so much bigger. I measure my success based on the happiness of my family, the freedom I have gained, and being an overall positive, happier person. The money we make is also great! But I could not have done it by myself, so I want to tell my coach, "Krista, Thank you!"

Takeaways

1. Get a good coach! It's so much harder to do things alone. Ask for help.
2. Find the coach that fits you and your style and who has built a positive community. Commit to doing what they coach you to do.
3. Listen to your instinct and not the opinions of others. Mute the distraction of other people's ideas of what you should do.
4. Make a plan and write it down. Put a time frame on it, do what you need to achieve it and follow through.
5. Be willing to be uncomfortable. It means you are growing!

LENKA DOYLE

Lenka Doyle Team
with John R Wood Properties
Christie's International

📞 239-823-9553

✉ Lenka@LenkaDoyleTeam.com

📍 Cape Coral, Florida

A final word from Krista...

Whew! Okay, if you've read through this entire book, you may be feeling overwhelmed. Don't let that stop you! Learning all this great stuff won't make a bit of difference to your business if you don't *take action*. You need to do something different than what you've been doing. What do they say about insanity? It's doing the same thing over and over and expecting different results!

Building a hugely successful real estate business based on the strategies I teach takes some time. There's no such thing as an "overnight success"—and if someone guarantees you instant success in real estate, run away from them as far and as fast as you can! It may take months of implementing these strategies to see real results. But if you stay consistent and persistent, results will come.

In this book, you've heard from people who are just like you. Just like you, they wanted something more from their business. Just like you, they looked for answers and found one of my books (or attended one of my events) and felt inspired—and maybe a little intimidated. But they took the next step. Then the next step, and the next. They started implementing and got the support they needed. Like Lenka Doyle wrote in her chapter, they made the *decision* that literally changed their lives.

People always say that a 1,000-mile journey starts with one step. So, one way to take action is to take one step at a time. Take one thing you've learned from this book and implement it, then move on to the next thing. You can eventually get where you want to go, but it will take much longer than it needs to, just like walking that 1,000-mile journey by yourself. Also, somewhere along the 1,000 miles, you're bound to get lost and probably discouraged.

Personally, I'd rather start a 1,000-mile journey with a plane ticket! I'd rather have a pilot who knows what they're doing fly me where I want to go. Yes, there's the upfront cost of the ticket, but how much time will it save me? How much faster will I get to where I want to be? And isn't it much more likely that I'll end up in the right place with an expert flying me there as opposed to walking that long journey by myself?

I'd love to be your pilot. I'd love to teach you more at my free 3-day event. To sign up, go to: **KristaMashore.com/Masterclass**.

FREE GIFT: BONUS RESOURCES & TEMPLATES
TOP PRODUCER
TOOLS UNLOCKED

My **pro tips** and *expert insights* on how to get started using these strategies and tactics in your business *right away*. Plus you'll receive access to over **25** additional tools, resources, templates and bonus trainings for FREE. Get started now, go to:

KristaMashore.com/TopProducer

KristaMashore.com/**TopProducer**

Made in the USA
Middletown, DE
13 September 2024

60908312R00172